THE SUING
OF AMERICA

THE SUING
OF AMERICA:

Why and How
We Take Each Other to Court

Marlene Adler Marks

Seaview Books
NEW YORK

The events in this book are true. Some of the names have been changed to protect the author.

Manufactured in the United States of America

Second Printing

Library of Congress Cataloging in Publication Data

Marks, Marlene Adler.
    The suing of America.

    Bibliography: p.
    Includes index.
        1. Justice, Administration of—United States.
    2. Actions and defenses–United States.   3. Trials
    —United States.   I. Title.
    KF380.M37   347.73'5   80-52412
    ISBN 0-87223-658-7

Designed by Tere LoPrete

Seaview Books/A division of PEI Books, Inc.

for Burton

Contents

Lawsuit, n. a machine which you go into as a pig and come out as a sausage.

AMBROSE BIERCE, *The Devil's Dictionary*

THE SUING
OF AMERICA

CHAPTER 1

Dreams and Promises

News item: A nine-year-old girl is raped on a San Francisco beach. Her mother sues NBC Television for $11 million, saying that the violence displayed on one of its programs indirectly caused the rape.

News item: A young mother, barred from breast-feeding her baby during her free time on duty as a firefighter, sues her employer, charging sex discrimination.

News item: A New York attorney brings a class-action suit against General Motors on behalf of "all persons everywhere now alive and all future unborn generations." He charges GM with polluting the air and seeks $6 *trillion* in damages.

Obsession with suing is part of the American character, and has been so for 200 years. We use lawsuits with extraordinary invention, and not always in the way that legal "authorities" would prefer. They satisfy needs no other mechanism fulfills. Every generation complains about the courts, the domination of lawyers in national affairs, the litigiousness of our citizenry. And still the lawsuits come, the camel's hump of American life, controversial but perhaps necessary for survival.

Today, everyone worries about lawsuit. It's the rare person who feels so protected and insulated from risk, or so insignificant, that he is not concerned that some chance act might land him in court. A cartoon in New York's *Village Voice* gives the general idea. It shows a man in an elevator giving advice to a friend: "You gotta remember one thing," the man says. "When you're married, work out financial matters as though you were in litigation—because someday you will be."

All sorts of people—including those who in a bygone era might have considered engaging in a lawsuit to be a public humiliation equivalent to a Scarlet Letter or a year in the stockade—are now palpitating for the court's attention. The diversity of suits is astounding: patients suing doctors, doctors suing lawyers, lawyers suing lawyers, parents suing teachers, and prisoners suing their jailers. Thanks to Lee Marvin and his former live-in lover, Michelle Triola Marvin, nervous paramours throughout the nation, who only yesterday, it seems, hid the "illicit" nature of their affairs even from friends and relatives, today feel privileged to shout it to the world in the form of a written contract, only later to sue in court. Ministers are taking out malpractice insurance because even they are subject to suit for mistakes of judgment. No one is immune. Attorneys representing such once nonlitigious groups as Chinese-Americans today brag that second- or third-generation young people are now standing up for their rights, and are more willing to go to court. We are one nation, divisible, in the courthouse.

"Conflict is useful," writes Paul Bohannon, an authority on justice in primitive societies. "In fact, society is impossible without conflict."[1] But Americans are not so sure. If suing is indeed part and parcel of the American character, it is not a trait we accept with an easy sense of pride. A frustrating ambivalence courses through what we clearly regard as "the lawsuit problem." On the one hand, we hate litigation, which, even as a moderate, nonviolent form of conflict, nevertheless implies hostility and aggression. A "mature" society like ours should no longer pulse with such anger, we suspect. But on the other hand, even as we sermonize about lawsuits, we're dependent upon them: This nation is deeply wedded to a belief in justice, and litigation is our major tool for achieving it.

We're caught between a rock and a hard place. Because we want to be both peaceful and just, simultaneously, we tend to act like hypocrites, discouraging the litigation of others, calling it "frivolous," while at the same time fomenting it when it seems our own rights are under attack.

This controversy about the baselessness of lawsuits is something of a red herring, a diversionary tactic. Unless we understand why Americans fight and complain, and why they choose the courts as the arena for their fighting and complaining, we can't do anything about changing our litigious habit—assuming we do have a habit, and that it's something we truly want to change.

A weird and remarkable assortment of lawsuits come at us wave upon wave through reports in our newspapers and magazines. The reader senses that these people are sending a message, but it's like interpreting smoke signals on a windy day. It is time for us to get closer to the source of these smoke signals, the American litigants themselves, and find out what's the problem.

Former U.S. Attorney General Griffin Bell, who set legal policy under President Jimmy Carter, worried in 1978 that "we just sue people and then find out later what we've got on them." Yet, under Bell himself, the number of lawsuits instigated by the federal government continued its upward spiral. According to the *1979 Annual Report* of the Administrative Office of U.S. Court, in 1978–79 the United States government, under Bell's authority, increased the number of lawsuits it filed by 37.6 percent over the previous year. For the first time in history, the federal government sued citizens more times than citizens sued the government.

Much of this increased case load is dictated by new anti-trust, environmental- and consumer-protection laws enacted over the decade of the 1970s, plus an increased willingness on the part of government to dun aging graduates for unpaid student loans. Still, it was Griffin Bell who gave a new respectability to exactly the kind of "shoot from the hip" lawsuits he otherwise found so objectionable. He brought an innovative but lightly researched lawsuit against the city of Philadelphia and its mayor, Frank Rizzo, charging "widespread and systematic police brutality."

Rizzo, who had served as the city's police commissioner, was just then going down for the final count on a long and controversy-plagued career. The politically explosive suit, one which jeopardized $10 million in federal funds, was prominently reported in national newspapers in continuing coverage from August to December 1979. This extensive reporting kept repeating the charges against the city, implying that the case was a piece of cake. But U.S. District Judge J. William Ditter was outraged by the suit, calling it a "regrettable move" that amounted to a "stacked deck." In rejecting the government's case, he criticized its lawyers for trying the case in the press and for making "sensational public statements which created the clear impression . . . that the defendants' guilt had been established beyond doubt."[2]

But by that time, Griffin Bell was gone from office, and it was left to Benjamin Civiletti, his replacement, to keep a stiff upper lip. This he did, defending the police-brutality suit as breaking new legal ground in insuring the civil rights of citizens against police overdiligence, and vowing to appeal.[3]

Of course, Bell was only following long-established precedent set by other U.S. attorneys general. Ramsey Clark, when he occupied that post under President John Kennedy, filed a massive antitrust suit against IBM on his last day in office. According to one adversary counsel, Clark admitted at the time that the case was weak.[4] Three presidents later, the government is still unable to rid itself of the IBM tarbaby; unwilling to drop the case for fear of appearing to capitulate, but not really prosecuting it either, for fear of losing.

The press, too, is at the least inconsistent in its approach to suing. Lawsuit stories are often presented to the waiting public as entertainment: "James Garner, Beaten, Broken . . . Now, Sued" ran the front-page headline of the *Los Angeles Herald Examiner;* "[George] Segal Is Being Sued and Loving It," said *The Los Angeles Times.* But they're also delivered as sermon: "The Chilling Impact of Litigation" (*Business Week*); "Why Everybody is Suing Everybody" (*U.S. News & World Report*). The media like to have it both ways: Television "docudramas" glorify and dramatize personal stories of litigants who win novel lawsuits like sexual harassment and job discrimination; then, having led the audience to believe that suing is socially acceptable and even beneficial, go on to decry our crowded courtrooms and Americans who sue too much.

The 1979 movie *Kramer vs. Kramer* has a typically mixed message. Joanna Kramer (played by Meryl Streep, in a role for which she won an Oscar) deserts her husband, Ted (Dustin Hoffman), and her child (Justin Henry), then changes her mind and sues Ted for custody of the boy—mostly as a means of exposing Ted as the inadequate husband she believes him to be. The lawsuit hits Ted just as he is fired from his high-level advertising position: He's been too busy taking care of the boy. Now, fearing the court will wreak vengeance upon him for his unemployment, Ted takes a new job for less money and clearly beneath his abilities. The pay cut provides further grist for the legal mill, allowing Joanna's attorney to humiliate him in court as a man not quite able to support his own child.

By movie's end, Joanna expresses shock at the brutality of the legal system. She has won her case—the judge has taken the child away from Ted and awarded custody to her. But Joanna, who was entirely willing to use the court to punish Ted when vengeance was her desire, now only wants what's fair: She decides on her own to permit Ted to keep the boy, as long as she has reasonable visitation.

With this heartwarming ending, the movie has let Joanna, and by extension the American public, have it both ways. When Ted is the "villain," an inadequate spouse and inattentive father, then lawsuits are condoned as a proper way to "get even." But as he reforms, the villain becomes the legal system itself. The movie thus ends on a classic populist note, however ill-deserved: "Power to the people," it says; without the legal system, they can find "justice" on their own.

Having received conflicting signals from our political leaders, the news and entertainment media, it's no wonder that the American public is confused about whether lawsuits are good or bad.

For almost everyone on the receiving end, lawsuits are scary. People, even big corporations, run away from them. Being sued—whether you are the average citizen or president of the United States—is like being sent a dead fish by the Mafia. It marks you as a misfit, a transgressor on others' rights. Griffin Bell once noted with irritation that he was named both professionally as attorney general and as an individual in lawsuits against the United States government. This pro forma naming, which rarely if ever put him at personal risk, nevertheless seemed to offend him. "A significant percentage of the pending suits against federal employees," he wrote, including himself in this category, "are frivolous."[5]

When Jane Fonda, the actress, sued twelve officials of the federal government for investigating her bank account during the Watergate era, she named President Nixon personally, believing that perhaps he had instigated the government's efforts to have her trailed, her phone tapped, and her mail opened. But U.S. District Judge Malcolm Lucas, appointed by Nixon to the lifetime post, took offense and removed Nixon's name from the case without even being asked to by government attorneys. Fonda's attorneys say he couldn't bear to call the case *Fonda* v. *Nixon* in open court. The case became *Fonda* v. *L. Patrick Gray* (Gray was head of the FBI at the time).

Being sued is like having a knife in the heart, a punch in

the abdomen—no one takes a lawsuit lightly. The senior counsel of Northrop Aviation thinks lawsuits in general are funny, or so she said one day in discussing the litigation phenomenon. She termed suing a peculiarity of the American public and a fascinating piece of human behavior. But lawsuits by disgruntled employees charging job discrimination against her company were another story: These she often saw as "frivolous," "outrageous," and the "acts of disturbed individuals who can't get along" in society.

Despite the fact that nothing mortal actually happens to people who are sued, there's a voodoo effect about lawsuits. We talk about people threatened by suit as being "under a cloud," or having a lawsuit "hanging over their heads." As long as a lawsuit is pending, financial assets are tied up, or at least watched more carefully; you are regarded as a risk by your fellow man, and certainly seen as one by lending institutions, who will be nervous about extending credit; and your work is often no longer trusted. Writers and artists who have been sued frequently report they cannot work at all while the suit survives. People who are sued generally view themselves as diminished. A businessman complained that a lawsuit by a competitor cut the sale value of his business by at least one-third, and that even though he eventually won, his reputation was muddied.

This all adds up to a lawsuit being a pretty powerful tool. In 54 percent of the cases surveyed in a New York City small claims court, the mere act of filing a case led to settlement. Whatever else had happened before—the phone calls, the pleading, the threats—apparently nothing worked as well as seeing that summons to come to court.[6]

The sheer number of cases being filed today, however, is gradually inuring us to the voodoo about lawsuits. Ten years ago, companies and individuals who sued each other absolutely refused to discuss their cases with the press. Lawyers for both sides used to say that they didn't want to influence the judge and jury. But what they really meant was that lawsuits were embarrassing—even for lawyers—and talking about a case, even if you were sure to win, was bound to create a bad public image.

Now, slowly, things are changing. People are beginning to see the public-relations value of talking about a lawsuit in the press. A case can be won with society at large, even if it is eventually lost with judge and jury.

Public relations seems to be at least one of the main reasons Sears, Roebuck filed suit against the U.S. government in February 1979. The nation's largest department store contended in its suit that the bureaucracy had created so many conflicting laws that Sears was forced to disobey at least some of them. The timing of that action was no coincidence: Sears was then facing a Justice Department indictment on the charge of discriminating against blacks and women.

For several weeks after the filing, public debate was divided on the merits of the case, which had been reported on page one of several metropolitan daily papers. And though the case was immediately dismissed as groundless (the indictment was handed down anyway), the tactic was a partial success, winning the company more publicity than it could probably afford to buy, as well as public support from some sections of the business community, some of whom were willing to buy copies of the company's complaint and briefs at $250 a set.

The controversy over America's litigation habits frequently centers on the allegation that too many bizarre and "frivolous" suits are filed. Justin Stanley, former president of the American Bar Association, once suggested that people who file baseless suits be either fined or held in contempt of court. Stanley was particularly irked by a suit filed by a county jail inmate in Tampa, Florida. The inmate sued an NBC network affiliate for $3 million over the station's televising of the World Series. It couldn't be a "world" series, the inmate complained, because only United States teams could enter.

Though the case was immediately thrown out of federal court, Stanley used it as an example of a suit that should never be filed in the first place. "We should no longer harbor the view that access to the courts is free to those who abuse their process," he said.[7]

Frequently, however, the difference between a serious lawsuit and a frivolous one is a matter of personal perspective. Lately, for example, we've heard about the difficulties endured by manufacturers regarding product liability suits. In one case, a woman using a public toilet in a restaurant stood up on the commode because the floor was too dirty. She slipped off the seat and hurt herself, then sued the toilet-seat manufacturer for having made shoddy goods. After a trial, she was awarded about $10,000, only to have it collapse upon high-court review on the theory that toilet seats are not made to be stood upon.

Manufacturers are screaming for legislative protection from product suits, hoping to immunize themselves against rising insurance premiums. They would have us believe that most of their cases are like the toilet-seat suit, a waste of taxpayers' money. Obviously, they would rather point to such seriocomic cases than to ones involving children whose pajamas catch fire. On the other hand, the consumer movement tends to worship litigation with a kind of blind faith. They (and their friends the trial lawyers) believe suing is a form of free speech, a potent political weapon without which the shopper might be all but ignored.

While these two competing interests—consumer and industrialist—remain deadlocked, the underlying social event is perhaps just as significant: Rather than boycotting, picketing, or using any of a host of other devices for getting manufacturers' attention, people are suing.

In discussing why Americans sue, we begin with the basic assertion that lawsuits initiated by private individuals (as opposed to corporations and government officials) generally have an emotional component, a need to win, to make bringing suit—and continuing to completion—worthwhile. The dream of victory, in all its manifestations, is the hidden agenda that brings Americans into court, often against the

advice of their counsel, and keeps them fighting their lawsuits long after all is lost. Court critics tend to disparage the
warlike "me against you" adversary system, but, like it or not,
winning is an all-too-human need. Man is a "games player,"
or *homo ludens,* according to the sociologist Johan Huizinga.
The first legal systems were contests, games, jousts with fate,
he informs us. In these ancient systems, Huizinga writes,
"Justice is made subservient—and quite sincerely—to the rules
of the game."[8]

Though modern man prefers to think of his efforts in
court as the pursuit of "abstract righteousness," quite often,
as we shall see, the old "games player" in us is urging us on.

Of course, some legal cultures are more games-oriented
than others. In attempting to solve our litigation problem,
many court critics look longingly at the example of the Japanese, who have one-twentieth as many lawyers per capita
as the United States, and a concomitantly smaller lawsuit
case load as well. But few among us, if answering honestly,
would prefer to adopt the Japanese attitude toward litigation if it meant facing the despair and helplessness that afflicted the fishermen of Minimata Bay. In 1956, the tiny fishing villages of this Japanese seacoast started suffering the
effects of mercury poisoning. Not only were fish dying, but
babies born to Minimata fishermen had severe nervous dis-
orders, wobbly heads, and rashes. The middle- and working-
class people of the cities were afflicted, too, as they ate the
fish caught in the bay.

Yet, imbued as they were with the time-honored tradition of *gamon*—the famed Japanese "grin and bear it" stoi-
cism—the victims categorically refused to sue, even after their
symptoms were positively linked to mercury dumping. And
rather than blame the industrial plant that did the dumping, the victims blamed themselves, believing, as some of
them later confided to an American researcher, that they
suffered radiation poisoning because they were "too greedy"
and like to eat fish too often. It took a full twelve years for
the self-blame of the victims to be transformed into intense

rage at their situation, and only then, in 1968, were the first lawsuits filed.[9]

In the United States, that twelve-year transition is commonly hurdled in months. Still, if we are proud that Americans in times of trouble know how to protect themselves—know how to get angry—we must also accept the fact that sometimes we get fighting mad about problems not really worth the bother. We sue for all sorts of reasons, and sometimes we pay a price.

There's an obsessional quality to the pursuit of justice; it tends to take over entire lives. For the person who needs to be right, and to have others assure him he's right (which is often a basic motivation behind litigation), the pursuit of justice can become an endless chase. Our lawbooks are replete with cases of people litigating the same case over and over again, adamantly refusing to accept an adverse judgment, always hoping the next judge will see things their way.

(Sometimes, however, relitigation is a strategy. The Internal Revenue Service, for example, has been known to encourage those taxpayers who object to certain IRS policies to litigate the question, rather than reach a compromise. "If the IRS loses at the circuit [trial] court level," wrote Donald P. Lay, judge of the federal court of appeals in Nebraska, in an article for *Judicature* magazine, "too often its response is not to file [an appeal] but to continue to litigate in other circuits in hopes of getting a different result. There are clear examples of cases where several circuits have unanimously ruled against the IRS, but it still refuses to accept the decision or petition for [appeal]."[10] The reason for this refusal is clear: If the U.S. Supreme Court rules against the IRS, the policy must be thrown out. Until the High Court rules, the IRS can claim the illegality only represents one judge's opinion.)

In all kinds of ways, lawsuits take their toll. Three U.S. soldiers sued President Nixon to stop the bombing of Cambodia in 1971. All three sacrificed high-paying, respected careers in the armed forces in order to do so, enduring the scorn of their commanding officers, ostracism by their peers, and misunderstanding by a great part of the American public. Still, they did what they thought was right and, years after their case ended, they do not regret their action.

That Americans continue to sue, despite the obvious and well-known hardships in the system, is at least partially attributable to the romantic image of litigation created by the national press. Suing is a public event. Participating in a case is a way to make a mark in history, to escape obscurity or anonymity, to be part of the national dialogue.

Of course, fewer than 1 percent of the estimated 22,000 lawsuits filed every day get reported in the newspapers, so stardom through suing cannot be taken for granted. Still, although this is impossible to prove, the image of the litigant as a potent David capable of taking on an endless variety of Goliaths is an inherent part of the role of suing today.

"Dogged Doctor Refuses to Give Up Case Against Big Farmers" ran the headline in *The Los Angeles Times* in its second annual feature article on the exploits of seventy-year-old Dr. Ben Yellen who pursued his lawsuit against Imperial Valley (California) landowners to the U.S. Supreme Court. Yellen wanted the Court to enforce a 1902 law which said that in order for a farmer to avail himself of cheap federal water, his farm could be no larger than 160 acres. Yellen lost, but *The Times* presented him as a folk hero. " 'I've got a lot of fighting to do before I turn up my toes,' " the "diminuitive physician" was quoted as saying.[11]

In their attention to what goes on in court—who sues, why, and what happens to them—the media infuse the act of suing with some of the homespun qualities of a country fair. The litigant is portrayed in the manner of a contestant in a pie-baking or cattle-judging contest—as an upstanding citizen, serious but slightly adorable. Regardless of what is at stake in the suit, the participants are rarely depicted as threatening our basic society. (Contrast this to the ominous and alarming portraits of newly discovered "revolutionaries" or "radicals" who eschew the courthouse, even if they espouse other intellectual, nonviolent methods.) Litigants get high marks for working within the system.

The relatively innocuous style of press coverage is quite in keeping with the general tone and purposes of lawsuits themselves. A lawsuit is essentially a social act, a *conservative* act. The purpose of the law itself, as Paul Bohannon has written, is to control conflict so that members of society can live together in harmony and social intercourse be continued. The domination of law and lawyers in American society indicated to the nineteen-century French journalist Alexis de Tocqueville that this nation would long be free of tyranny. For however angry both sides may be, their willingness to come together in a court of law signifies that they have some degree of faith in the rules of our society.

But however conservative a lawsuit might be, it is often too radical a tactic for certain segments of the American public. After the fiery summers of the early 1960s, Congress created the Office of Economic Opportunity, with a legal-services branch of 2500 attorneys ready to represent the poor. These new lawyers were immediately successful in their lawsuits against government agencies—lowering barriers to qualify for welfare, for example. But these successes angered the very congressmen who had voted to establish the new organization; they saw these lawyers as revolutionaries out to destroy the system even as they were using it. Mark Arnold, assessing President Johnson's War on Poverty for *The New York Times* magazine, called the legal services program among the two most effective innovations of the era (the other one was Head Start for preschoolers).[12] In 1974, President Nixon attempted to gut the legal-services program, only to be stopped by court order. The controversy over taxpayer financing of lawyers for the poor (part of a larger question of this country's dedication to economic equality and justice) continues in muted form to this day.

A lawsuit functions as news, as a three-sided communication between two opposing factions and the members of the society in which the dispute is occurring. Even if a case is never reported in the press, the participants do their best to publicize their problems themselves, hoping to gather to their side the moral support of an approving public.

In simple agricultural societies where everyone seems to know everyone else, news travels fast along an informal grapevine. When a wrongdoer is identified, the weight of public opinion may cause him to change his ways. But in complex industrial societies like ours, press coverage becomes more crucial. In fact, it may actually substitute for a sense of "community" which otherwise is lacking. Laura Nader, the anthropologist, suggests that the major problem of our day is that people who sue do not know and have no access to the people and institutions they hope to effect. A woman who took a hormone that later caused cancer may have to sue a drug manufacturer in Switzerland. An automobile passenger in Oklahoma, burned in a crash, may be suing an auto manufacturer in Detroit. Bureaucracies are faceless, and the chance to make an impact is slight. Press interest in a lawsuit and the issue it presents helps even the score, not only by coverage of court proceedings but by identifying, through pictures and interviews, the people and procedures being criticized. Press coverage provides the face-to-face contact that all communities need in order to make justice work.

The Sunday *Times* of London had an "insight team" investigate the worldwide thalidomide tragedy, in which the sedative drug, when given to pregnant women, caused hundreds of malformed babies. Only in the United States, the insight team concluded, did the victims of thalidomide get anything approaching a just compensation. Our laws, they said, made it easier to prove the drug had caused the atrocities. Our attorneys, too, were more willing to take these cases, because they shared a percentage of future proceeds. But the press, they found, was the key.

"The American press did not do much investigating of the thalidomide disaster," they write in the book *Suffer the*

Children, "but the American lawyers involved in thalidomide cases all give credit to the newspapers for helping them to thrust their cases into the public mind—in precisely the way that was banned in Britain."[13] Getting the case into the public mind, of course, influenced the potential jury, which eventually returned a generous verdict.

It's important—and perhaps surprising—to recognize that these high-profile lawsuits that monopolize the press, and consequently shape the public's basic ideas about justice, comprise but a small percentage of all the litigation in our courts. Individuals rarely use the courts to further what might be called their "destiny." It is only recently, over the past two decades, that historians and social scientists have begun digging up musty court records, piecing together the role of suing in American society. But the picture now emerging is of a court that is basically the province of big business, organizations, and governments. Despite the advances of the Warren and Burger courts in allowing individuals greater opportunity to sue, statistics suggest that the individual American appears in court when he either gets divorced, has an automobile accident, or is sued by an organization or the government.[14] The picture commonly held of a nation at war and using the court as its battlefield does not emerge from the statistics now available.*

But so dominating and convincing is the battlefield image that researchers are surprised when their findings contradict it. In one study of state courts in three midsize American cities, one sociologist reported his surprise that few if any headline-making types of cases had been filed. Cases of fraud and deceit, libel and slander, and taxpayer suits alleging abridgment of civil rights did not appear among the 7800 cases surveyed. Products liability and medical malpractice——also in the news—amounted to only 1 percent of his sample. And public-interest lawsuits—the cases that aim to stop the

---

* For a breakdown of the federal court case load, see *Management Statistics for United States Courts,* 1979, and case-load descriptions from the various state courts.

building of bridges and the leveling of mountains—amounted to only 3 percent of his survey.[15]

This study only confirms what courtwatchers everywhere soon learn: Courts are basically used by corporate entities. The big business of courts is debt collection and contract compliance (making people live up to their business promises). Organizations sue, individuals tend to be sued. When individuals take on large and powerful entities, they rarely win, because, as sociologist Marc Galanter writes, the very legal system itself is designed so that "the haves come out ahead": That is, the repeat users—those same large corporations and governments—have the inside track just from their sheer knowledge of the system; the "little guy," despite the media image to the contrary, has an uphill battle.[16, 17]

The domination by business interests is apparently an old story in American litigation history. In seventeenth-century New Haven, the pattern was that the wealthiest classes initiated the most suits. And the richest class of all—the merchants —generally started more lawsuits than all the other classes combined. Then as now, when poor people showed up in court, they were there as defendants.[18]

While business concerns continue to dominate our courts today, Lawrence M. Friedman and Robert Percival, two Stanford University legal anthropologists, note with alarm the growing caseloads of lawsuits that aren't really arguments at all. Examining court business in two California cities over an eighty-year period, the two professors found that the courts are increasingly occupied with routine administrative procedures, such as uncontested divorces and automobile-accident cases in which insurance companies settle before trial. "Neither of these types of cases are 'true disputes' between two contending parties," they write. "No doubt courts are still very useful, but they are almost totally unused by ordinary individuals to resolve *personal problems*."[19]

The picture emerging from scholarly research, then, is in almost complete opposition to the rather sexy David v. Goliath image coming at us from the media. But as it turns out, neither picture is a lie. The courts in America today operate on two separate and distinct levels: one being the bureaucratic, debt-collecting, business-oriented sphere; the other a symbolic, somewhat romantic sphere of "justice" as this nation wishes it to be. Statistically, Friedman and Percival may be right—the courts are rarely used by so-called ordinary individuals. But symbolically, it is clear that these same "ordinary" individuals feel intimately involved with the actions of courts, some of them feeling that the courts are *too* much involved in private affairs. A Boston judge orders school desegregation; a woman's group undertakes a massive sex-discrimination case; a jury rules that AT&T is a monopoly and must pay $1 *billion* to a competitor who was hurt by its practices. These cases make up a small percent of the court docket, but interest and affect thousands of "ordinary" people.

It is in this symbolic sphere that the media play an important role, by helping to create the sense of community within which the court can operate. When people feel detached from each other, when a legal decision seems irrelevant to anyone other than the individual affected, then the court's work becomes relatively meaningless. By dramatizing the power of judges, the media imbue them with authority; by publicizing and interpreting judicial rulings, the media broadcast the principles that (at least for that moment) are to be lived by in our society; by personalizing the plaintiff and defendant of any case, they help create the sense of duty and obligation which define justice as a two-way street; and by following up on the appeals, reversals, and inevitable ineffectiveness of any particular case, they build or defeat expectations about the nature of fairness and equality.

The press thus creates within our culture at least the appearance of what scholars call "bicentric" or "multicentric" power, in which two or more warring or opposing factions are of approximately equal strength.[20] The appearance of multicentrism is probably crucial to the continuation of our belief in justice. The use of lawsuits is an affirmation that the individual *can* fight against big corporations, the government, his own employer, the faceless bureaucracies that rule his life—that he has equal power against his adversaries through the courts. If we didn't think so, if we truly believed we were powerless and that the "haves" really do come out ahead, we probably wouldn't bother to litigate at all. But we might very well revolt.

In a far less serious manner, gossip is an inherent part of "justice," too. Through lawsuits, the powerful are brought low, and the meek, in Andy Warhol's words, get their fifteen minutes of fame. We all note with interest when Virginia O'Hare wins $850,000 from her doctor because he moved her belly button two inches off-center. Newspapers and television cater to this love of gossip. The New York *Post,* in typical tabloid fashion, filled us in on every available detail of Ms. O'Hare's case, even showing us pictures of her belly button, which, according to testimony, was moved because she underwent a "tummy tuck" in order to have a "nice, flat, sexy belly" rather than the round breadbasket she had before the operation. We talk about her, we stare. And is Ms. O'Hare embarrassed by the exposure? Hardly. For a moment she is a national hero, her award against her doctor treated like a winning ticket in the Irish Sweepstakes or a lucky pull on a one-armed bandit in Las Vegas.

Of course, the glare of the public spotlight makes the courts doubly attractive to litigants who have a performing frame of mind. Michelle Triola Marvin, whose name has come to symbolize legal rights for unmarried lovers, spent years trying to become an entertainer before her lawsuit thrust her into the public spotlight. With long dark hair, wide eyes, she advanced an image that was part Annette Funicello and part Elizabeth Taylor, yet her singing career proved eminently forgettable and she was consigned to bit parts, mostly in "B" movies.

Michelle might not have sued her former lover, Academy Award–winning actor Lee Marvin (*Cat Ballou*) to gain stardom for herself. (She legally adopted his name when she started singing professionally.) But people should be held responsible for the attorneys they select. Michelle took her woes to Marvin Mitchelson, a Los Angeles attorney known for his publicity cases involving the wives of big-name stars (among them Tony Curtis, Rod Steiger, and Alan Jay Lerner). When he handled Rhonda Fleming's divorce, the press was in attendance for weeks. Mitchelson introduced into evidence a pack of love letters the actress's husband had sent. For days during the trial she cried both on the stand and in the pressroom. Mitchelson, well-dressed, blond, and cornily sincere, held her hand the whole way, making sure courthouse reporters didn't miss a tear.

And so, by retaining Mitchelson, Michelle was almost certainly casting herself in the role of scorned lover, the kind of part director Mitchelson knew best. She claimed that Lee had promised her half of everything he earned during the nearly six years they lived together. She insisted she gave up her singing career at his request, and was his wife in all but name.

It so happened that live-in love was a big issue for feminists during the late 1970s. Michelle soon found herself the woman of the hour, the champion of legal and social rights for unmarried lovers everywhere. Her epic "palimony" lawsuit played for eleven media-packed weeks during the spring of 1979 in the Los Angeles Superior Court.* By trial's end, Michelle was nationally famous, a star of *People* magazine, the *Enquirer,* and the California *Family Law Reporter.* As they say in the movie business, she had true "crossover" potential, meaning she had appeal to audiences of many stripes.

Incidental to her newfound fame, Michelle also ended the trial with a judgment for $104,000 against the actor, which kindhearted Judge Arthur K. Marshall had awarded her so she might "rehabilitate" herself. That $104,000, however, remained a paper judgment for at least two years, while Lee appealed to a higher court. Michelle's financial plight came

* *Marvin* v. *Marvin,* 18 C. 3d 660, 557 P. 2d 106 (1976).

to light in the summer of 1980, when she was arrested for shoplifting in Beverly Hills.

As for Mitchelson, he may be remembered as the first member of his profession to be shown taking a bubble bath in his office on the television show "60 Minutes." He obviously had no concept of invasion of privacy. His five-year investment in the Marvin case more than paid off in new clients rushing to his antique- and art-laden offices. Within a year, he was handling the affairs of Bianca Jagger (wife of Rolling Stones' star Mick Jagger) and the wife of an Arab sheik whose estate was reportedly worth more than $1 billion. Nevertheless, Mitchelson asked the state of California to pay him half a million dollars in legal fees for representing Michelle, claiming his lawsuit was a public service. His request was denied.

Lee Marvin claims he also profited, in other ways. The trial, he says, taught him how to lie—"Everyone lied." He also had the judge's opinion that the actor had never promised Michelle he'd give her half of everything. Michelle made that claim, but Lee insisted she mistook "hunger for love." Lee wanted his victory pure, or so it seems. His appeal insists that Michelle is not entitled to anything from him, including a contribution to her rehabilitation.

Moreover, the trial gave his career a hefty boost. Lee, whose ancient ancestor Matthew Marvin was the first chief justice of the state of Connecticut, was cast in the role of courtroom "heavy," a one-man stand-in for old-style male chauvinism of the love-'em-and-leave-'em variety. This, of course, was precisely the rough-and-tough sort of chap he'd played in dozens of films throughout his career, and now he played it to the hilt. When Michelle testified about his drunkenness, he had witnesses talk about her other boy friends. He made her testify about her abortions, her limited singing talent, her laziness. Did he love her in 1964 when they traveled together down to San Blas, Mexico? "No," Marvin said crustily. "The fishing was bad." He made it appear he had never loved her at all.

His courtroom performance was a stellar success. He had been a popular screen personality for more than two decades, but now he became truly famous, as the writer Jimmy Breslin commented, for being "involved in a lawsuit with a woman." Cabdrivers hailed him as their hero. In the days after the trial ended, he couldn't walk down New York City streets without getting his hand shaken every few minutes by admiring strangers. Thanks to this lawsuit, Marvin's once-slumping box-office drawing power was on the rise and he again was being offered starring roles at the $2 million per picture to which he'd grown accustomed.

The fact that a lawsuit like this one can have capricious side effects for both participants is part of the reason why litigation in America has such a patina of disrepute. The Marvin case in particular earned snickers from the press and from attorneys alike (both groups remaining fascinated by it nevertheless) as a "media circus" or a pure concoction of an imaginative attorney's mind. Marvin Mitchelson's reputation with his peers probably wasn't helped much when he admitted in the *National Law Journal* that Michelle's case had problems that he had suspected would make it difficult to win.[21] For more than half a decade Mitchelson had pressed forward with this case, insisting that Michelle—and, by extension, all unmarrieds—be allowed her day in court. But with this latest admission he confirmed what court observers had long thought: that the case itself was a weak thread on which to hang such a strong right.

We Americans prefer to take our disputes seriously, if we have to take them at all. But the curious fact is that almost all lawsuits may be said to have "ulterior" motives—that is, goals other than the ostensible ones written on the legal complaints. Obviously, a suit to collect a debt might be supposed to seek just that. But even here, watch out: The annals of our appellate courts tell many stories of debt collection where the debtor later complained that the real goal was to ruin his reputation or even wipe him out of business. The fact that someone is willing to file suit is often an indication that he or she is either really angry or really hungry for something. Intense emotions are involved, and, once raised, are not easily quelled.

Furthermore, because suing is such a public act, more than the hopes and dreams of the actual parties are at stake. Michelle Marvin's problems, for example, had meaning far beyond the level of gossip to scores of women and men who have been in her position. Before women's liberation, Michelle might have been embarrassed to bring her case to court, fearful of being castigated as a loose woman or a gold digger. But by a coincidence of timing, her case was transformed to the level of sociology. By 1978, even the all-male California Supreme Court was forced to recognize that upwards of two million people nationally were living together in what was formally known as "sin." To deprive these individuals of their right to sue, as was the rule throughout the nation until Michelle Marvin came along, was to condone an injustice. The court, which traditionally had made it its duty to promote the sanctity of marriage and discourage people from flouting society's moral code, could no longer force its views on a growing minority who, for various personal reasons, chose alternative life-styles. Within two years of Michelle's victory, seventeen other states had followed suit, granting unmarrieds the right to go to court to enforce broken promises.

Behind the scenes, a number of special-interest groups were hoping that Michelle would win. They filed petitions with the California court, attempting to convince the justices that Michelle's was not an isolated instance of a lover left holding an empty bag of troths at an affair's end. Lovers routinely act poorly toward each other after the passion dies, but these lobbying groups—among them feminists, antifeminists, and homosexuals—argued that something should be done about this dastardly state of affairs. The cure, these advocates implied, was to let them fight it out in court.

These groups might have had to wait decades to accumu-

late sufficient political clout to achieve passages of laws granting unmarried hetero- and homosexual couples the right to
sue to have their contracts protected. But by appealing to the
court, and using the Marvin lawsuit as their vehicle (and letting the press focus and change public opinion), they short-
circuited the political process.

Yes, of course, the Marvin case was an "entertainment," an
example of the "bread and circuses" of public life which some
might take as a sign of corruption and social decay. It offered
the diversion of a rich and famous movie star being exposed
as something of a lout, and gave the masses an inside view of
Hollywood life and mores. But because it also reflected the
hopes and desires of thousands of average citizens, causing
them to mobilize behind its flag, the case takes on some of the
more significant aspects of "theater" as perhaps the Greeks
knew it: a modern morality play, with a Damon Runyon
touch.

Whether in fact we are the most litigious nation on earth
has never been documented, but we accept it as fact because
we've heard it so often, and having heard it so often, we assume it must be bad.

But interestingly, Dov Levine, a High Court judge in
Israel, told me *his* people are "the most litigious on earth," a
character trait he traces to the argumentative nature of tal-
mudic debate. And the Barotse of Northern Rhodesia like-
wise are prone to suing, as are many of the other tribes in
Africa. The Zapotec Indians of Mexico not only have great
numbers of disputes, they have at least three levels of courts,
including recourse to the supernatural, to make sure their
problems get solved.

Whether or not we actually litigate more than any other
people, we are unquestionably vocal about and sensitive to
the impact of lawsuits on the "justice" system, our economy,
and ultimately on our nation's social fabric. Inevitably, part

of this sensitivity stems from the highly visible role of attorneys, whom Tocqueville praised as the only true members of the American aristocracy, but who otherwise are traditionally and universally scorned (since the time of Shakespeare) as provocateurs unworthy of public trust.

With more than 400,000 lawyers, the villainous image must inevitably fit some, though the vast majority of American lawyers never see the inside of a courthouse other than to fight their own traffic tickets. Most of their time is spent either writing wills or engaged in business negotiations designed to avoid the necessity for future litigation. Nevertheless, the public image of the profession is of a troublemaking breed, promulgating litigation where otherwise only peace would reign.

Lawyers are their own worst enemies in this regard, having a masochistic tendency toward muckraking in their own backyard. They appear to get pleasure out of writing books and articles informing the public how bad they are, how exorbitant are their fees, and how unethical their standards. (See, for example, *Verdict on Lawyers,* edited by Ralph Nader and Mark Green, and Laurence Tribe's article for *Atlantic,* "Too Much Law, Too Little Justice.") [22] It should not be forgotten that attorneys advocating reform may be careerists, too, standing to gain financially and prestige-wise from their stance.

Concentrating on the alleged villainy of the legal profession, however evil may be its ways, only heightens the swashbuckling image that attorneys secretly relish and that the public enjoys—at least when viewed from afar. Periodicals catering to lawyers suggest the kind of fantasy worlds some attorneys inhabit. *The American Lawyer,* a monthly publication with a jazzy, muscular reporting style, imbues even the limpest branches of the profession with a sexy, tough-minded masculinity. ("Bond Counsel: New Race for the Riches"; "The Houdinis of Libel Law.") Trial lawyers, of course, are the stars. They have the brain and brawn of big-league athletes, at least according to their own mythology. "D.C.'s Toughest Litigators" was a story about the Washington, D.C., law firm Howrey & Simon. A front-page exposé of "New York's Healthiest Big Firms" made the sports image explicit: A full-page drawing depicted six lawyers dressed as baseball players in New York Yankee pinstripes, waving their hats in victory at a far-off adoring crowd. This approach apparently strikes home with the tabloid's attorney readers. *The American Lawyer* reports an 80-percent renewal rate and concentrates its readership in the thirty-five-to-fifty-five age bracket.

Criticizing the bar for creating litigation is a political dead-end. For one thing, lawyers are legislators, too. For another, both the bar and the public are fond of the trial lawyer as a national hero: Paul Bunyan with portfolio. Everyone loves Clarence Darrow. Abe Lincoln, lawyer, is an American fairy tale. These two giants are part of the reason thousands of young people flock to law school each year.

David Reisman, a Harvard professor trained as a lawyer before becoming a sociologist, suggests that many young lawyers are attracted to the profession by an "obsolescing image" of the work that lawyers actually do. Motivated by a dream of themselves as country lawyers or trial lawyers à la Darrow, he writes, these young people may believe that "trying a case . . . is somehow more real" than the work they ultimately find themselves doing at the desk of a major corporate law firm. Government lawyers, in-house counsel (full-time legal advisers to major corporations), and insurance lawyers, who make up so much of the breed, Reisman writes, may "feel themselves not quite lawyers, not quite independent professionals."[23]

As long as the trial bar continues to occupy high ground, litigation will figure prominently in the American arsenal of social weapons. The first colonists attempted to outlaw lawyers, thinking that way they'd eliminate lawsuits. This movement faded fast—the colonists needed lawyers' services more than they feared them. The message from those early days no doubt is binding upon us today: We can, and should, reform the legal profession, but nothing short of revolution will eliminate it.

The continuing controversy about the role of attorneys in fomenting litigation obscures an equally important problem regarding the nature of justice in America. Specifically, what does the American litigant seek when he comes to court?

To read the historians, love of lawsuit was planted with the first ears of corn, the first grains of wheat. No sooner had the Pilgrims landed at Plymouth Rock and marked their homesteads than they found themselves before a magistrate arguing about deeds and land titles. The educated colonists learned to love the law almost as a second religion, not merely because it aided them in their fast-growing businesses, but also as a form of diversion. Law was the science fiction, the pop psychology, of the day, subject to endless debate and tavern chatter. Far removed as they were from the intellectual and artistic salons of Europe and London, the colonists made their own love of law the subject of great philosophical ferment. This ardor coincided with a vogue for simplified legal writing in England (where most law applicable in the colonies was written), which made the law easily understood even by less-well-educated Americans.

"Generally, in our colonies," wrote Dr. William Douglass, "particularly in New England, people are much addicted to quirks in the law." A "very ordinary country man in New England," Douglass said, knew enough law to pass as a "country-attorney" in England. The most popular "simple" lawbook was Blackstone's *Commentaries on the Laws of England*. Edmund Burke, visiting the colonies just before the Revolution, was surprised to discover that nearly as many copies of the tome were sold here as at home, though the colonies had about half the population.

The colonists loved the law for its intellectual stimulation, but they enjoyed the court for its drama and fun. Life in the colonies was a pretty grim affair. The nearest neighbor might be acres away, and anyway, the religious groups that had come here for liberty were humorless, straitlaced folk who censored most forms of entertainment. Harsh winters, inhospitable soil, sometimes unfriendly (or at least terrifying) Indians only deepened the furrows on the serious New Englander's brow.

Into this bleak existence came the courthouse—a lively break from the dismal ordinariness of colonial living, a breath of springtime for these gossip-starved souls, calling for an unbuttoning of even the stuffiest shirt. John Adams's diaries bloom with delight at the opening of court in the mid-1700s. The court and all its personnel traveled from village to village, town to town, cutting a circuit throughout the state of Massachusetts, and finally arriving in Adams's adopted town of Braintree at the first festival of spring, about the second week of May. The town came alive with anticipation, and as the judges and lawyers arrived, horse races, evening dances, and general partying broke out on their behalf. A school holiday was declared when court met, and so many out-of-towners came to see the courtroom fights that all the rooming houses in town were completely filled. Writes Adams's biographer:

> Court week meant the end of winter, the end of snow and silence and bitter unremitting cold. . . . [The lawyers] came by chaise and on horseback, their briefs and lawbooks in their saddle bags, their servants behind on their horses borrowed from spring plowing. One and all —judge, lawyer, plaintiff, defendant, and juryman—were pleased to be in town, primed for courtroom triumphs or a little quick money from the business picked up on the outside.[24]

John Adams, who was then a schoolteacher, was so attracted to the ceremony and vitality of the legal debates that he spent his whole week's vacation in the courthouse watching the proceedings, then adjourning with the lawyers, judges, and court retainers to the local bar for still more discussion of the law and the merits of the cases just heard.

And when court week was over, social life in Braintree curled up and died. Adams's spirits "went down and stayed down." "I have no books, no time, no friends," he wrote in his diary one mournful day when court had packed up. "I must therefore be contented to live and die an ignorant fellow."[25]

It's easy to see why courts were so popular, and why the clergy looked upon lawyers as the devil's advocates. The clergy initially endeavored to hold down the influence of the courts by serving as judges themselves. They were, in fact, the only ones qualified to serve in the post, for the new country lacked a trained judiciary and at least the clerics were educated in canonical law. The nation's first law school, Litchfield, in Connecticut, did not open until 1784, so throughout the colonial years and most of the eighteenth century, lawyers were ill-trained, unorganized, and unprofessional, and the lay judges were even worse. (John Adams referred to his untrained brethren as "wigmakers" and "shoemakers" who brought "dirty and ridiculous litigations.")

Nevertheless, when Tocqueville visited the new nation in about 1815, he was profoundly impressed by the role of the law, and litigation, in American life. Legal argument, Tocqueville wrote, "is substituted for [religious] faith, and calculation for the impulses of sentiment." Not only does law substitute for religion, he declared, the courts are the inevitable resting place of most political action as well. "Scarcely any political question arises in the United States," he wrote, "that is not resolved, sooner or later, into a judicial question."

The law permeated American society. It was the language of the Republic, taught at universities, not as training for a profession but because law was a key to theology and philosophy. Historian Daniel Boorstin has written that the law to this new nation was the language of "dreams-come-true." The lawsuit, he suggests, served as a legal test for how well the nation was living up to its original goals, and constituted a "conserving narcissism not often found among non-primitive nations."[26]

With respect to lawsuits, our nation has changed little in two hundred years. We still have that "conserving narcissism," that desire to keep the faith. The Declaration of Independence, quickly translated into the Bill of Rights, is still interpreted as a legally binding promise to citizens about the quality of life. No mere utopian ideal, these articulated guarantees of life, liberty, and property are continually, daily tested in courts throughout the land. Unlike most legal systems, writes Graham Hughes in *The Conscience of the Courts,* "standards of fairness and equality are built solidly in the heart of the [U.S.] legal system, so that in the United States it is often difficult to make a sharp distinction between what is moral argument and what is legal argument. . . ."[27]

In our own post-Freudian era, it is equally difficult to distinguish between what is legal argument and what is merely psychological release for the litigant. The law still remains the language of "dreams-come-true," but today we tend to define those dreams in psychological terms. Not content merely with religious and political (in the sense of Democrat versus Republican) uses of the courts, today Americans have transformed the lawsuit into an all-purpose outlet for the expression of all sorts of emotions and goals. In the late twentieth century, the lawsuit is a popular vehicle of protest and grief, of social and political reform (in a wider sense of reconstructing our institutions), an insurance policy in the event of catastrophe, and a tool of vindication and harassment. Lawsuits mirror American life, reflecting the litigant's hopes and dreams.

This book looks into the mirror. It will explore some of the dominant emotions and passions that have generated our most notorious cases, acknowledging, of course, that human beings are complex and may have several motivations working at any one time. The purpose of isolating these emotions is not to insist that this or that reason alone is behind the suit, nor to recommend that courts be used for therapeutic purposes, but rather to explain how the legal system and human emotion work hand in hand.

To the extent possible, this reflection purposely excludes the role of attorneys, except where they sue on their own behalf. There has already been considerable examination of this profession's domination of our society; for the moment, it is the American litigant himself who interests us.

CHAPTER 2

Protest

Sit-down strikes, wildcat walkouts, rioting, picketing, petitioning, boycotting—all are weapons in the American arsenal of protest. The trouble with all of these methods is that, to be effective, they require huge groups of people. A sit-down strike by just one person won't do. A wildcat walkout of three workers seems pathetic. A lonely picket looks like a kook. A single name on a petition is ridiculous. A boycott staged by five won't make a dent in a manufacturer's sales report.

The lawsuit can be a unique weapon of protest. One person alone can work a minor miracle. When the Dodgers moved from Ebbets Field to Los Angeles in 1956, for example, two angry residents of the City of Angels protested the building of a new 50,000-seat stadium at taxpayer expense. Their suit challenged a secret deal by which the team received from the city 300 acres of public lands for the arena, plus half the revenue from oil on the property, should any be found. The taxpayers thought city fathers were too generous. Their lawsuit fanned the flames of controversy surrounding the baseball deal, culminating in a popular referendum in which the stadium won by only a slim margin. After the election, the lawsuit continued. Eventually, the two taxpayers lost their case,* and the arena was ready at Chavez Ravine for the 1959 season in which the Dodgers won the National League cham-

* *Louis Kirschbaum* v. *Housing Authority*, 51 C2d 857 (1959). *Julius Ruben* v. *City of Los Angeles*, 51 C2d 857; 337 P. 2d 825.

pionship. But by then the protesters had stalled construction for a full four years (a delay that also caused a $3-million increase in building costs) .[1] Twenty-five years later, when the Oakland Raiders football team decided to transplant to Los Angeles, a similar situation arose. This time, lawsuits filed by small groups of disappointed fans in both cities helped delay the move for at least one full season.[2]

The "protest" type of lawsuit appeals to the "no man is an island" facet of the American personality. Litigants think they are performing a public service by taking their government to task, and insist their cases prove this country is still "of the people, by the people." Protest lawsuits, however, are often based on a naïve notion of the judiciary as miracle worker, and consequently they may be fruitless in material results. Still, suing is a remarkable vehicle for airing public grievances. The lawsuit begins by expressing the isolated emotions of a lone disgruntled individual, but at its best strikes a chord in the public at large.

While these attempts to interfere with the "business as usual" of government may strike bureaucrats and their lawyers as a nuisance, concerned citizens continue to care enough to invest in and bring these lawsuits on principle. Three million dollars in additional costs for Dodger Stadium may seem a high cost to bear for citizen vigilance, but, in the long run, apathy is costly too. One noted legal scholar, writing on protest-type suits, notes that most people are too "indifferent" to government activity to litigate particular actions. It is unfortunate that some people interpret indifference as being in the public interest.

The attraction of the protest lawsuit derives from the fact that anyone can bring it and everyone can understand its message, which is usually a cry of "No!" at some allegedly untoward public act. Frequently people who have never before taken an active role in their government or civic life decide that *now*, this moment, they must speak out, lest some terrible wrong occur or go unpunished.

Abraham Lincoln Wirin, former head of the American Civil Liberties Union in southern California, made it a habit to file lawsuits in his own name whenever the action of government agencies—notably the police—offended him. In 1955 it was revealed that the Los Angeles police had concealed microphones in the attorney room at the local jail, where they eavesdropped on prisoners talking with their counsel. The court had recently declared wiretapping without proper judicial authorization to be illegal. Wirin filed suit, claiming that Police Chief William H. Parker was using public moneys to buy the mikes, furthering an unlawful act. Parker said it was none of Wirin's business how the police spent the city's money. But in 1957 the California high court said that Wirin, merely in his role as taxpayer, had the right to insist that no public moneys be used for these purposes. The wiretapping stopped.*

In protest suits, the dream of legal victory takes a back seat, at least initially, to the unencumbered necessity of saying one's piece. The litigant is so anxious to get into court, so eager to do *something* to register his dismay, that he often doesn't think beyond the moment. During the gasoline shortage in the late 1970s, for instance, the 900,000-member International Association of Machinists (IAM), one of America's largest labor unions, filed a lawsuit against the Organization of Petroleum Exporting Countries (OPEC).† It was a landmark action, accusing the thirteen Arab and South American member nations of fixing the price of oil in violation of U.S. antitrust laws. The IAM sought the return of billions of dollars in overpayment caused by the price-fix scheme. The IAM seemed never to have considered that this audacious act could cause a war.

The case was instigated by the union's energetic president, William W. Winpisinger. One day, while visiting with some union officials, "Wimpy" wondered aloud if there wasn't

* *Wirin* v. *Parker*, 48 C 2d 890, 313 P 2d 844 (1957).
† *IAM* v. *OPEC*, 78-5012 AAH (U.S. Dist. Ct., L.A.).

something America could do about the oil crisis. Inflation caused by rising oil prices was eating into his membership's wages.

James Davis, short, nervous house counsel to the union, mentioned an attorney acquaintance, an antitrust expert with solid academic credentials who had been waiting several years to file a lawsuit against OPEC. Wimpy was at this time trying to instill some activism into his aging and tepid constituency. A lawsuit seemed like a good idea. Davis introduced Wimpy to the lawyer, Richard I. Fine of Los Angeles.

Fine was an expert in foreign commerce, and had served on an American Bar Association committee investigating the legal impact of the 1973 Arab oil embargo. It was his opinion that American consumers—including the federal government, which itself bought OPEC oil—could bring antimonopoly lawsuits against foreign governments in U.S. courts. Such suits were authorized, he said, by a little-known law called the Foreign Sovereign Immunities Act, passed by Congress in 1976. To Fine's frustration, the government had refused to sue. But in 1978, when Fine met Wimpy, there was an immediate meeting of the minds. Lawyer and client were one. A lawsuit was prepared.

At first the lawsuit was treated as something of a joke. The press ignored it when it was filed at the end of December 1978 in downtown Los Angeles federal court. Only as the hearing date rolled around the following spring did anyone start to consider what the case could mean. Jimmy Davis, the glad-handing union attorney, insisted to whomever would listen that the lawsuit was just what the nation needed. "By the time we get through," he promised a reporter, "the entire country will be joining this suit." Davis extended an open invitation to any city or group that bought oil directly from OPEC to join the action.

When cities actually did start lining up behind him, the State Department started paying attention. The federal government, published reports suggested, was terrified of what an independent and "creative" judge might do in a case like this. Government fears were further aggravated by a story running on page one of *The Los Angeles Times* just one month before the first hearing on the case. The story, headlined "900,000 Unionists Take OPEC Suit Seriously," was written by Charles Maher, the *Times*'s new legal reporter, who had spent weeks investigating the suit, talking to law professors and antitrust experts. He concluded that the suit was legitimate.

"The suit may at first glance seem a Quixotic enterprise," Maher wrote, "but it is no joke. And if it is a publicity stunt, as some may suspect, it is a costly way to get publicity."[3]

The story laid out the peculiarities of antitrust law as it applied to foreign nations doing business in the United States. In essence the law said that if you do business here, you are bound by our laws. Further, Maher implied that if OPEC ignored the suit, the IAM could win a victory in the form of a default judgment. If a judge ordered a default, then all that remained was for the IAM to seize OPEC's bank accounts, airplanes, and other assets until the sheiks were ready to set oil prices on some rational basis.

The *Times* article was a godsend to the IAM. Carrying copies of Maher's story, Jimmy Davis went around the country enlisting cities to lend their name to the effort. A *Sacramento Bee* reporter was impressed: "For those waiting in line at gas pumps who think 'there ought to be a law,' an attorney in Los Angeles believes he found one." The *Bee* ran a major story on the case, alongside a picture of Davis.[4]

Cleveland and New Haven quickly joined the suit. Baltimore and three other cities soon followed. But at the Los Angeles City Council, the lawsuit was an object of terror.

"This sounds like a great thing," said Council President John Ferraro. "But it's a gamble. If [the Arab nations] get mad at us, it's like stepping on Superman's cape. . . . If he gets mad, what will that do to us?" Council members didn't know which was worse—joining the suit and incurring the wrath of the oil ministers, or not joining and thereby risking the loss of huge financial rewards if the suit was a winner.

After two months, the council voted to join—thus bringing to seven the number of cities supporting the IAM.

President Jimmy Carter didn't know how to regard the suit. Some of his advisers suspected Wimpy was trying to embarrass him, for Wimpy was actively pushing Senator Edward M. Kennedy to challenge Carter for the 1980 Democratic presidential nomination. Now it seemed the lawsuit was turning into a populist revolt. The State Department was aghast: It couldn't have a union and a few small cities running U.S. foreign policy. "U.S. May Help OPEC Fend Off Price Fix Suit," warned the L.A. *Times* in a June 20 story, quoting government attorneys.[5] Embarrassing and politically disastrous as it might be, the administration preferred to have OPEC win the lawsuit rather than risk war. The Carter administration, in fact, was considering filing a "friend of the court" brief, hoping to convince the judge he had no jurisdiction and should dismiss the action.

The New York Times appreciated the administration's position, but barely concealed a giggle in its June 24 editorial: "For one poignant moment last week," it said, "Jimmy Carter had a chance to experience the humiliation that the OPEC cartel daily inflicts on his country. For a president [attempting to carve out a position on the OPEC suit] it should have been the moral equivalent of the gas line."[6] But the New York paper did agree that the United States could not afford to have the IAM win its lawsuit, warning that a legal victory could be economically disastrous. Economists in London and New York were predicting that if the union won, Arab oil sheiks would withdraw their holdings from U.S. banks, resulting in the worst financial havoc since 1929.

There was dramatic tension in Judge A. Andrew Hauk's courtroom on June 25 when the first hearing was held on whether the judge should even hold another hearing on the default question. The seats were filled with the press, with random members of the public at large, and with American attorneys ashamed to admit they represented the interests of Arab oil nations. These last were in the courtroom to warn their clients of any impending ominous moves. When Judge Hauk announced he indeed would hold a default hearing in August, reporters ran for their telephones in the hallway, the attorneys stretched and yawned, and the spectators were jubilant. "It's a great victory for us, the people of the United States," said one elderly courtwatcher. "It took guts to hear this case, and this judge is not afraid to do it."

But when the August 20 hearing was held, the results were anticlimactic. It's often this way in lawsuits: a big buildup for a trial that fizzles out. Perhaps theatrical disappointment is built right into the adversary system: one side prodding the law into ever more inventive and creative directions, the other side resisting that change. A lawsuit can be a dream or a nightmare of the world to come, one that may never (and in some cases should never) come true. Richard Fine's dream of using the Foreign Sovereign Immunities Act to solve the oil crisis was one such daring dream. Judge Hauk, over four days and nights of hearings, entertained Fine's notion, but then rejected it. The case was thrown out. Hauk said he had no jurisdiction to issue a default, since the OPEC leaders never met in the U.S. when oil prices were set. After hearing expert testimony on the question of price-fixing, the judge concluded that the Arabs alone were not to blame for the crisis; U.S. companies slapped a surcharge on foreign oil, further victimizing the American consumer. So going after OPEC would solve nothing.

Hauk said he originally thought the case was "flaky," but finally complimented the attorneys, saying it was a "good case to bring" if only because it focused national attention on the energy problem.

And so the OPEC suit ended. The plaintiffs lost. But winning was never the point. The OPEC suit was street theater of a peculiarly American variety, in which the frustration of the "common man" almost triggered an international crisis. The OPEC case gave the public no easy answers, and some might call it a waste of time and money. But then, perhaps this is just what the public wanted: a graphic demonstration that, in the oil crisis, there are no simple answers. If it did nothing else, at least the lawsuit put to rest the notion that we could *sue* other nations into doing things our way.

Most protest cases fall into the basic category of "taxpayer suits"—actions by taxpayers to halt waste and unlawful use of public funds or property. The taxpayer suit has been with us since 1847, when one Mr. Adriance sued the mayor of New York City to stop him from appropriating $5000 for uniforms for the first local regiment of volunteers to the Mexican War. By the time Adriance received a court hearing, the bill for the uniforms had already been paid. Nevertheless, the fact that a judge heard his case—and agreed to stop disbursement of other funds upon Adriance's complaint—is regarded as a legal landmark.*

The taxpayer suit as a legal innovation has not had entirely smooth sailing since that time. The common law, which we inherited from England, does not permit such actions, holding that it is up to responsible elected and appointed officials to prosecute on the public's behalf. In 1856, soon after Adriance's victory, New York clamped down on taxpayer suits, ruling that a Mr. Davis, an interested citizen, could not sue to halt construction of New York's Broadway subway line.† As taxpayer suits spread nationwide, judges did their best to check them, fearing, as one West Virginia judge wrote, that "the door would be open wide to multitudinous suits filling the courts with litigation."

Despite judicial concern, Americans have returned to the taxpayer suit again and again. It's a form of litigation bathed in the pure glow of democracy. Ronald K. L. Collins and Robert M. Myers, two legal scholars, call it "one of the more effective forms of therapeutic devices genuinely available to public-minded citizens wishing to cure those ills which plague the body politic."[7]

* *Adriance v. Mayor of New York*, 1 Barb 19 (1847).
† *Davis v. the Mayor of New York*, 14 N.Y. 514 (1856).

New York set the style for taxpayer litigation. When "Boss" William Marcy Tweed ravaged the city during the 1860s, a special state law was passed encouraging citizens to sue to stop Teapot Dome abuses. Tweed's ring filched about $30 million from the city, and since the ring included prosecutors and city attorneys, there was no chance that the authorities would take action on citizens' behalf.

A decade later, as the Populist-Progressive reform period began, the taxpayer suit again became popular, along with the better-known initiative, referendum and recall. In Illinois, for example, taxpayers in 1888 successfully sued to stop an illegal state contract authorizing without bid the sculpting of eight "electro-bronze" statues of state heroes intended to grace the capitol building.*

This spotty history preceded Lonn Berney as he embarked on his taxpayer suit against H. R. Haldeman.

The story begins one evening in February 1978 when Berney was watching the CBS evening news with Walter Cronkite. What he saw on the screen made him sick. The TV news camera was on location in Brentano's bookstore in midtown Manhattan, only a few miles from where Berney lived, and the cameraman was panning over mounds of books. H. R. Haldeman, former White House chief of staff to President Richard Nixon, had just published his memoirs of the Watergate years, *The Ends of Power*. The black-and-gold books were piled high in Brentano's, one of New York City's largest bookstores. Clearly audible in the background was the chiming of cash registers ringing in the sales.

Haldeman and his fellow Nixon commandant John Ehrlichman had left office in 1974 under a cloud of suspicion. They were soon indicted for multiple offenses stemming from their involvement in the break-in at Democratic headquarters at the Watergate Hotel in June 1971. Later in 1976, they were both convicted of one count of lying under oath. But

* *Littler* v. *Jayne,* 124 Ill. 123, 16 N.E. 374 (1888) .

never since leaving the White House had the pair ever answered the questions that the public was eager to hear the answers to even half a decade later: What did they know about the Watergate cover-up, when did they know it, and when did they tell Richard Nixon? Haldeman and Ehrlichman had kept their lips sealed—until now. In *The Ends of Power,* published by the New York Times Book Company, Haldeman charged that Nixon personally launched the Watergate bugging operation, and that Nixon was part of the cover-up of the crime from the very day that the burglars were arrested.

Haldeman's book certainly could have led to Nixon's impeachment, had he remained in office, and had he not been pardoned by President Gerald R. Ford. But coming four years after Nixon stepped down in disgrace, all the book could do was sell copies and cause a flare-up of old bitterness. The deal to publish *The Ends of Power* brought Haldeman and a ghostwriter a $140,000 advance against sales. Here on CBS that February evening, the camera showed money changing hands, and piles of books beginning to move.

Watching the news that night, Lonn Berney knew he had to do something. John Dean had already published *Blind Ambition,* for a $300,000 advance against sales, and it had quickly climbed to the best-seller list. There were also the proceeds from the television "docudrama" based on the book. Jeb Stuart Magruder led the Watergate pack to the publishing hustings with *An American Life: One Man's Road to Watergate,* and now it seemed that every imprisoned defendant except John Mitchell was having his say and listening to the cash registers ring. John Ehrlichman disguised his Watergate story as fiction, and his novel *Company* starred Jason Robards as president when it was translated into the television series "Washington Behind Closed Doors." Nixon would sell autographed copies of his memoirs, *RN,* at $250 a throw when his book finally appeared.

Berney was burning. Convicts, all of them (except Nixon, and this seemed to Berney a mere technicality), and they were making fortunes off their Watergate misdeeds. Berney was a thirty-year-old lawyer with a large ego and a low tolerance for duplicity. He went to his lawbooks to see what could be done.

He knew he was inordinately angry about Haldeman, and as he sat reading cases he examined his reaction. Why was he so upset at this late date? John Dean's book had not particularly bothered him when it appeared the year before. Dean had been the White House attorney who first helped cover up Watergate, but ultimately, he testified, he had told Nixon there was a "cancer growing on the presidency." Dean's turn of phrase was rich—it made Watergate sound like *Macbeth*—and Berney approved of Dean because eventually the young man turned government evidence and brought his case before a Senate investigative committee. As for Magruder and his ilk, Berney felt they were merely cogs in the wheel.

But Haldeman was a different story. Berney was plainly offended by him. Haldeman, Ehrlichman, and Nixon. He had an endless store of anger and unrelieved venom toward these men who had turned the White House into a den of felony. When he thought about them, Berney momentarily lost his breath—and this was years after they were out of office. Perhaps he suffered from a naïve faith in the electoral process, but, as a lawyer, he considered that Haldeman, Ehrlichman, and Nixon had what attorneys call a "fiduciary relationship" with the American public—a relationship based on responsibility and trust. In their fiduciary capacity, these three officials were supposed to do what was in the best interests of the public, not use that trust for their own private gain. In publishing *The Ends of Power* and reaping the profits, Haldeman was doing just that. He was using secrets learned while in public office for the mere purpose of lining his own pockets. Facts that he had refused to disclose to the Watergate Committee he was disclosing now for his own pri-

vate gain. It was immoral, unethical, and—Berney hoped—
illegal.

The next morning Berney went to his crowded and un-
fancy law offices around the corner from New York's City
Hall. It was a casual, hang-loose office, where everyone from
secretary to law partner worked in jeans. This morning,
though, he felt a rare tension among his staff. Everyone he
met was angry about the Haldeman book.

At a meeting early that day, Berney and his partner, Norman L. Cousins, started tossing around the idea of filing a
lawsuit against Haldeman. There was nothing surprising or
unique about their discussion. All over the country, attorneys
for years had been conjecturing novel lawsuits against former
Watergate principals, searching for creative ways to make
them accountable. Fictitious lawsuits were the topic of cock-
tail-party banter wherever lawyers met. But the suits that
were actually filed after Watergate were suits by people who
had had direct contact with Nixon's malfeasance. Some 1200
antiwar demonstrators sued him after they were falsely arrested at a rally in 1971. Years later, they settled for about
$600 each. The Democratic National Committee sued Nixon
and the Republican National Committee for spying on them.
The Democrats settled for $775,000. Reporters and White
House staffers whose phones were tapped also sued, with
varying results. But by 1978 there had been no one from the
general public who had spoken out in rage and disgust at
what was widely perceived as the strain on our government
and the abuse of faith summarized in the word "Watergate."

In the Berney & Cousins office, an informal poll revealed
that everyone wanted to "do something." It was hard to go
about normal business, the staff was so incensed. But action seemed impossible. Haldeman was no longer in public
office; he was a private citizen and could no longer be fired
or demoted or otherwise hurt in any official capacity. Strictly

speaking, from the legal knowledge available at that time, it seemed as if nothing could be done.

Nevertheless, Lonn Berney could not be stopped. Even if his lawsuit did nothing, he wanted it filed anyway. He wanted to go on record as being against thievery from the public trough. If H. R. Haldeman's book was going to earn a lot of money, Lonn Berney felt that he was entitled to a share of those winnings, for he was a taxpayer who had footed the bill for Haldeman's salary. As a taxpayer, he had made it possible for Haldeman to hold the job through which he got the secrets that he was now selling. If this line of reasoning was not the law, Lonn Berney thought, then it *should* be the law.

Berney and Cousins decided to file a taxpayer's suit, a decision they probably knew was risky. While any taxpayer can file a lawsuit, the ones that have the best chance of victory are cases in which the litigant has a direct stake in the results of the misappropriation of funds. Berney would have a lot of trouble on this score. For one thing, no funds were actually being appropriated by the government and given to Haldeman; the profits from the book were coming directly from consumers. Berney's conception that Haldeman had breached a "fiduciary relationship" with the American public, and was now profiting from that breach, had never been tried in court. It was a new legal theory, one that the young attorney was adapting from business law where corporate officials have precisely this sort of trust relationship with stockholders. But government and business are two different worlds. The prospects were not bright for convincing a court that this new theory applied to H. R. Haldeman's book profits.

Furthermore, taxpayer suits had fallen on bad times. During the Vietnam War, scores of lawsuits were filed to declare the bombing of Southeast Asia to be illegal.* The question

* Among the various Vietnam War taxpayer suits, see *U.S.* v. *Richardson,* 418 U.S. 166 (1974).

of who had a right to bring suit, and for what purposes, occupied considerable court discussion while the killings continued unabated. Ultimately, most of these suits had proved
futile. Taxpayers who did not like the war on principle, and
did not want their dollars going to support it, were thrown
out of court unless they were soldiers on duty. Berney and
Cousins knew that modern judges generally dislike taxpayer
suits because it's not always clear who has standing to sue and
who is a naïve interloper using the court to express a political
opinion. Consequently, attorneys resorted to them only when
there was no other basis for getting a hearing.

Lonn Berney believed he had no other basis for getting his
views before the public. And so the taxpayer suit, shaky as it
might be, was worth a shot. This was more than a legal
theory, after all; it was an emotional statement, an act of the
heart. As an emotional statement, the taxpayer suit was per-
fectly qualified to carry his message. It was simple, direct,
and would tell everyone exactly where Lonn Berney stood
in relation to Haldeman's book. He was a taxpayer and he
wanted a return on his dollar.

Now that they had decided on a course of action, the question was: Who should be plaintiff? Berney and Cousins
could not step forward themselves, nor could any lawyer in
the office. The cynical nature of the press and the legal profession would cause the suit to be immediately branded an
attorney trick, a publicity stunt without validity. While attorneys are as prone to outrage at political events as any
other citizen, their relationship with the courts and the
public is controversial, to say the least, and fraught with misunderstanding. Most attorneys therefore are content to be
handmaidens to the actions of others, holding the cloak of
nonlawyers as they enter the legal arena. They rarely enter
the fray on their own behalf, lest they appear self-serving.

And so . . . who else could sue? Debra Jenkins, a sweet-
faced, ponytailed former psychology student was working as
a legal secretary in the office. She was twenty-four years old,
a veteran of antiwar and other social-reform protests of the

1960s, and somewhat soured on political action. Like everyone else in the office, Jenkins took offense at Haldeman's
book, and "saw red" at the notion that he was to reap some
profit from it. Would she be willing to put her name on the
lawsuit? she was asked.

"I never thought of the law as helping society," recalls
Jenkins (who was so thrilled by the experience that, after the
lawsuit was concluded, she entered law school). "I always
thought it was real estate and wills. But I was really angry at
what I'd seen on television. Haldeman made me sick. So
when Lonn said there was something we could do, I said,
'Why not?' It's something we all believed in."

Debra Jenkins thus agreed to perform the role that lawyers call "the attractive plaintiff." Like many other suits dependent upon media exposure, the protest case deals in symbols. The person bringing suit comes to personify in the
public's mind the issues he is presenting for a hearing. The
plaintiff need not be beautiful, merely someone who represents and evokes feelings shared by the average American and represents those feelings in their most palatable
form.

In one case, a young couple with a child were evicted from
their apartment and sued the landlord for the right to remain. They were media naturals, and when they appeared
on major national and local news shows to tell their tale of
woe, almost immediately a tenants'-rights protest sprang up
around them, loudly proclaiming that families with children
suffered housing discrimination. The situation was soon rec-
tified by legislation.

The "attractive plaintiff" need not be human. The snail
darter, a tiny fish on its way to becoming extinct, served the
purpose in lawsuits aimed at halting construction of a dam
in the Tennessee Valley. Whales, eagles, and porpoises also
do the job nicely.

On February 22, 1978, about three days after the publication of *The Ends of Power,* the lawsuit entitled *Debra Jenkins* v. *New York Times, Times Books and H. R. Haldeman*

was filed in New York Supreme Court.* Jenkins typed up the complaint herself and the proper legal papers were issued. H. R. Haldeman was served with a notice of pending litigation at his temporary headquarters in California, where he was serving his time in Lompoc State Prison.

As an act of public protest, the case had yet to find its audience. *The New York Times* had not yet picked up the story, and only about eight people in the country, including Haldeman himself, knew that litigation was in process. Still, the very act of filing a suit is part of a subtle ritual. Many litigants experience a mixture of excitement and relief just from the mere act of going down to the county courthouse and watching the clerk assign a case number to their legal papers. It is at this moment that the battle is joined, the enemy has been exposed for all to see, but in a polite and socially acceptable manner. Debra Jenkins and Lonn Berney had put a white-gloved hand firmly on the shoulder of a man they thought was going to run away with something belonging to them. Haldeman couldn't ignore their suit for fear of losing by default. By accepting service he acknowledged the existence of the suit, which gave Berney and Jenkins the validation they were seeking.

This recognition plays a crucial role in lawsuits between strangers. When a person feels himself victimized by the acts of some unknown, invisible force, the natural response is to strike back—but at whom? The lawsuit lets you fly right to the top, to the chief honcho him/herself if need be, with access to that person of authority guaranteed. One of the first requirements of the litigation process is the serving of legal papers on the person named in the suit. If you sue Richard Nixon, either he or his duly authorized representative (usually his attorney) must accept service and voluntarily appear in court.

As it turned out, the Haldeman suit won for Berney and Jenkins more than just the acknowledgment that they existed. Within days of the filing, the case took on the trappings

* *Jenkins v. Haldeman,* 78 Civ. N.Y. 1451 (1978).

of a crusade, a political version of faith healing, a promise of restoration of faith. An almost religious frenzy erupted in those who read about it. On March 2, 1978, two weeks after the filing, when Debra and Lonn appeared on "The Today Show," they were introduced as beguiling "citizens with a message":

"If you're one of those people who are annoyed about ex-convicts or felons cashing in on their misdeeds by writing books that we pay for, and they keep the royalties, join a woman . . . who is going to do something, she hopes, about H. R. Haldeman."

Berney and Jenkins sat side by side, answering questions put to them by Jane Pauley, the show's host. Berney outlined the case and suggested how Haldeman might respond. He predicted the former White House aide would probably defend himself by claiming that the First Amendment guarantee of free speech gave him the right to publish whatever he wanted. "I don't think it's relevant," said Berney about the First Amendment. Debra Jenkins suggested that this case was just the beginning. "You would sue former President Nixon as well?" Pauley asked. "Yes, I would," replied Jenkins.

Response to the lawsuit grew and grew. Newspapers all over the country picked up the story—the UPI wire carried it—and Jenkins, who prized her privacy, was awakened at four in the morning to talk to journalists from as far away as Australia and New Zealand. If there were holes in the hastily conceived lawsuit, reporters either didn't find them or ignored them. Berney didn't even know there was actually a New York State law prohibiting exactly the kind of unjust enrichment he was protesting. A reporter from the New York *Post* kindly called to give him the word that the so-called Son of Sam statute had been on the books for the past six months. It was passed the previous August of 1977, as a result of the hectic jockeying for the movie and book rights to the story of David Berkowitz, an accused mass murderer known as the .44 caliber killer. The law said that revenue from the sale of any tales of misdeeds would be held in escrow, awaiting any lawsuits by victims of the crime or their heirs. The profits might be used to pay the accused's attorneys fees, but otherwise would not be released unless the suspect was cleared of charges, or in four years if no civil lawsuits resulted.

The legal validity of the case, however, was not the reason for its intense public appeal. Like a pin in a filled balloon, the lawsuit exploded years of unarticulated fury at the behavior of the Nixon gang, and gave vent to a widespread craving for vengeance. Almost immediately the lawsuit was out of Berney's hands and taken into the hearts and minds of an apparently eager public. Mail poured in from all over the country. Stanley Marcus, president of Neiman Marcus and the Carter Hawley Hale stores in Dallas, wrote: "Congratulations on the filing of the lawsuit against H. R. Haldeman and his publisher. You have rendered a great public service and I sincerely hope you prevail."

Berney and Jenkins became the grass-roots experts on the responsibility of public officials—and this was clearly the red-hot issue of the day. "We're not saying to anybody, 'Don't write that book,'" they said in the *New Yorker*'s "Talk of the Town" section. "We're merely saying, 'Don't profit from it.'"[8]

Lonn Berney had a long way to go in proving his novel concept's legal validity. In preparing for court, everything that made the Haldeman case a favorite with the American public caused it to lose the respect of the legal profession. The emotionalism of this cause's true believers offended lawyers and judges, who like to keep their carnivals well starched. Clark Gurney, Haldeman's lawyer from a well-respected Wall Street firm, immediately tried to get the case out of state court and into federal on the grounds that Haldeman was in California and Jenkins was a New Yorker (the federal court having been established to solve legal problems between citizens of differing states). This was good strategy: Federal judges just might be friendlier toward a former president than state judges, who, after all, are merely appointed by a governor. And federal judges might be less impressed by the New York State "Son of Sam" statute, allowing Gurney more time to shoot down the taxpayer-suit theory.

Gurney seemed as offended by the media's clamoring after Berney and Jenkins as Berney and Jenkins were about Haldeman's book. In April, Gurney sent transcripts of "The Today Show" and copies of the *New Yorker* article to Federal Judge David N. Edelstein, who was to rule on moving the case out of state court. It was "with grave reluctance and deep regret," Gurney wrote Judge Edelstein, that he had to report that "a member of the bar" had taken such liberties as to discuss the case with the media. Gurney insinuated that Berney's appearance on the show and interviews in the media violated various canons of professional ethics guiding attorney behavior. He seemed particularly incensed that Berney had told Jane Pauley that Haldeman might want to use the First Amendment guarantee of free speech as a defense in a future trial. Gurney also suggested to Judge Edelstein that Debra Jenkins was not a bona fide client but merely a legal secretary roped into bringing a lawsuit by her publicity-seeking boss.

Berney viewed Gurney's letter as akin to a threat to have him reprimanded by the Bar Association unless he dropped the case without further ado, and he was furious. "I told them I wouldn't stand for that kind of crap," he fumed. He regarded Gurney's move as the high-pressure tactic of a silk-stockinged lawyer trying to scare off the opposition.

To Berney's pleasure, Judge Edelstein refused to hear the case, deciding he had no authority to do so, and returned it to the New York State Supreme Court where it had originally been filed. It was a tactical victory for Lonn Berney: He would have a New York judge ruling on a local statute—the ball was in his court.

And now a wonderful thing happened. With the refusal of Judge Edelstein to remove the case to federal court, Haldeman's attorneys began talking settlement. They no longer disputed Debra Jenkins's right as a taxpayer to bring the action, no longer cared to argue the validity and applicability of the "Son of Sam" law. They wanted to negotiate: Just what did Lonn Berney want? Amazingly, a case that began as purely an emotional release, a mere statement of frustration, a yearning to *do something,* seemed destined to get results.

It is one of life's little ironies that Lonn Berney, the would-be political "radical" who detested H. R. Haldeman as a symbol of the corruption of power, should feel sympathy and understanding for him once he sat across from Haldeman's representatives at the bargaining table. From Berney's new vantage point, Haldeman looked quite transformed—a man stripped of power, desperately needing the proceeds from his book so he could pay the attorneys who had represented him in his criminal case. Those legal fees would total $128,-987.* His advance from *The Ends of Power* had been $140,-000—and he had to split this amount with his coauthor.† Haldeman, Berney saw, was impotent, perhaps even desperate. He was a man no longer in charge of his own life, a man in hock to everyone.

In the years after the 1978 settlement, some would suggest that the fact that Haldeman made any income at all from *The Ends of Power* was an outrage and a violation of public trust. Others would have preferred to see the case decided by erudite opinion of the U.S. Supreme Court so there would be a final ruling on a taxpayer's right to sue in future similar cases. But Lonn Berney, thinking like a lawyer now, rather than an outraged citizen, recognized that there was little more to be won by proceeding to trial. Chances were he would never get the kind of victory he

---

* Haldeman deducted his attorneys' fees on his tax returns. A deduction of $12,737 was disallowed in California in 1980, and Haldeman sued the state income-tax board, insisting he was entitled to it. (See *Los Angeles Times,* March 26, 1980.)

† The New York Times Book Company sold serial rights to *The Ends of Power* for more than $1 million.

sought—a statement that public servants who engage in crimes must turn their profits back to the taxpayers.

"We got everything we wanted," Lonn Berney said a year after the case ended. What he got was a consent decree, a formal settlement consisting of assurances by Haldeman that the profits from *The Ends of Power* would go for attorneys' fees and for a meager living allowance. Berney was satisfied that Haldeman would not use the money to live the good life ("No swimming pools," he insisted.) And so the case ended, quietly, without public fanfare.

Says Berney: "I believe what Justice [Felix] Frankfurter said, 'I can hate what a person does, but it's quite different from hating the person.' With Haldeman, when he was far removed from me, I sued him, I hated him, I hated what he did. But when I came to know and understand him, I didn't want him to benefit from the book to the extent that I didn't want him to be enriched, but I did feel for him as a person."

Timing is critical in a protest suit. Juanita Anderson and Madge Van Horn, two Fremont, California, political activists, have sued Richard Nixon on much the same taxpayer grounds as Debra Jenkins used to sue Haldeman: They want Nixon's revenues from his memoirs, *RN,* and from the five-part David Frost television interviews, totaling about $1.3 million, to be returned to the National Treasury.* But because they waited too long, filing their case in 1979 when Nixon had already been out of office six years, their lawsuit has gotten nowhere. It has neither attracted tremendous media attention nor engendered any response from Nixon himself.

Anderson and Van Horn had high hopes for their suit. They thought that (then) U.S. Attorney General Griffin

* *People* v. *PORN et al.* v. *Richard Milhous Nixon,* No. 79-4129, Northern District of California.

Bell might pursue the action for them, as is possible when private persons take on litigation in the public interest. But Bell did not act, and the two women and their attorney, William Jennings, were left on their own.

An endless round of appeals began. Nixon won one procedural round after another, even shifting the case to federal court, where some of his own appointees were on the bench. Several years after starting her case, Madge Van Horn is disgusted. "The old routine is that if you bury something long enough, everybody will forget about it," she says bitterly.

Perhaps, having once been an ardent Nixon supporter, it's her intense disappointment in her former hero that keeps her going. Gas prices and the cost of food are what people care about now. To everyone but Van Horn and Anderson, Richard Nixon is history. These ladies keep the vigil of their lawsuit.

"When my grandchildren ask," says Anderson, "I want them to know I did what I thought was right."

CHAPTER 3

Grief

When critics comment that the American courthouse resembles a church and our judges function as lay priests, they are usually implying that this is a bad thing and that too much power resides in the judiciary. But, power aside, these churchlike trappings are precisely what attract certain people to court to solve their problems. They find in the liturgical formality, the Latinate "legalese" spoken by attorneys, and the august black prelatic robes of the judiciary an environment that is at once comforting and healing, quiet and sobering. The religious hush that falls over the courtroom while it's in session further certifies that they have arrived at a sanctuary.

This may be at least one of the reasons why suing has become a part of the way we mourn. Calling the lawyer comes soon after calling the undertaker—in some cases, the lawyer comes first. In October 1978, a Pacific Southwest Airlines jet crashed en route from Chicago to San Diego, killing 151 persons. It was the nation's worst air disaster to date. By the very next day, the heirs had already contacted attorneys. Lawsuits against the airline were filed within a week.

This kind of lawsuit is filed during a time of personal agony and places special burdens upon the legal system. During the course of his lawsuit, the litigant will expect more from the court than justice as we generally define it. He'll seek an answer to the awesome and infinite question "Why me?"

"Why me?" is the anguished question Job asked God when his faith had been tested through a torrent of misfortune. Modern Jobs do not turn to the Lord for an answer, they turn to the courts.

"Why me?" leads to lawsuits asking "Why was my wife paralyzed after surgery?"

"Why me?" leads to "Why did I lose my husband in that airplane crash?"

"Why me?" leads to "Why did my innocent child get crushed to death at a rock concert?"

"Why me?" leads to "Why did my son kill himself?"

Modern popular wisdom has it that the use of the lawsuit in times of personal crisis has something to do with the decline of the old belief in "fate." "People are suing today because they want to blame someone for everything that happens to them," one law student commented. "They don't believe in fate and bad luck anymore."

But it is not so much the belief in fate that has changed as it is how and where we come to terms with it. Mourning is a ritual that one does not pass through overnight. Whether or not one seeks to go public with one's mourning by way of lawsuit may well depend upon what other avenues are available for the expression of grief. Those who lack a strong support network—family or close friends—during this period of upheaval sometimes find in litigation the succor and distraction they seek. Lawsuits are not designed to help a person through times of psychological distress, but in a surprising number of ways they pinch-hit quite adequately.

Even those who do have the aid they need may opt to sue. By now, suing is an approved method of acting out grief, though we have yet to formally acknowledge it as such. Other cultures may, in the face of death, have a huge bonfire and burn the loved one's belongings. We do not. Instead, we sue on the loved one's behalf, and keep his memory alive.

A Long Island woman died leaving a large estate to be

divided more or less equally among her husband and two adult children. Despite the apparent fairness of the split, within months each of her heirs had retained attorneys and begun suit. Why? The husband wanted *half,* not a third, because he'd been such an exemplary spouse. But the daughter wanted her father to have nothing at all; she insisted her mother never loved her father, so why should he profit from her death? Father, son, and daughter each claimed intimate knowledge of what their wife/mother wanted done (the son wanted the will enforced as written) and would accept nothing less than having it their way. Their ensuing lawsuit was more than a mere exercise in greed. By suing, they garnered extra years in which to demonstrate their loyalty and devotion to mom, the woman they all loved so well. In a sense, their lawsuit kept her alive.

The opportunity to hold on to the past is one of the chief benefits of a "Why me?" suit. The litigants are engaged in a stalling tactic, though few of them recognize this consciously. They can't help their stalling; it's just too painful to move on. Elisabeth Kubler-Ross, a psychologist who has done pioneering studies in the area of death and dying, has identified five phases that a dying person and those who love him pass through, though not always in fixed sequence. Briefly, these five are denial and isolation, rage and anger (which Kubler-Ross dubs the "Why Me?" phase), bargaining, depression, and acceptance. The filing of a lawsuit generally coincides with the "rage and anger" phase, long before the bereaved is ready to accept his loss. The mourner resists, fights back, holds on. He refuses to pick up the pieces of his life, partly out of grief, partly out of guilt at having survived. He finds in a lawsuit the perfect excuse for postponement.

Litigation thus becomes a crutch, leaned upon until the pain heals. The very slowness of the legal system gently guides the mourner back to life at a leisurely pace, past rage and anger and on through the other stages of grief until he arrives at final acceptance.

Litigation provided just such a brace for the West Vir-

ginia survivors of the Buffalo Creek dam disaster, in which
125 people died and 4000 of the 5000 residents of the southern Appalachia mining valley were left homeless. In the
course of their two-and-a-half-year lawsuit, Buffalo Creek
survivors literally came back to life. They went from isolated
despair, to anger, to bargaining (in the settlement phase of
trial), past depression, to ultimate acceptance of their loss,
much as Kubler-Ross might have predicted.

The dam burst on February 26, 1972. It was one of the
worst man-made disasters in United States history. Tidal
waves of twenty to thirty feet careened at speeds up to thirty
miles an hour. A turbulent torrent of black sludge carried
men, women, and children along so fast that they were
knocked unconscious. Houses, cars, and dead children sped
by. A whole way of life was destroyed. Even those who were
untouched by the waters were witnesses to scenes of horror.
Buffalo Creek was a tight-knit community where everyone
knew everyone else, and that day some people stood help-
lessly in groups looking on as their friends died in the valley
below.

When the waters settled, unrelieved mourning descended
on the valley of Buffalo Creek. The isolation stage had begun. "The children neither laughed nor played," writes
Kai T. Erikson in *Everything In Its Path,* a book about the
effects of the flood. "The adults acted as if they were surrounded by a sheath of heavy air through which they could
move and respond only at the cost of deliberate effort. Everything seemed muted and dulled."

Alienation seemed to affect everyone. A few men could go
back to work in the mines, but most were in shock and off
the job for months. One of the few exceptions was Charlie
Cowan, a fifty-six-year-old gas station owner. Cowan's station was the town meeting place, and he himself was something of a folk hero, having brought a lawsuit against several
coal companies to recover for strip-mining damage to his

property. After the dam disaster, Charlie alone seemed to have the energy and resourcefulness to take action. He called Arnold & Porter, a prestigious Washington, D.C., law firm (former Supreme Court justice Abe Fortas was a founding partner), and started wheels turning for a lawsuit against the dam's owner, the Buffalo Mining Company, which also owned several coal mines where the dam victims had worked. Cowan remembered that Arnold & Porter had just won a big victory for disabled miners and widows against their own union. Cowan and a few other townspeople now wanted the firm to take on the mines directly.

Arnold & Porter would do better than that. Gerald Stern, chief counsel on the case, took aim not only at the Buffalo Mining Company but at its parent conglomerate, the Pittston Company, an oil-and-gas concern traded over the New York Stock Exchange. Pittston called the flood an "act of God" for which it could not be liable.

Suing Pittston was good strategy since the lawsuits thereby involved citizens in two states: New York and West Virginia. As explained earlier, in our discussion of the Berney suit against H. R. Haldeman, "diversity of citizenship" cases can be heard in federal court. For Buffalo Creek litigants, this would provide an escape from a state court where judges might be politically beholden to mining interests. Suing Pittston also meant the probability of more money for the victims. A West Virginia jury might be more inclined to dig into the pockets of a wealthy New York company, whose sales in 1972 totaled $682 million, than one of their own, whose purchase price represented one-thirtieth of that figure.

The first lawsuit (handled by a West Virginia–based law firm) was filed in April, just two months after the flood. It was the first sign that the community was reviving. "Anger is increasing among the 5,000 survivors," *The New York Times* reported. "Young miners don't have the patience to wait for the courts to settle their claims, they say they want to close down the mines until the claims are settled."

Some miners settled with the company on their own, at

bargain-basement prices. The coal company paid between $4000 and $8000 to each survivor who agreed not to sue in the future. It was a trifling sum; the homes that had been destroyed were valued at a minimum $20,000. Furthermore, evidence was slowly being gathered that could lead to the conclusion that officials within the Pittston hierarchy knew the dam was dangerous; the company had doubled its liability insurance coverage just days before the dam burst. "They should have volunteered to rebuild all the homes, refurnish them, and give the survivors something for their hardship," insists Charlie Cowan. "If they'd done that, it would have cost the company far less in the end."

But Pittston was fighting the survivors, not helping them. The company even claimed that the miners themselves knew the dam was unsafe and so were at fault for not moving away before it exploded. Some people had no choice but to settle for their pittance; they needed money immediately. Everyone seemed to feel the settlements were an outrage. A group of local ministers publicly urged the company to see that area residents received "justice" and adequate payment for their losses. Their pleas fell on deaf ears. Pittston told the survivors not to retain attorneys—it would do them no good; those who brought lawyers with them to negotiations would not get a penny more than those without, they promised. The way company lawyers treated the townsfolk was "criminal," in the view of one angry disaster refugee.

Still, it took considerable energy to get angry. When Gerald Stern, the Arnold & Porter attorney, arrived at Charlie Cowan's gas station to talk to his future clients, he found them "crushed." "Their whole demeanor demonstrated how overwhelming this disaster had been," Stern wrote in his account of the lawsuit, *The Buffalo Creek Disaster*. "It was hard for them to sit up straight or to talk for long periods of time. . . . Tears came quickly and often."

With so many people in different stages of the grieving process, not everyone was ready to bring suit at the same time.

About 400 survivors, representing 250 families, sued Pittston in September 1972. They demanded $52 million—$11 million in property loss; $20 million in "psychic injuries" from nightmares, headaches, and the like; and $21 million to punish the company for its gross negligence in building a faulty dam. By August the following year, 200 more people were ready to sue, and the damages asked for rose to $64 million.

But the fact that they were finally ready to sue didn't mean they could now talk about what had happened to them. They were too numb to speak. These survivors still lived with the effects of their loss every day: They had trouble sleeping; rain made them nervous. Psychologist Robert Jay Lifton, an expert on the aftereffects of disaster, describes such symptoms as part of the "survival guilt" syndrome, especially that aspect he terms "death anxiety."

It took Roland Staten many months to be able to talk about what happened. When he did, it was quite a story, told to lawyers in the form of a deposition:

> As I was climbing out [of the window of my house] the water just sort of picked me up and I was on the roof before I even knew it with [my son].
>
> My wife, she was hanging on the edge of the roof and she—as I tried to help her up, she was kind of heavy—she was about five and a half months pregnant, and I picked her up or tried to pick her up with my left hand and holding my son in my right hand. And he was screaming and carrying on and as I tried to pick her up, why, I just lost my grip, you know, just the roof of the gable of the house, the way it was made, and her pulling on me too and I went back in the water with [my boy] in sort of a lurch, you know, and my wife says, "What are we going to do, what are we going to do?" and I said, "Just hold on to anything you can find, anything," and by that time the water was so deep and so much force, why I was 20 or 30 feet from her.

When I looked back and saw her she said, "Take
care of my baby." And by that time I was gone. That's
all I heard. That's the last time I saw her.[1]

Within moments, Roland Staten's boy was gone too. The
water had pulled him under.

For Roland Staten, being able to talk about his wife and
son marked an obvious improvement. Soon he and the
others emerged from their isolation, growing increasingly
angry. Pittston had built a faulty dam. The miners, talking
among themselves, complained that Pittston had known the
dam was going to collapse but didn't tell them. They'd let
their families die, they said. But it wasn't just the collapsed
dam that made them angry; the miners and other survivors
now raged against all the real and imagined abuses they'd
been made to suffer over the years at the hands of Buffalo
Mining. They complained that their bosses maintained unsafe work conditions and treated the workers like slaves.
"The coal companies didn't have any respect for the men,"
one survivor told Kai T. Erikson.[2]

Now, after the flood, Pittston was acting no better. It
housed the survivors in meager trailers, grouping them ran-
domly. It didn't occur to the company that former neighbors would want to live near each other, but this omission
was just about the last straw for the distraught community.
The survivors complained that the trailers were like "con-
centration camps." One displaced resident told Gerald Stern:
"There isn't one family in our trailer park that we were
really close friends with, and so we feel like we're in a strange
land even though it's just a few miles up Buffalo Creek
from where we were."[3]

As painful as these living conditions were, the anger these
survivors now focused on their bosses was probably what
kept the lawsuit alive. Their anger enabled them to with-
stand years of financial and emotional deprivation while the

suit continued. As long as they could get angry, they cared about life. And that rage also motivated the attorneys to work faster to get Pittston to the bargaining table. "While they suffered in these trailer camps," writes Gerald Stern, "we pressed forward." Whenever Stern felt particularly good about how the case was going, he'd recall that down in West Virginia the survivors heard the beat of rain on the flat tin roofs of their trailers, reminding them of the flood. They saw themselves as "condemned prisoners," he knew, and he worked just that much harder.

Stern himself had little contact with the townspeople, however, after the lawsuit began. He was in Washington or in the courts plotting strategy. Other attorneys from Arnold & Porter were enlisted to get the survivors' stories in depositions and interrogatories. Arnold & Porter wanted to impress upon Pittston that although many of these survivors had not personally been touched by water, they had indeed suffered psychic injuries that impaired their ability to lead normal lives. Psychic damages were still novel and controversial in the early 1970s and many lawyers and judges believed that unless a litigant walked into court in a cast, he hadn't really suffered. But Arnold & Porter lawyers believed the injuries of their clients were real, because they met the people. The recollections contained in the depositions were so heartrending that the attorneys grew exhausted and depressed after just a short stay in Buffalo Creek.

As for the townspeople, now that their anger was aroused in a fight against the mines, they took an avid interest in their suit. Though waiting for the verdict was a hardship, they hung together. Their mutual stake in the lawsuit kept the flood vivid in their minds as an important legacy to uphold. The lawsuit became a major event, as big in some respects, Gerald Stern later wrote, as the disaster had been, at least to those who had not lost any relatives. Meetings were held throughout the litigation. A "disaster committee" was formed of townsfolk who kept in close contact with attorneys.

The survivors entered the next two stages of mourning

simultaneously: bargaining and depression. When Robert Jay Lifton, who earlier had analyzed "survival guilt" in postwar Hiroshima, visited Buffalo Creek at the request of Arnold & Porter attorneys, he found the survivors struggling vainly to give the flood some meaning. Buffalo Creek was a man-made disaster, far more difficult to accept, Lifton suggested, than acts of God. Lacking a God to bargain with, the survivors became depressed, feeling their lives and their agony were pointless. But thanks to the ongoing negotiations with the hated coal companies, they were at least partially shielded from feeling the full impact of their depression. Their lawsuit made their pain feel valuable.

The case was also of great moment to those valley residents who were not litigants. Six different companies worked neighboring mines, and bosses at these companies sided with Pittston. Attempts seem to have been made by these companies to discourage litigants from suing: Word spread through the mines that those who sued Pittston would lose their cases. About 200 people who were contemplating suit never filed. Hundreds more never even consulted attorneys in a quest for their rights.

In the end, these rumors worked to Pittston's advantage. About 3000 victims who did not file suit received settlements totaling $12.5 million. The 654 litigants who went to court shared $13.5 million, of which attorneys received about $3 million.[4] By going to court, survivors averaged about four times better than they would have if they'd settled with the companies on their own.

"I would have waited three years," says Charlie Cowan. As it turned out, it only took two and a half. On July 6, 1974, a week before the trial was scheduled to begin, Pittston agreed to the $13.5-million settlement figure. While on the average this meant approximately $16,000 per litigant after the deduction of legal fees, many did quite a bit better. Those, like Roland Staten, who suffered one or more "wrongful deaths" got the state limit of $110,000 for each loss. Several people received close to half a million on behalf of their lost relatives. Pittston eventually settled because it feared a trial would be embarrassing. Internal company memoranda showed that Pittston employees had discussed the unsafe dam several months before it collapsed, though nothing had been done. Other evidence clearly suggested that the mines had been operating in violation of federal safety standards. A jury armed with such information might have made mince-meat of them. Since Pittston was traded as a commonly held stock on the New York Exchange, publicity attendant to this case was already working havoc with the company's financial situation. It was cheaper to settle, even if it did mean tacitly admitting fault.

The ending of a lawsuit that had occupied such a major part of their lives was celebrated by Buffalo Creek residents at a party in the school gymnasium. For a poor town about to inherit so much money, the affair was somber. "Life's been rough," says Charlie Cowan. He used his approximately $40,000 to rebuild his house and store. "I just try to put it [the disaster] out of my mind, not think about it," he says. The completion of the lawsuit, writes Erikson, was a kind of "graduation."

It propelled people into the future at the very mo-ment it was placing a final seal on a portion of the past. The time had come to seek new housing, to make over-due decisions, to put the many pieces of a shattered life back together. A painful period of suspension was over, but that put people in the position of no longer being able to act as if their fates were hanging on an attorney's competence, a judge's sense of fairness, or a jury's compassion. So it was a cruel time as well as a comforting one.[5]

Acceptance arrived for most. But some people just didn't want to let go. For them, the end of the lawsuit was a sad occasion; it signaled the loss of camaraderie, the end of battle.

A few people were still angry and wanted to keep on fighting; they complained that $13.5 million hardly hurt Pittston, which at that time grossed $42 million annually. Others griped that Pittston should do more than pay out damages; it should rebuild the town, provide recreation so people could take their minds off the tragedy. For a time, this carping threatened to rechannel survivors' anger from the coal companies to the attorneys. The Disaster Committee stayed active, and became a political force. Within a year of the lawsuit's settlement, the Disaster Committee began a move to incorporate Buffalo Creek so that "the people," and not the mines, could run the government. When the move to incorporate failed, some townsfolk blamed this, like most everything else, on Pittston and its reputed political connections.

But for most survivors, two and a half years was probably long enough to stay angry. This is not to imply that their rage was immediately dispelled just because a settlement of the case was reached. But as Erikson has implied, that settlement did indicate the need to lift the onerous veil of the past. Residents of Buffalo Creek took their money and built houses, bought cars. Some blew all their cash within the first year, and later regretted it. The town may not have fully recovered, but life did go on.

Would Buffalo Creek survivors have relinquished their hold on their tragedy any sooner without their lawsuit? Charlie Cowan thinks not. He regards those who settled privately with Pittston in the first sad days after the dam burst as tragedies themselves: They have nothing, not even money. This, of course, is one voice. But it does seem clear that those who missed out on the Buffalo Creek litigation snubbed a major mass event that changed the lives of everyone it touched.

Although money is usually a goal in lawsuits of grief, it is not the only or even the major one. The dream of making a fortune in court usually moves to the forefront of a case only after all the emotionalism has been drained out of it. When the suit is first filed, the litigant is so occupied with his loss that money may hardly have any place in his thoughts at all (although his attorney never forgets it). Typically, the "Why me?" litigant is involved in a mystery: Why did this horrible tragedy occur? Who could have stopped it? As a survivor in the early throes of grief, he "enjoys" his lawsuit because it caters to his fact-finding obsession. Mourners crave repetition of the details of death and injury, and they get it in enormous quantity as the case proceeds. In deposition, in discovery, and in trial, the facts are replayed, ordered, reconsidered. The survivor sees himself as a detective now, ferreting out new clues. Soon he may satisfy himself that the loved one died because a doctor did not arrive promptly at the hospital. Or because the medicine was administered by an unfriendly nurse.

This obsession with getting all the facts may explain the popularity of medical malpractice cases. If complications occur after surgery, the concerned family will necessarily reexamine the quality of care given by the hospital and the physicians when they start their Sam Spade routine. They may sue the doctor or the hospital or both, claiming that those in charge were grossly negligent and functioning at standards far below those of the rest of the medical profession. Sometimes completely innocent people are sued; sometimes it's an obviously culpable party. On the occasion of his loss, the mourner does not particularly care about accuracy.

Yorick Spiegel, an expert on the anger phase of the grieving process, explains that these anguished people "crave an explanation" but not necessarily the "right" or logical one. During this stage, Spiegel writes, "it can be more important in some cases to let the mourner find a helpful or conceivable cause than to insist on the objective reasons which led to the death." Often, that "helpful or conceivable cause" becomes the focus of a lawsuit against the doctor or the hospital.

A Michigan man, for example, didn't know exactly which doctor said, "Oops, I cut in the wrong place," while the man was undergoing prostate surgery. But he thought he heard someone say it, a fact that became significant when he discovered one of his testicles had atrophied due to a poor blood supply. He sued the hospital and the attending surgeon, insisting that someone was to blame. Eventually, as the case proceeds, he may indeed find the person who said "Oops" and perhaps be compensated for his injury. But those possible results are probably beside the point, at least in the heat of the lawsuit's first filing. Suing functions in this case as a fact-finding process, an important part of becoming accustomed to loss.

This obsession with facts leads people to insist upon suing even when they are told they cannot prevail. George and Pat Martinez knew at the outset they had little chance of succeeding in their suit against the state of California, but they felt compelled to continue with it as their only way of discovering who in the government hierarchy was responsible for the death of their daughter.

On August 1, 1975, fifteen-year-old Mary Ellen Martinez was murdered in remote Tecolote Canyon near San Diego. Richard June-Jordan Thomas kidnapped the girl and tortured her, then raped and murdered her. The killing was entirely senseless—but then, Thomas was clearly out of his senses. Five months before the murder, he had been released from a California prison where he was serving a twenty-year sentence for attempted rape of two young girls in the very same canyon area. When he was sentenced in 1969, a psychiatric examination had concluded that Thomas was a mentally disordered sex offender beyond rehabilitation. It recommended Thomas be put away and never let out.

This much about Richard June-Jordan Thomas's horrible career was immediately available to George and Pat Martinez through radio and newspaper reports which were issued in waves during those summer days following Mary Ellen's death. "She was a good girl," George told local journalists who were closely following the story. They had two other children, but Mary Ellen was the star of the family, "like a precious piece of art," her father said. Mary Ellen's death was more than an isolated blow. The family had recently moved to California from Arizona, where George had been having trouble finding work during a recession in the construction trades. Arriving in San Diego, he discovered that unemployment there was the highest in the state. George Martinez was almost continually unemployed from the day of his arrival. California was not good for the Martinez family. With the loss of Mary Ellen, they seemed to hit rock bottom.

In the first days of their mourning, the shocked Martinez family relied on journalists and police detectives to answer their questions. Thomas was held for murder (and later found guilty and sentenced to death). Pretrial inquiries showed that the state knew Thomas was dangerous even as the parole board was taking steps to free him. The board had been warned that there was every likelihood that if Thomas left prison he would strike again. Despite this knowledge, the board let him out, for it was in a "Catch-22" situation: State law mandated that only people who could be rehabilitated could be treated in a state mental hospital. Thomas was beyond psychiatric help, so he could not be treated. Since he could not be treated, said another quirky California law, he had to be let free after a minimum incarceration. In 1975, Thomas left prison after serving five years of his sentence. Five months later, Mary Ellen was dead.

A lawsuit was not George Martinez's first thought. He was overwhelmed by the task of just keeping his family in order. With no money, no job, deep into his grief, his impulse was to flee California (and he would return to Arizona in 1979, even before the U.S. Supreme Court uttered the last word on his case). But Thomas's criminal trial was not yet over. Martinez wanted to see for himself how justice would be carried out. He and Pat were filled with questions that the news stories had missed: What happened after Thomas left prison? Was he closely supervised? Why was he permitted out by himself? Where was his parole officer? Why hadn't the state notified the public that a dangerous person was in the San Diego area? They hoped the trial would answer these burning questions. But it didn't. Thomas was convicted of first degree murder in April 1976, but, despite the conviction, George Martinez knew little more than he had before the trial.

He began to ask questions. Who on the parole board had decided to let Thomas out? Which psychiatrists had screened him? What positive information about the man had been given the board which caused them to reconsider the conclusion of the 1969 psychiatric examination—that Richard Thomas should never see daylight outside the prison gate?

No answers were forthcoming. George Martinez received a $2500 "victims' allowance" from the state of California, and, from the point of view of state officials, the case was closed.

By the time George and Pat reached the San Diego offices of Don McGrath, a personal-injury and business lawyer, they were already talking about changing the law. The law that most upset them was one granting state officials immunity from lawsuit for the untoward results of their negligent acts. Because of this immunity, state officials could afford to be cavalier to the Martinezes, and the snubbing they received made George and Pat not only angry but also fearful. "We don't want this to happen to anyone else's daughter," they told McGrath. "We don't want this to happen again."

George, who had no experience whatever with political matters, thought the best thing to do was organize a political campaign. He wanted people throughout California to sign petitions to the legislature demanding an end to state immunity. But Don McGrath, who had been active in Arizona campaigns for Senator Barry Goldwater and other Republicans, didn't think this was the best route. "I think the lawsuit is the only way to vent your spleen, get your frustrations out, and have something good come out of it," he told Mary Ellen's parents.

The goal, McGrath said, was to make the parole board publicly accountable for letting Richard Thomas out of prison. A petition would never do it. A lawsuit might. He reasoned that petitions are futile: One or two people working by themselves have little chance of rallying enough citizen support to influence the legislature. That worked only when thousands of people faced the same problem, like high taxes, or a flood careening through their canyon. For the isolated outrage, lobbying through petitions wasn't worth the cost of the ink.

Of course, McGrath couldn't be too optimistic about winning a lawsuit either. A challenge to overturn the immunity of state employees on constitutional grounds was a one-in-a-million long shot. It was traditional that government employees were immune from blame for the results of their actions. The policy stemmed from the concept "the king can do no wrong." But while the infallibility of the king was an idea long gone, governmental immunity still generally remained, because without it no state worker would feel free to do his job—especially a risky job like serving on the parole board—for fear of suit. "We put these people on the firing line," said one proimmunity attorney. "Parole officials, for example, have to go by their instincts, their feel for human behavior. This is not a predictive science. So when they call a shot, it's with the full knowledge that it might be wrong. But to call them to task personally for their mistakes would make it impossible for them to do what they think best."

McGrath warned the Martinezes that, since there was a good chance the case would be thrown out of court, they of course could not expect to receive any financial damages. Why sue, then? McGrath said that while they could not expect a legal victory, they could certainly draw attention to their problem. If influencing the legislature was their goal, this was the way to go. The plight of these grieving parents suing the state over the death of a child was novel and stirring. The media would love it, the public would be roused, and concerned legislators might respond, too. Who knew, maybe somebody would get them some answers. Moreover, even if the parole board won its case, there was a good chance the members would be scared enough by the filing of the suit to proceed more cautiously in the future.

George and Pat Martinez listened to McGrath and decided to sue. They signed over to him the $2500 "victims' allowance" they'd received from the state, which would just about cover costs up to the first level of appeal. After that, McGrath said, his firm would advance all costs.

They waited until the Thomas criminal case was over and the time for his appeal had expired. Thomas was convicted April 13, 1976. On May 25, Mary Ellen's parents and siblings filed a "wrongful death" suit against the state of California and six personally named members of the parole board, demanding damages of $2 million.* They charged that state officials were responsible for Mary Ellen's death through their "reckless, willful, wanton, and malicious" freeing of Richard Thomas.

As predicted, the filing immediately caught the eye of the media. The Martinezes were interviewed extensively on statewide radio and television. Pat Martinez told reporters that the purpose of the suit was not the $2 million, but to make sure that what happened to Mary Ellen never happened again. Few who heard her voice on the air could doubt her grief. She was now fighting the state for the rights of parents everywhere. Soon they had reason to be optimistic. The California Supreme Court ruled in July that a psychiatrist who knows his patient might hurt someone has a legal obligation to warn the potential victim.† While this was not precisely McGrath's point, this new decision contained a

---

* *Martinez* v. *State of California*, U.S. Supreme Court 78-1268 (1/15/80) , 85 Cal Ap 3d 430, 149 Cal Rptr 519 (1978) .
† *Tarasoff* v. *Regents, U.C.*, 17 C3 425 (1976) .

heartening suggestion that the court wanted to insure the safety of the innocent individuals against the acts of dangerous persons.

The goal, of course, was to get to trial. Both McGrath and the Martinezes knew it would be a real victory if they could pierce the internal workings of the parole board and question face-to-face the people who decided Richard June-Jordan Thomas should be set free. But by November 1979, the case had been thrown out of court as baseless. Governmental immunity was upheld first by the trial judge, then by the court of appeal. The California Supreme Court denied a hearing. McGrath had complained of six different ways in which the state had erred, all of which he said contributed to Mary Ellen's death. But the state courts said that even if McGrath was correct and the state was culpable, it was not liable for damages.

Almost $6000 had been eaten up in printing costs and travel expenses in a case that had never presented its first witness or a single piece of evidence. The U.S. Supreme Court, however, agreed to hear argument on the case.

State governments throughout the nation must have feared Don McGrath's logic, for many of them filed friend-of-the-court briefs urging the Court to uphold their immunity. McGrath was clearly outnumbered. In his corner was only a tiny organization attempting to represent the legal rights of thousands of victims of crimes. Accustomed though he was to being a maverick, Don McGrath felt alone.

"The analogy I make in this case," McGrath argued to the justices, "is the situation where a zookeeper has seven cages and eight tigers. He has to let one of them go. When he does, somebody gets killed, but the zookeeper says, 'You can't sue me' because the courts have given him immunity from liability. It's as if the court was telling people to go ahead and sue the tiger." McGrath argued that the Martinez family was left unprotected. Under the common-law concept of immunity, they could not sue a parole-board official, but must take action, instead, against Richard June-Jordan Thomas;

since he alone raped Mary Ellen and killed her, he alone was considered responsible for his acts. But Thomas, a mentally disordered sex offender, hadn't worked in years, if ever. He was penniless. And further, McGrath didn't believe that Thomas alone was responsible for the death of Mary Ellen. Some government officials were negligent in letting him go free from prison, and McGrath believed that every person should be held responsible for his grossly negligent acts. Hiding behind immunity encouraged people to mess up.

The nine justices were not swayed by such logic. In January 1980, the U.S. Supreme Court perceived the problem two ways. First, as a states' rights issue: Did the state of California have the right to make its personnel immune from suit? Justice John Paul Stevens, writing for a unanimous Court, said it did. Second, did the state of California actually do anything that led directly to Mary Ellen's death? Again, Justice Stevens said no. Richard Thomas had not been an employee of the state when he murdered Mary Ellen, he had simply been freed by the state, an act too remote from her death to be considered a direct cause of it. Parole is an administrative function, Stevens wrote, like setting speed limits at 55 mph rather than 45. Of course more people will get killed at the higher speed, but this, the Court said, was not the fault of the state but of the drivers.

Perceiving the issue this way, the justices ignored George and Pat Martinez and their need to confront the people who had so radically changed their lives. "Maybe we're wrong," Don McGrath said. "Maybe there was good reason to free Thomas. But we should have the right to know. Just let me get to court so I can ask the people why they did it. If I'm wrong, I'll admit it."

It was never to be. Five years after Mary Ellen's death, her parents' action seems to have accomplished nothing. Most lawyers would term the case a loser, but the Martinezes feel differently. "I thought they would collapse," Don McGrath said. But they did not. "Either way, we're winners," George

Martinez told reporters on the eve of the U.S. Supreme Court ruling.

Some people would call this mere rationalization, but Martinez appeared to be serious. They had raised the issue, they'd gotten people interested in the problem. On behalf of Mary Ellen, a case had gone all the way to the U.S. Supreme Court, and George Martinez had gone there, too. No longer was he the forlorn, unemployed, unsophisticated construction worker he had been when he entered McGrath's office. He may have learned nothing more about Mary Ellen's death, but he knew quite a bit more about the way government worked, the way the world worked, too. George Martinez packed up his family and moved back to Arizona. He was ready to get back to work of his own.

Lawsuits triggered by grief are rife with potential for abuse. From the mourner's standpoint, a lawsuit can seem like a reasonable and in some senses therapeutic response to tragedy. From the view of the person being sued (perhaps unjustly), it can spell tragedy anew.

The need to blame someone is strong, and, psychologists tell us, normal, even in the most natural deaths. *The First Year of Bereavement,* a study by Ira D. Glick, R. Weiss, and C. M. Parkes, followed a group of widows through their first year alone. For the first month or so, they got along splendidly with everybody. But by the second month, many of the group were fighting with their in-laws, reinterpreting behavior of the husband's family, in essence blaming them for his death. If such bitterness and anger arises naturally between family members who have enjoyed a history of respect and intimacy, it's easy to see why this period elicits more hostile and aggressive actions—including lawsuits— when the mourner deals with complete strangers.

Some societies, recognizing how natural blame-finding is during grief, have institutionalized it into a ritual. Among the Lo Dagaa in West Africa, as Yorick Spiegel writes, the death of anyone but infants and old people is regarded as murder. After a death, the whole society bends to the task of finding the assailant. The cause of death may be disease or some external act, human or supernatural. Every avenue is explored. But despite the community's best efforts, frequently no "murderer" is found. This doesn't bother anyone; the purpose of the ritual is not really to find a murderer but to enact the search.

The Lo Dagaa have discovered the therapeutic value of blame-finding, but when the "search for the guilty," as Spiegel calls it, takes place in the courts, good therapy can make bad law. The fact is, a mourner is emotionally unfit to initiate a lawsuit, and he should be protected from his impulse to do so during the first stages of his anguish. While he may need to blame someone, anyone, an unfounded accusation in a lawsuit can be emotionally, professionally, and financially devastating to the defendant.

We may have grown accustomed to using the courts to assuage grief, but that is not their intended purpose. A lawsuit involves a cold calculation of loss, often in terms of dollars and cents. In the United States, the legal counterpart of the search for the guilty is the "wrongful death" suit or other similar private lawsuits based on "torts" or private wrongs. These actions try to disregard the grief, not cater to it. The concept of wrongful death, which we inherited from English common law, is based on the idea that a person is a commodity of monetary value. When a person is wrongfully killed or otherwise injured as the result of another's mistakes, the law says he or his heirs must be financially compensated for the loss. A murderer can be sued, for example, by his victim's wife or children and held responsible (assuming he has an income) for the wages the victim had been earning and might have continued to earn. But the mourner is not interested in money at this stage. He wants psychological relief. That he is able in numerous ways to get that relief from suing does not mean that it is always in his—or his society's—best interest that he do so.

Since bereaved people cannot reasonably be held responsible for the effects of their lawsuits, the legal system must insulate itself from them. One way of doing this would be to insist upon a minimal cooling-off period before any death- or injury-related lawsuits can be filed. Mourning is generally completed within a year. It may be too much to expect that outstanding claims wait so long to be filed, but some period of time is obviously called for. The litigant can file an intention to sue, a simple piece of paper that will protect his legal rights, but, otherwise, all use of the courts should cease. In this way, the grieving party gets a period of time in which his total attention is directed toward his loss and toward resuming his life. The diversion of a lawsuit, with its attendant aggravations and salting of new wounds, is avoided. Obviously, cooling off runs counter to our culture's concept of racing to the courthouse as soon as possible so the opponent can see the plaintiff suffer. But under the circumstances of this type of case, the race seems unnecessary and brutal.

Given time to heal her grief, Marie Pruetzel may no longer have needed the outlet of filing lawsuits in the aftermath of the suicide of her son, Freddie Prinze.

On January 28, 1977, Prinze, a 22-year-old comedian and television star, committed suicide following a lengthy depression. He had talked of suicide for several months. "I love you, Kathy," he said in a goodbye telephone call to his estranged wife. "I love the baby. But I need to find some peace."[6] Putting down the receiver, he fired a bullet into his brain.

But though Prinze may have been suicidal for some time, his mother nevertheless couldn't believe he did it. He was at the top of the entertainment world, earning $25,000 a week at Caesar's Palace. Sure, Freddie had been depressed, and he was taking alarming amounts of Quaaludes and snorting cocaine. But why had he done it? Why couldn't anyone stop him?[7]

In the days after his death, magazines and newspapers retold the story of Freddie's sad life at the top, and the events that preceded the final gun blast. Prinze had been seeing a psychologist—actually a prominent hypnotherapist and medical doctor—for more than a year. The day before the suicide, the doctor had met with the young comedian and removed from his possession some Quaaludes and a gun. Prinze asked the doctor, "What am I? Am I psychotic? Schizophrenic? What am I?"[8] According to one magazine account, the doctor replied, "You're none of those things, Freddie. You're just an immature little boy." The next day, Prinze asked for the gun to be returned. The doctor complied. The next night, Prinze killed himself.

Three months after Freddie died, his mother filed wrongful-death suits against both the therapist and an internist who, she charged, had been writing prescriptions for Prinze's sedatives. These men could have saved Freddie, Marie Pruetzel charged. The internist wrote the prescriptions, she stated, knowing her son was an addict; and he never even checked his vital signs.

Her lawsuit is a classic case of a "search for the guilty."

Suicide is always shocking and tragic for those who are left behind. "Survivor-victims of such deaths," writes Edwin S. Schneidman, a psychiatrist specializing in the subject, "are invaded by an unhealthy complex of disturbing emotions: shame, guilt, hatred, perplexity. They are obsessed with thoughts about the death, seeking reasons, casting blame, and often punishing themselves." Our common-law heritage doesn't help the survivor's self-image, either. The common law insisted that suicide was "self-murder," and considered it a capital offense. One who killed himself while in full possession of his faculties (this was always a tricky point) forfeited all his worldly possessions, leaving his family pauperized. Consequently, the surviving heirs had a great stake in proving that the suicide was psychologically unbalanced when he pulled the trigger, didn't know what he was doing, and in no way intended to commit the act. It was more than a good name these legatees were defending;

they were trying to save themselves from the poorhouse.

Our modern laws no longer consider suicide a crime, and most of the risk in admitting that such an act took place is gone. However, vestiges of legal punishments do remain. In some states, the life-insurance policy of one who commits suicide is void unless the policy was in effect two years before the death. In many smaller respects as well, a social stigma remains.

Thus, profound sociological and psychological responses (mainly of the subconscious variety) may have been at work when Marie Pruetzel filed her suit. Even assuming for the moment that the two doctors were indeed negligent, it would not be surprising or unnatural that Freddie's mother may have found in the vehicle of a lawsuit an emotional outlet for the entirely appropriate, normal, and predictable feelings of guilt and remorse (like those described earlier by Schneidman) aroused by her son's suicide.

"In this lawsuit Mrs. Pruetzel is asking the doctors why didn't they stop Freddie Prinze from taking his own life," says George MacDonald, a lawyer representing the internist. "Well, we can ask her the same thing. She was in contact with her son for the full month before he died. Why didn't *you* stop him, Mrs. Pruetzel?"

The demand for justice in Freddie Prinze's death combines all the elements of a traditional "Why me?" suit, with the added anguish peculiar to the trauma of suicide. There is present the same anger and rage on the part of survivors, the same search for the guilty, the same need to reenact the death to find new clues to how it could have occurred. Perhaps most important, there is obvious refusal to let go of the deceased and accept that he is, in fact, dead.

A "Why me?" suit is a postponement of that inevitable acceptance; it prolongs the moment of truth as long as possible. But it can't prolong it forever. Regardless of the outcome of the Prinze trial, the truth must inevitably be accepted if the mourner is to get on with the business of living.

CHAPTER 4

Political and Social Change

For those Americans who seriously seek and work for political and social change, litigation can often be the fastest route. While a ruling in their favor does not guarantee overnight changes, legal sanctioning of their cause undoubtedly speeds the process.

The "cause" case, in turn, elevates the litigation process to a level of wholesomeness and idealism that otherwise seems lacking, for the issue in "cause" cases is not vengeance or profit for oneself but the pursuit of the public good—a "better America."

Involvement in "cause" lawsuits thus makes people feel good, useful, even patriotic. Their respectability cuts across party lines, and in fact has nothing to do with the goals of any one particular suit. The aim may be "progressive" reform, "conservative" defense of the status quo, or some brand of radicalism in either direction. That's irrelevant. In the twenty-fifth anniversary of the landmark U.S. Supreme Court school-desegregation case, *Brown* v. *Board of Education, Topeka, Kansas,* those who had participated in the case—both pro and con—recalled it as being the high point of their lives, like being on Mount Sinai when the Commandments were delivered.

Our love of the "cause" suit is bound up in the timeworn but still beloved American clichés it evokes: fighting the good fight, nonviolent protest, and looking out for the underdog.

Our "cause" litigant sees himself as the spiritual son or daughter of the Founding Fathers, insisting that his suit is making America live up to its promise.

Superficially, these cases resemble "protest" suits, since the rhetoric of outrage and reminder of America's legacy is often the same. But the protester has no great revolutionary goals; he reacts to an isolated incident, then disappears from view. The policy suit, on the other hand, is always reaching for the moon. Some reformers dream of litigating the United States into a socialist nation; others will be satisfied only when tax laws are more equitable (or nonexistent), or rivers are cleaner, or there are no nuclear power plants in operation. It is the grandeur of the vision that separates the protest case from the cause variety.

Imbued with missionary zeal, the social reformer (to use the term most generally) is willing to pursue his cause endlessly, without respect to cost. He goes to any and every tribunal willing to hear his case, fighting not for himself but for an image of America to which he has at least temporarily dedicated his life.

Litigating social change will never be entirely out of style, but the Golden Age of cause lawsuits may in fact be over by now. It may be seen as framed by two race-relations reform suits: the 1954 desegregation case, *Brown* v. *Board of Education,* and its 1979 reverse-discrimination counterpart, *Allan Bakke* v. *Board of Regents, University of California.* Though race led the way as a reform issue, almost every other aspect of national life was swept up in its tumultuous wave. The Golden Age coincided with a period of great social and political ferment—including the Vietnam War protest movement, the women's liberation movement, the environmental-protection movement, and the rise of self-proclaimed minorities. During this period, American society undertook a sweeping redefinition of moral wrongs, and in rapid-fire manner went about making them into legal wrongs as well. Discrimination on the basis of race, sex, or age, for example, is no longer just bad manners; it is now seen as material deprivation of the

Constitutional rights and privileges of various groups of citizens. Environmental pollution is not merely inconsiderate but a crime against the planet and its inhabitants. Breach the pollution laws and you're looking for a suit.

There have been other "progressive" eras in our history, but in this Golden Age the court has led the way as never before. The modern cause litigant is well aware that the court, when stirred to social activism on behalf of a worthy litigant, can have a thrilling power to alter our national perceptions of justice and of citizen responsibility for the welfare of our fellowman. In filing his lawsuit, the cause litigant is asking the court to perform its magic once again.

The cause lawsuit begins with optimism. The litigant truly believes that right is on his side and that he cannot help but prevail. But he soon learns the hazards of the trade. Rather than providing push-button justice and the arrival of Heaven on Earth, going to court is a lesson in "the science of exigencies," as Theodore Parker called politics: No victories are pure, no defeats are total.

During the recent so-called Golden Age, social scientists began studying the impact of Supreme Court decisions: who obeys them, and why they do so. In 1962, the U.S. Supreme Court outlawed prayer in public schools. It was a highly controversial decision, calling for the change of long-established practice, especially in the southern states. Six years after the decision, many southern states still refused to alter their practices regarding school prayer, and some schools impishly increased the daily dosage.

The big question for researchers was not the aggressive flouting of the law where public opinion was unanimous, but the more subtle "inertia," or passive resistance, that occurred in many midwestern states. Kenneth Dolbeare and Phillip Hammond, professors of political science and sociology, respectively, surveyed 250 schools in a typical state they dubbed Midway. Their findings: In general, the public at large tends to be unaware of U.S. Supreme Court actions. And even when they are aware, they take their cues from their own public leaders. In the school-prayer case, these Midwest leaders, sensing the ambivalence of the populace, refused to do anything—buck-passing was the order of the day. Since no official took a position ordering school prayer to cease, it continued. Civil-liberties groups in Midway all felt strongly that school prayer must end, the researchers discovered, but the small-town setting discouraged argument and confrontation of any kind, including litigation to force compliance with the Supreme Court order. Apparently no lawsuits were filed at least for the first five years.[1]

Dolbeare and Hammond's research suggests the limitations of lawsuits that aim at a true make-over of American society. We change our ways when we want to or are literally forced to, these researchers suggest, and the most well-intentioned Supreme Court decision may never overrule old established and dearly held custom unless that force is applied.

If cause lawsuits cannot produce miracles, they do have other significant benefits. In the words of Stuart Sheingold, professor of political science, cause suits "make democracy work." As Sheingold explains in *The Politics of Rights: Lawyers, Public Policy, and Political Change,* by going to court, people who are otherwise excluded from conventional politics can have their views expressed. A lawsuit is successful, Sheingold says, when it changes the "balance of power" in how decisions are made.[2]

Going to court does not short-circuit the political process, it merely widens the gate and allows more people into the game. The same pressures, need for compromise, and defense of unpopular positions which mark any political venture are present in lawsuits, too.

On the road to reform, litigation may be only a way station. During a long-drawn-out school-desegregation trial in Los Angeles during the 1970s, a new group, Bustop, demanded and received the right to appear in court representing parents who were against busing for school integration. Bustop appeared at every hearing, its lawyers cross-examined witnesses and were quoted widely in the press on every judicial ruling. After a year of court proceedings, they and their views became widely recognized. But when Tom Bartman, the Bustop lawyer and strategist, won a seat on the Los Angeles school board, the group's court appearances noticeably decreased.[3] The antibusing group was no longer an outsider in the political process. With a seat on the school board, they were part of the establishment, and they needed the court no more.

More than almost any other kind of case, the policy-change suit demands a willingness to accept countless defeats in the fond hope that some judge someday will understand and approve the cause. The relative success or failure of these cases depends upon so many considerations, there's simply no way of predicting which will stand, which die, only to rise later from their own ashes. We can isolate a number of requirements that all policy-change suits share. But even when all of these are satisfied and operating at their optimal level, there's no guarantee that the suit will be a winner.

The plaintiffs may be serious, dedicated, and in the game with the intention of winning, but they can do nothing more than translate their tale of woe into the form of a written complaint if they lack the right to sue—that is, the right to be in court. This right can be granted in a variety of ways. It can be granted directly through specific law, as in the 1964 and 1974 Civil Rights Acts, which expressly give blacks, women, and the elderly the right to sue as victims of discrimination. Or it may be granted indirectly, in that a right may exist, but be difficult to find.

For example, in the late 1960s, before there were laws protecting the environment, an upstate New York environmental group was looking for ways to protest the construction of a nuclear power plant at Storm King Mountain in Cornwall. In order to sue the Atomic Energy Commission, the group sleuthed out a little-known section of the AEC charter which made the commission responsible not only for promotion of the nuclear power industry but for the public safety as well. The group then cited safety violations in the disposal of nuclear wastes, for radioactive waste materials were polluting the waters and endangering the lives of fish. The suit lost,* but at least the group got into court.

When rights are not granted specifically through laws, they can be inferred out of a general sense of justice. A homosexual group in San Francisco felt they had indeed arrived at a point of respectability when in 1979 the California Supreme Court permitted them to sue a public utility.† The gays charged that they'd been victims of sex discrimination in hiring; the utility countered that gays weren't an identifiable class of people who could be discriminated against, and therefore could not sue. The California court sided with the gays, saying their plight was as bad and as obvious as that of blacks and women when it came to hiring bias, and so they should share the same legal rights to enter the courthouse. The gays felt complimented to be joined by the court with such eminent company as blacks and women.[4] They have not yet won their case—and in fact may never do so—but the sympathetic words of the court, adjudging them to be an identifiable minority, were still music to their ears, reinforcing their resolve to fight on for their rights.

Policy-change lawsuits basically function as a lobbying tool. They're the back door into a political system that might otherwise be closed. Nevertheless, there are times when a group may indeed have a right to sue, but still find the door slammed in its face. This occurs when judges believe a case to be either a waste of time (so-called frivolous cases) or a "political" question that they dare not touch. The "political" bar to a hearing can be particularly painful. Since policy-

---

* *Scenic Hudson Preservation Conference* v. *FPC*, 354 F 2d 608 (2d Circ 1965).

† *Gay Law Students Assn.* v. *Pacific Telephone & Telegraph*, 24 C. 3d 458, 595 P. 2d 592 (1979).

change suits inevitably ask a court to pass judgment on the acts of presidents, or Congress, or state legislatures, if a court won't hear the case, there's nowhere else to go.

As late as 1956, the U.S. Supreme Court held that it did not have the power to decide whether Tennessee's election maps give more weight to the votes of farmers than to those of city dwellers. This decision capped decades of bipartisan organizing in the southern state, where the legislature for fifty years had flouted its own law demanding reapportionment according to population. But the Supreme Court ruled that reapportionment was a "political" problem, and rejected the cry for judicial help.

But this time, the Tennessee reformers would not take the Court's "no" for an answer. Instead, they tried a new legal tack. Rather than challenge the legislature in state court for violating local law, the reformers hit upon a "new" legal theory which was slowly becoming popular and well known: that the illegal acts of state governments—such as the refusal to obey the Tennessee reapportionment law—were not merely a "political" question but a violation of the United States Constitution—specifically the Fourteenth Amendment, which says that no state may deny a person the equal protection of the laws. The so-called equal-protection amendment was passed in 1866 in order that the federal government might control state treatment of former slaves. But there was no reason why that amendment could not or should not be interpreted to protect *all* citizens from any and all sorts of state abuses.

In May 1959, Charles W. Baker, chairman of the Shelby County Court in Tennessee, headed a list of plaintiffs suing Secretary of State Joe C. Carr and a host of state officials, in a complaint filed in federal court. The suit demanded that Tennessee maps be reapportioned in such a way that Carr and everyone else in Tennessee would have "equal protection of the laws." The litigants had documents showing that, the way present maps were drawn, a voter in a rural county had five times the representation of a voter in the city. "That is not only taxation without representation," one plaintiff's attorney wrote, "but slavery."[5]

In December, a three-judge federal court dismissed the case as a "political" question. While the court agreed that equal-protection rights were being violated by the acts of the legislature, it would not involve itself and tell them what to do. The case was appealed, and finally came before the U.S. Supreme Court. There, attorneys for the would-be reformers appealed to the justices, pointing out that if the Court refused to act, there was simply no place else to get relief.

The Court understood the argument, and was impressed by the equal-protection theory. In March 1962, it ruled in *Baker* v. *Carr,* for the first time, that legislative apportionment was indeed an issue that judges could and should hear.*

On this seemingly minor point, the history of voter equality was constructed. Two years later, in a second case, *Reynolds* v. *Sims,* the U.S. Supreme Court would rule that legislatures must be apportioned according to population.† (Although the Court had an opportunity to make this ruling in 1962 in *Baker* v. *Carr,* it apparently was not yet ready to do so.) "One man, one vote" became the law of the land.

The success of a cause lawsuit also involves the difficult question of whether the "judicial climate" is right for a case and the goals it represents. The reformer knows that his long-range goals are not particularly popular—if the cause were popular, it would be law. And so he appeals to the court, hoping that, by granting a sympathetic verdict, the judge will lead the way toward convincing the public. Strategically, the reformer's goal is to reach the court at a moment when it will give his otherwise "way out" views some respect and understanding.

Timing can be crucial, as antislavery forces discovered during the 1850s in taking up the cause of Dred Scott. Scott was

* *Baker* v. *Carr,* 369 U.S. 186 (1963) .
† *Reynolds* v. *Sims,* 377 U.S. 533 (1964) .

a slave who moved with his owner, an army surgeon named John Emerson, from Missouri, a "slave state," to Illinois, a "free state." The abolitionists, who had concocted the Scott case almost out of whole cloth as a test on the slavery issue, wanted the U.S. Supreme Court to say that Scott's move from Missouri to Illinois made him a free man.

The case first began when Emerson died. Scott and his family were left to Emerson's wife to hold in trust for their daughter, but Mrs. Emerson wanted no part of slave ownership and abandoned them all. Needing someone to support him, the slave went back to a prior owner's son, one Peter Blow, who couldn't afford to keep him. Blow, not knowing what else to do, brought the case to a lawyer, who hit upon the idea that, if Scott was shown to be a free man, he could sue John Emerson's estate for past wages.

The lawsuit for past wages began against Emerson's estate in 1846.* Scott lost one trial, won another, and then lost in the Missouri Supreme Court (the state where he claimed legal residence and citizenship), which ruled finally that, since he was still a slave, he could be owed nothing.

Mrs. Emerson was by then remarried to an abolitionist congressman from Massachusetts, who desired to press on with the question of Scott's freedom. (By one account, Scott himself cared not at all whether he was slave or free, as long as his family was supported.) Her new husband arranged an artificial sale of the slave to John Sanford, who was Emerson's brother-in-law and executor of the doctor's estate. Once the sale was complete, it was arranged that Scott would sue Sanford for his freedom.

The case made its way up the judicial ropes and arrived at its desired destination, the U.S. Supreme Court, in 1856.† But by that year, the political air was poisoned by the slavery question. Scott himself immediately became a mere pawn in the game between North and South. Five of the nine justices

---

* See Julius J. Marke, *Vignettes of Legal History,* pp. 81–104, and Don E. Fehrenbacher, *The Dred Scott Case,* pp. 241–48.
† *Scott* v. *Sanford,* 19 Howard 393 (1857) .

were from slave states, and, in a previous lawsuit on slave-related questions, the Court had upheld the rights of states to do as they wished. Thus, while abolitionists were impassioned in their dream of changing the Supreme Court's collective mind on this aching question, the timing was always against it.

The end result was even worse than the abolitionists could have anticipated. The proslavery justices, buoyed by the election of a southern-sympathizing president, James Buchanan, decided to use *Scott* v. *Sanford* as a major statement protecting the rights of slaveholders. In 1857 they issued their 7–2 opinion, going about as far as they could in denying basic rights to blacks. Relying on the position of slaves at the time the Constitution was written, Chief Justice Roger B. Taney wrote that Negroes were "beings of an inferior order, and altogether unfit to associate with the white race, either in social or political relations; and so far inferior that they had no rights which the white man was bound to respect."[6]

The Dred Scott case is an example of extraordinarily bad timing. The case became a major presidential-campaign issue that split the Democratic party and indirectly led to the election of Abraham Lincoln, who said he would vote to overrule the decision if given an opportunity to do so. It also caused a precipitous decline in the prestige of the Supreme Court, which previously had been regarded with awe.

As for Scott himself, the details of his life are somewhat obscure, but his lawsuit appears to have brought him little but grief. Sanford, his new owner, died soon after the decision. Scott and his family were freed, thus losing their only means of support. A year after the decision, in September 1858, Dred Scott died of consumption, in dire poverty, ignored.

Since timing is so crucial, the shrewd strategist tests the political winds before bringing his case into court. This is what the American Civil Liberties Union has attempted to do with the Supreme Court under Warren Burger. The ACLU is one of the nation's oldest law-reform organizations and uses the courts on a daily basis. Yet it took this group nearly six years to become convinced that it would be better to have no decision at all on some key issues than the total defeat it might suffer under the Burger Court. Under Earl Warren, Burger's predecessor, the ACLU won the vast majority of its cases. Warren Burger, aided by four other conservative Nixon appointees, dropped that success rate to less than 50 percent. As a result, the group decided to stop cases before they reached the federal High Court. In fact, it ceased relying on litigation as its major tool and instead began to lobby Congress directly. "If you lose in the Supreme Court," one ACLU attorney said in announcing the new strategy, "you're cooked as far as the whole country is concerned. You've set a bad precedent that applies nationwide."[7]

Political and social-change suits aim to alter the balance of power, to get from the court something that is presently impossible to achieve elsewhere. Unlike the "protest" case, where one person or group can temporarily change the political atmosphere more or less on their own (with, of course, assistance of attorneys), in reform cases much work remains to be done behind the scenes. This behind-the-scenes labor may include lobbying the legislature, fund raising to defray legal costs, building a grass-roots movement, or even providing legal research and secretarial services. Without such organizational support, the most righteous legal case may end in failure.

The establishment of a strong and dedicated organization changed the Karen Silkwood case from a lonely "why me?" complaint of a grieving father and two children into a significant and effective means for building a movement to fight nuclear power.

Karen Silkwood died in November 1974 in a mysterious car crash on a deserted stretch of Oklahoma highway. The twenty-eight-year-old lab technician had worked at the Kerr-McGee plutonium plant outside Oklahoma City, where she was a union activist. In the days before she died, she had be-come convinced that she was contaminated with radiation and believed she had confirming evidence that her apartment was contaminated with small amounts of plutonium. At the time of the crash, she was on her way to meet a union official and a science reporter from *The New York Times* to docu-ment her charges that Kerr-McGee maintained unsafe work-ing conditions. She was said to have compiled a number of documents to serve as proof of her charges, and to have car-ried them with her in an envelope when she left for her meeting.

Silkwood's car ran (or was run) off the road. The car was found, but the envelope was missing. When two federal in-vestigations, by the Justice Department and the Atomic Energy Commission, failed to find proof of wrongdoing by Kerr-McGee, Karen's father, Bill Silkwood, and her young children filed an $11.5-million lawsuit, contending that the company had negligently caused her contamination.

This lawsuit was of immediate interest to a host of groups: The women's movement, the unions, and the then-burgeon-ing antinuke forces all saw in Karen's death a martyrdom for their own particular causes. The Karen Silkwood story be-came a hot property, the rights to which were contested by would-be moviemakers representing each viewpoint. Jane Fonda and *Ms.* magazine competed for the prize. Two male "radical" filmmakers camped out at Bill Silkwood's door, and even went fishing with him in an attempt to hook his daugh-ter's biography.

Ultimately, the antinuke forces came to dominate the pre-trial fund raising, and when the trial began in spring 1978, Howard Kohn wrote in *Rolling Stone* that "the primary issue in the trial is negligence. But anti-nuclear forces view the Oklahoma City courtroom as an epicenter of their fierce na-tionwide struggle."[8]

The antinuclear organization helped keep the Silkwood lawsuit alive; without its support, Bill Silkwood, a $15,000-a-year painter, might have had to settle. Kerr-McGee offered him $1500 for $5000 worth of his daughter's belongings destroyed when Kerr-McGee sent workers in to decontaminate her apartment. As it was, Bill Silkwood recalled, "If the company had offered me the full $5000 like they should have, I'd probably have taken it."[9]

The Silkwood supporters were of inestimable value to the small and struggling legal staff preparing the case. These volunteers picked up where Justice Department and congressional inquiries into the Silkwood death had left off. Two Catholic priests, Bill Davis and Wally Kasuboski, became the legal investigators, though they lacked any experience. They and other of Silkwood's friends followed up every lead, and while their work was primarily aimed at the forthcoming trial, it assisted the antinuke movement as well. Evidence regarding nuclear safety "irregularities" was leaked to the media years before the trial began. The movement used Silkwood as a symbol, and marked the fourth anniversary of her death with a well-publicized demonstration. Nationwide mailings, aimed at getting financial support for the trial, linked Karen's alleged contamination with the overall problem of nuclear poisoning. (Who, if anyone, caused Karen's actual death remained a mystery.)

All that hard work came together in a spectacular $10.5-million jury verdict in May 1979. A judge for the first time ruled that a nuclear plant could be held responsible for low-level contamination of its workers, and, based on that unprecedented ruling, a jury made a landmark award to the Silkwood heirs, nearly $10 million of it in so-called punitive damages, aimed at punishing Kerr-McGee for its actions. A page one *New York Times* headline termed the verdict a "setback to the nuclear industry."[10] (Kerr-McGee promptly filed an appeal.) But the court system alone was not uniquely responsible for that verdict. It might never have been achieved without the dedication of the Silkwood support group, using the case for its own reform purposes.

*   *   *

Reform cases are based on symbols: a little black schoolgirl deprived of equal education; a dirty river; a nuclear power plant that almost melts down. These symbols fill the role of the "attractive plaintiff," described earlier. They function in the policy-change suit much as in the protest variety, selling the case both to the court and to the world outside.

Ralph Nader, who has become a symbol of consumer rights, is among the most famous and persistent self-styled "attractive plaintiffs." During the early 1960s, Nader was trying to get congressional attention for a pet project—automobile safety. He protested the construction of General Motors' Corvair model, calling it a hazard and asserting that its steering column came off. But Nader's audience remained limited until he discovered that he was under constant surveillance by General Motors "spies." Nader filed a lawsuit, charging GM with invading his privacy. In March 1966, the president of General Motors personally apologized to Ralph Nader and gave him a check for $425,000 in settlement of the suit. Having established himself in that one lawsuit as a champion of consumers, Nader used the money to establish Nader's Raiders, which became Public Citizen, a consumer-oriented watchdog group. Nader continued to use himself as a symbol, publicizing such issues as airline overbooking by suing in his own name.

Sometimes, however, the use of an "attractive plaintiff" as a means of publicizing a case can do more harm than good. In trying to stop construction of the Tellico Dam in the Tennessee Valley, environmentalists seized upon the tiny snail darter, a guppylike fish that was threatened with extinction. The snail darter may have seemed an unlikely choice to play the role of "attractive plaintiff," but the press, at least initially, embraced the fish as the symbol of the antidam movement. One writer called it "a finny little David fighting the Goliath of modern progress."[11] Advocates of the dam, on the other hand, called the fish a "useless minnow," and gathered some support for their cause from others who were similarly appalled that a public works project costing millions could be jeopardized by a tiny fish whose existence had just been discovered.

In the end, despite numerous court victories, including at least one at the Supreme Court level, Congress passed a special law exempting the Tellico Dam from the Endangered Species Act. The dam was authorized for construction. The snail darters were transplanted, but most of them died in their new homes. Few if any of the fish remain.

Given the respect afforded social-change suits, it is not unnatural that people who enter court for private and personal reasons are often swept up in the reform-suit spirit. This appears to have happened to George and Pat Martinez, the couple discussed in chapter 3 who sued the state of California when their daughter was murdered. Theirs, as we have seen, was the classic "why me?" suit, full of anguish and disbelief and obsession with the details of death. But once the "why me?" aspect of the case was exorcised, husband and wife began to see themselves as reformers. They became deeply involved in the broader legal issue of their case, the question of whether governmental employees should be immune from suit.

Because such immunity existed in California, the Martinez case was thrown out of court. But George and Pat Martinez went beyond the lawsuit. They spoke out on the issue, testifying before Congress and discussing it with various state senators. State employees whose negligence causes harm to others should be accountable in court for their actions, they insisted. They did not succeed in building a movement around their cause, but their political foray as attractive plaintiffs did point up a problem that exists within the law and they themselves grew from the experience.

In many kinds of lawsuits, lawyers can have purely mercenary interests and still do a fine job. Not so in "change" cases. Litigation of this type generally offers little in the way of financial reward; it promises only years, if not decades, of hard labor before the first ego-gratifying favorable decisions come filing in. Consequently, the lawyer who gets involved in a lawsuit to end an injustice must totally believe in the cause. A lot of attorneys can sympathize, many more can be brilliant technicians, but more than sympathy and technique may be required. What many of these reform cases demand is the inspiration of a lawyer who knows the hardship of his case firsthand. This lawyer will fight the good fight not only for his client but indirectly for himself.

Without the vigorous, dedicated efforts of black attorneys working on their own behalf as well as in the interest of their whole community, the movement for civil rights against the villainous Jim Crow went nowhere. In 1927, Kelly Miller, a leading Negro intellectual of his day and a leader at all-black Howard University, criticized his colleagues for permitting whites to serve as the voice of Negro needs. "No man of one group can ever furnish leadership to people of another," Miller said.[12]

Miller's view became the dominant ideology behind the growth of Howard University Law School during the 1930s under the direction of Dr. Charles R. Houston. And it was probably not mere coincidence that when Houston's students (among them the future United States Supreme Court Justice Thurgood Marshall) came before the bar, blacks began winning their first victories on the way to real justice. Black attorneys saw indignities nonblacks couldn't see, and possibilities to bend the law which nonblacks might not try.

Similarly, the road to equality for women may have been blocked by the underrepresentation of women as lawyers. Generally, Americans define the strength of their case by their ability to find a lawyer who will handle it. Before there were women lawyers, or black lawyers, or lawyers with a bent toward environmental and welfare cases, the courts were dominated by (and to some extent continue to be dominated by) Caucasian male lawyers with a business orientation who had the court's attention all to themselves. American women were barred from law schools until about 1900. Though they were free to study law under a male attorney, various statutes deprived them of their right to practice even if they could pass the bar exam.[13] The roadblocks, both legal and sociological, were not totally removed until the 1960s. And once they were, the courts were flooded with cases involving the threshold issues of hiring discrimination, equal pay for equal work, and unfair credit laws.

This notion of the "empathetic lawyer" offends many attorneys. It violates their belief in themselves as professionals, as nonpartisan hired guns. Gerald Spence, who became chief trial counsel in the Silkwood case, was initially reluctant to sign on in this lawsuit because there were too many "movement lawyers" involved in it—lawyers who fight a case because of their political or emotional commitment to the cause. "I didn't want to just become another antinuke," Spence said after the $10.5-million verdict was in. "I didn't want to become a movement attorney. I don't think movement attorneys tend to be effective."[14]

A continuing argument rages between these two camps: the cool, analytical, uncommitted "hired gun" on the one hand; the impassioned, dedicated "movement lawyer" on the other. But the fact remains that for four years "movement lawyers" filed the papers, did the research, mobilized and deployed the volunteers, and kept up the morale of the grieving Silkwood family. They believed in the *cause,* not just the case. Were it not for them, there would have been no suit for Gerald Spence to try.

A legal victory is such a high it's easy to think that the Kingdom has come and everything will now be perfect. Alas, one lawsuit does not a revolution make. The hard work often begins *after* the winning judicial pronouncement is in. Twenty-five years after *Brown,* the nation still struggles with school integration. "Politicians and the middle class never had the guts to make the change," one disgruntled advocate commented while commemorating the lawsuit's silver jubilee.[15] There has been a plethora of reform-type suits over the past decades, and the results of even the biggest successes have been sobering.

In the early 1970s, an environmental group called the Wilderness Society filed suit to halt construction of the Trans-Alaskan Pipeline,* which was to bring oil from Alaska to the U.S. mainland. The society wanted the oil line to contain safeguards for the wildlife of the area, and in due course an injunction was issued halting construction, and protections were written into the blueprints. A settlement was reached, and the pipeline builders consented, on paper, to allowing various groups to oversee construction to insure that environmental protections continued.

So far so good: It appeared that the Wilderness Society had won a major victory. But as building resumed, the victory was shown to be hollow. The developers were sophisticated and worked their way around their own agreements, never precisely breaking the pact, but not permitting effective overseeing to be carried out, either. Federal monitors did not see two-thirds of all construction activity, though they were supposed to see it all. Almost one-fifth of the environmental protections written into the settlement were ignored.

The Wilderness Society could do nothing about any of it. They had no clout in Congress, where approval of the pipeline construction was granted. They had no funds, so they couldn't oversee the building of the line themselves. Even when joined by three other environmental groups, the Wilderness Society could barely scrape together funds for a single plane excursion over the frozen Alaskan site. Because they had concentrated all their efforts on winning the battle in court, never thinking ahead to the political realities of making their victories stick, the Wilderness Society eventually was defeated.[16]

This is precisely the point where many reform cases get stuck. "Litigation often leads to paper victories," concedes John Denvir in a Law Review article on public-interest

* *Wilderness Society* v. *Hickel,* 325 F. Supp. 422 (D.D.C. 1970).

suing. "The lawsuit is a success, but the social evil is essentially untouched."[17]

The truth is, after years of fighting for piecemeal victories, so-called public-interest groups get tired. They've concentrated on the lawsuit so long they forget the suit is merely a lobbying tool, not the end in itself. After winning the legal battle, the political struggle is sure to follow. Reform suits are political acts in legal clothing. Losers smell this and don't take defeat lying down.

This was especially clear during the early days of welfare-rights litigation. Lawyers would win major victories on behalf of their poor clients, only to find there was no way to implement the decision. Once, a San Francisco judge ordered a state agency to increase rent subsidies for the poor, but because the legislature refused to allocate the money, the increases never went through.[18] In Chicago, similarly, a federal judge in 1969 ordered that low income public housing be scattered throughout the city rather than isolated in an area then known as the Negro Ghetto. It was a great victory for the six poor people who brought the suit,* but the city balked and for years refused to build any new low income housing rather than obey the court's will. As these suits illustrate, reform battles must be waged simultaneously on many fronts. For the true reformer, the fight is never over.

A lawsuit that stopped construction on the Century Freeway for almost a decade contained all the elements for success, from the "right to sue" to the "zeal to go on." For years it appeared that total victory was at hand, that David would indeed kill Goliath. But in the final assessment, though both sides probably got all they could from the suit, neither got precisely what they wanted.

Ralph and Esther Keith know what a real victory would mean: no freeway, ever. Since 1947, the Keiths have lived in the same three-bedroom house in Los Angeles County, not

---

* *Gautreaux* v. *Chicago Housing Authority,* 296 F Supp. 907 (1969) .

far from International Airport. They raised their son and daughter there in relative quiet, and only once did they get involved in local politics—when they helped oust some conservative members of the school board. Then, in 1964, they learned that a proposed freeway, a 17.2-mile stretch of Interstate 105, would go right through their bedroom.

Ralph Keith, a determined, middle-aged meteorologist, was troubled by the news. He didn't think the freeway was necessary. His job was measuring the air quality in the Southern California Basin, and he was concerned by the dismal, smoggy air as it presently was. California had plenty of freeways already; any more of them might endanger the public health.

The Century Freeway had been in the planning stages for more than a decade, the last phase of California's pioneering highway system which had begun in 1947. But although the money had been already allocated and state officials regarded construction as accomplished fact, Ralph Keith's sense of logic told him it did not have to be so.

For six years, Ralph and Esther fought the freeway. They attended public hearings, wrote letters, and tried to mobilize their neighbors. Their big stand came on March 4, 1970. It was a day Esther Keith will never forget. At 10:20 in the morning, two representatives of the state Division of Highways pulled up at her front door and demanded to be let in. Their plan was to assess the value of the Keith home, so the state could purchase it and start the ball rolling for freeway construction.

Esther Keith, who is proud of her reputation as an "adamant woman," muddied their plans. She locked her screen door and refused to let the highway men in. "They stood at my front door for three-quarters of an hour," Esther says. "They threatened me, and were verbally abusive. And when that happened, I knew I'd never stop fighting them."

The right-of-way assessors remained outside and debated with Esther Keith about her legal position. They argued back and forth. Finally, she recalls, they said they would stand in front of the house and make their assessment from there, thus guaranteeing a lower price. Esther wouldn't budge. "Go ahead," she told them. "See if your assessment holds up in court." The two men walked away.

Phone calls and letters from the state followed. Ralph Keith began to write about his confrontations with the Century Freeway in a local newspaper. They began collecting letters from their neighbors who'd had similar dreadful experiences. One neighbor told Esther that when he challenged the price that the state was offering for his home, the right-of-way man said, "You're just lucky we're willing to pay you. If this were Russia, we'd just put a gun to your head."

Soon their organizing got the attention of the Western Center on Law and Poverty, a public-interest law firm funded by the federal government. The Western Center had received complaints from poor and old people who were also being harassed by the state, and they were considering a lawsuit challenging the entire right-of-way process. The Keiths were elated: Someone had heard their plea.

Suing the state proved beyond the capacity of the struggling Western Center. But it was a case tailor-made for the newly created Center for Law in the Public Interest, a privately funded law firm eager to do environmental work. In 1971, the Keiths agreed to be plaintiffs in a proposed suit that would challenge the Century Freeway as a noise and safety hazard. That suit, *Keith* v. *John Volpe* (then U.S. secretary of transportation), was filed the next day.* By that time, all the homes adjacent to the Keiths had been removed. Signs reading "Private Property—Keep Out" surrounded the Keith property.

The first years of the Century Freeway suit coincided with the best years of the environmental movement. "Save the earth!" was the rallying cry of groups like the Sierra Club, the Wilderness Society, and Friends of the Earth. The nation celebrated "Earth Day" in 1970, and only a year earlier passed the National Environmental Policy Act, which dedicated the

* *Keith* v. *John Volpe,* 72-355 HP (U.S. Dist. Ct., L.A.) .

federal government to "create and maintain conditions under which man and nature can exist in productive harmony." Some law firms, like the Environmental Defense Fund and the National Resources Defense Counsel, specialized only in environmental work. Other firms, like the Center for Law in the Public Interest, now representing Ralph and Esther Keith, regarded the environment as one of many interesting, socially progressive issues. They were interested in discrimination cases, stockholder rights, and the care of drunks, too.

In many respects, the six lead attorneys at the Center exemplified the new "glamour image" of the public-interest lawyer in the Vietnam era. The oldest, Rick Sutherland, was thirty-four. The youngest, Mary Nichols, was twenty-seven. All of them had been *Law Review* editors at prestige schools, including Harvard, Yale, and Boalt Hall. All were impressively good-looking. Crucially, four of them had left lucrative careers at one of Los Angeles's most prestigious law firms, O'Melveny & Myers, for an uncertain future with a firm dependent on grants and private donations. Though at first they were rejected for funding by the Ford Foundation, a last-minute change of heart brought forth the final $75,000 grant that enabled the Center to open its doors to the Keiths in 1971.[19] Once the suit was agreed on, the attorneys began putting in ten- and 12-hour days of preparation.

By the time the Center was ready to attack the Century Freeway in May 1972, a large coalition had begun to grow around the suit. Several small cities in the area, which opposed the freeway for the havoc it would cause in their residential neighborhoods, signed up as plaintiffs. The Sierra Club joined, too, protesting the freeway as environmentally unsound. And the National Association for the Advancement of Colored People challenged the freeway as a blight on some of Los Angeles's best black neighborhoods. The Century Freeway would pass right through Watts's most affluent area, the so-called Blodgett Tract, and indeed the area's most valuable homes had already been destroyed. When the state had first given the go-ahead for construction of the freeway ten years earlier, right-of-way purchasers had immediately bought up and razed the Blodgett homes. It had been an enclave of middle-class respectability in a welfare ghetto. In destroying Blodgett, the heart of the community was cut out. "It's no accident," says one resident of the area, "freeways always cut through the most affluent black areas, where there are prime working families and the most stable people." In filing suit, the NAACP hoped to insure the rights of middle-class blacks who still lived along the proposed freeway route.

Center attorneys agreed with the Keiths that the Century Freeway was unnecessary. If they had their way, the freeway would never be built. But, realistically, they couldn't promise the Keiths (or any of the other plaintiffs) such a permanent solution. The best they could do was insist that the freeway conform with the National Environmental Policy Act. Obviously, a concrete stretch of freeway, which would only add noise and pollution to the area, was not a condition "under which man and nature can exist in productive harmony," as the act required. But caution was necessary. A judge might disagree with the attorneys' interpretation of the law. At that point the act was only two years old, rarely tested (or read), and there was no way of knowing how some fine-print clause might be interpreted by a judge if challenged in court.

And so the lawsuit argued before Judge Harry Pregerson that May day in 1972 asked for a very simple thing: a halt to construction of the freeway until the state filed an "environmental-impact statement" on how the new road would affect local communities. This statement was clearly required by the act, but the state, assuming that the freeway was exempt because it was ten years on the drawing boards, had never bothered to comply. On July 7, after two months' deliberation, Judge Pregerson, a well-respected Johnson appointee and a former marine who won a Purple Heart in World War II, issued his order: Stop the freeway. "This is the most resounding decision involving a freeway anywhere," rejoiced a Sierra Club representative. The state had already acquired one-third of the 6000 parcels of land on the estimated $530-million project. In the judge's forty-two-page decision, he specifically cautioned plaintiffs not to think he was stopping the freeway forever. "Whether or not it will ever be built remains for the appropriate federal and state administrative agencies to decide," Pregerson wrote.

Despite this disclaimer, it did seem that time was on the side of "no freeway." For one thing, there was an immediate six-year stall while the Department of Transportation wrote its environmental-impact statement. For six years, the seventeen-mile stretch of land remained untouched. The extent of this delay was a surprise. When Pregerson had first issued his stop-the-freeway injunction, the state had complained it would cause a loss of six months. For unknown bureaucratic reasons, the study took twelve times that long, and cost $5 million.

As work on the environmental study continued, the political climate of the state seemed to favor "no freeway," too. The Keiths were excited by the election in 1974 of Jerry Brown as governor. A former Jesuit student (and later boy friend of rock star Linda Ronstadt), Brown campaigned for his first term on a new "era of limits" in government spending. The Keiths assumed freeways were included in Brown's proposed cutbacks. Esther Keith swears she heard him expressly promise (in "the one clear statement that he made") that his election would mean "no Century Freeway."

Once Brown became governor, they grew increasingly optimistic. His appointee to the Department of Transportation, Adriana Gianturco, immediately placed a lid on new freeway projects. Indeed, there were so many cutbacks in state highway programs that Brown seriously considered loaning California construction workers to Saudi Arabia for public-works ventures. Last, but hardly least, Brown appointed Mary Nichols, a Center legal associate, to the Air Resources Board. This board would have to approve the state's environmental-impact study of the Century corridor. Ralph and Esther thought they were blessed: How could they lose?

Both the lawsuit and the freeway construction remained at a standstill until 1977. Most of the cities in the seventeen-mile corridor hadn't wanted the highway in the first place, so in the first years of the injunction, the mayors and businessmen along the route were more or less content with no activity. But as the years stretched on and the grass began to grow in the vacant fields where homes had already been razed, the natives grew restless. Homeowners who were yet to be bought out were in limbo; they weren't sure what to do with their land. Should they even bother to repaint? And if there was no freeway, would their homes be worth more? Meanwhile, land values adjacent to the vacant lots plummeted. Local officials in towns all along the proposed freeway strip began to complain about crime and vandalism in the abandoned areas. They wanted action: If there was to be a freeway, get on with it already, they seemed to say.

Thus, the political climate, once so favorable to "no freeway," began to change. First, John Byork, a city councilman from the beleaguered and financially shaky city of Lynwood at the farthest end of the freeway corridor, began mobilizing political support. He appealed to his congressmen—Charles Wilson and Glenn Anderson. A committee calling itself Fourteen Congressmen for the Freeway put pressure on the federal Highway Administration. Although the Keiths have letters from Wilson and others insisting that federal money would never be allocated to the project, the highway bureaucracy now began to make noises as if the money would be forthcoming as soon as the injunction was lifted.

By 1977, when Jerry Brown ran for reelection, times had changed. The environmentalists were no longer as popular. The theme in these days of recession was "jobs"—specifically, construction jobs. Brown needed the union vote, and he wasn't going to get it by being antifreeway, since freeways meant employment. Brown felt the heat from politicians in the freeway corridor. Even the black community, which originally had reflected NAACP concern at the freeway's destruction of prosperous black residential areas, now favored the freeway for the jobs it would bring. The assemblywoman from Watts, for example, looked at the ruins of the Blodgett Tract, which she represented, and knew that if there was no freeway, that area would never be rebuilt. "It's difficult for me to be against the freeway," Assemblywoman Maxine Waters said in 1977. "I'm thinking maybe at least I'll be able to unpack some jobs in the area and insure that one possible decent thing comes out of it."

But Brent Rushforth, the Center attorney representing the Keiths, refused to bow to political pressure. "I think this freeway is hardly inevitable at all," he said that summer. "If I were to bet, I'd bet that the freeway will never be built."

Rushforth had several novel suggestions for alternatives: The seventeen miles could be turned into a big public park; or the homes that had been removed could be rebuilt; or the area could be turned over to private enterprise for factories. But along the vacant corridor, alternatives to the freeway were no longer seriously considered. This made Rushforth angry. "I believe the light ought to go on in the mind of bureaucracies of the absurdity of building a freeway," he said. "I think the project as proposed is an absurd project, lacking imagination, and has enormous inadequacies in terms of air-pollution control."

If the light did go on in the mind of the bureaucracy, as Rushforth urged, it was a very dim bulb. Ever since Brown's election, the antifreeway contingent had been waiting for him to veto the project. There was no reason he should be beholden to it, they reasoned, since it was a project he'd inherited from his predecessor, Ronald Reagan. When Brown didn't veto it, the Keiths and others like them put their faith in Brown's liberal, antigrowth appointees. But this faith, it turned out, was misplaced, too.

As predicted, Mary Nichols, the former Center attorney now on the Air Resources Board, found the state's environmental-impact statement to be inadequate: The effects of the freeway would be disastrous, she wrote. But despite her ruling, events didn't go forward as scheduled. The Keiths say they were told that Tom Quinn, chief of the Air Resources Board and a Brown appointee, would kill the freeway based on Nichols's report. But, mysteriously, a reexamination of the Nichols report was ordered instead. The air-pollution problem along the freeway corridor now was reexamined in the light of evidence supplied by the Department of Transportation (the same department that was under attack in federal court). This evidence showed that the freeway would have little or no effect on air quality, and might even improve the rest of the environment. With this new report now approved by the state, there was nothing to be done. The freeway would go through.

These political realities were apparent to the Keiths and their lawyers even before the first hearing on the adequacy of the state's impact report. Tactically, they could challenge the statement, present expert witnesses with contrary evidence. But there was only a slim chance of success. Fighting an environmental-impact statement is extremely difficult. During the six years since the case began, environmental law had become big business and the Environmental Protection Agency had been challenged in hundreds of cases. The sorry news from the courts was that the law is very weak. Once an environmental statement is completed, it is hard to knock down. The burden is placed on those who would challenge a project—people like the Keiths—to question the report; the state or other project organizer is assumed to be correct.

To launch such an attack on the Century Freeway report would cost possibly millions in hearings and appeals, and the Center, conceding now that the freeway would probably be built, felt this would be wasteful.

They did not simply abandon the fight, however. If there was to be a freeway, at least it should be a "human" project: No more harassment of homeowners—they should get a fair price for their houses and land; and the communities the freeway would cut through should profit also, with jobs and job training.

John Phillips, the Center attorney in charge of negotiations, began a three-month settlement process that eventually assured these goals in writing. His biggest victory was in housing. In an era when Los Angeles was suffering a housing shortage, 4200 homes would be destroyed by the freeway. This struck him as cruel and abrupt, so, in a unique piece of political maneuvering, he got the federal government to agree to contribute $250 million to build low-income replacement homes. All this was not as good as "no freeway," everyone knew. But it was better than nothing.

In October 1979, the injunction halting construction of the freeway was finally lifted. The *Los Angeles Times* nevertheless termed the outcome "clearly a victory" for the Center for Law in the Public Interest, insisting they got everything they wanted. The newspaper counted as part of "everything" the environmental studies and housing analyses that were part of the six-year stall, and praised the Center for helping to scale down the freeway from ten to eight lanes, with some sort of rapid-transit system to be erected in the middle.

Judge Pregerson, too, considered the case a victory for the plaintiffs. He ordered the state to pay the Center $2.2 million in attorneys' fees, citing the enormous public benefit that was derived from the Center's work. Thanks to this case, the judge said, the freeway blueprint changed from a rather typical mundane highway of 1950s vintage to an up-to-date, multiuse freeway with minimal noise and air pollution. The estimated cost of the project: $2 billion.

"What the Center set out to do is stop the Century Freeway," says Richard Rypinski, the attorney representing the state throughout the negotiations. "And there will be a freeway. So if there's a victory, it's only a partial one."

The victory is only partial for Ralph and Esther Keith, too. "There's even less of a reason to build this freeway today than there was in 1972," Esther said in 1980. "We shouldn't be building roads which encourage people to use their cars."

But neither Ralph nor Esther sound particularly upset with the way the case ended, and in at least one respect they feel victorious. A crucial part of the settlement imposes indirect court supervision over the state's buy-out of housing. If a pattern of abuse emerges, the court will know it.

"Most things in life end in compromise," says Ralph without a hint of acrimony in his voice, "and that's what happened to us."

Nevertheless, a full decade after Esther Keith refused to let state employees assess her house, the Keiths still have no intention of letting them inside. They figure it will be four more years before they absolutely have to.

"This is Custer's last stand," says Esther. "And there are sure a lot of Indians."

C H A P T E R   5

Money

For all the talk of why so many Americans sue, the dominant underlying reason remains a simple one: money. Sure, we want to express our feelings, to protest and to vent our grief, to seek vindication and to influence social or political events. But just as often, if not more often, we sue to get the cool, hard cash.

Money lawsuits should be viewed for what they are—business investments. But we rarely regard these suits with appropriate objectivity. A money lawsuit actually bears close resemblance to making a bet at the track or investing in a stock, but Americans don't see it that way. When our favored horse doesn't win the race, we don't demand the turf be changed. When our stock fails to perform, we don't call the New York Stock Exchange. But when our money lawsuits fail, it's justice itself that isn't working. This confusion of the desire for money with the search for justice creates problems.

This type of lawsuit begins with a controversy: Jones says Peters owes him something; Peters either broke his promise to perform a service, or won't pay for services already rendered. To end the controversy, Jones must take affirmative steps to force Peters to make good. These steps—starting from the first demand phone call—are his investment. If Jones decides to take the matter to court, signaling he is after high stakes, the required investment grows, both in time and money. Hiring an attorney, he must either pay for the services up front or agree to pay a certain percentage of the amount eventually recovered. These are the rules of the game, like paying the entry fee at the track or paying a stockbroker his commission. Attorney services are the "seed money" of the suit. Without them, the investment may not bear fruit.

It happens on occasion that a person with an outstanding claim says it isn't worth the investment, and lets the matter die. Often, a claimant does think it's worth it and would like to proceed, but can't afford to. In either event, the person may naïvely blame the system, believing that he should get what is his without any cost at all to himself. This poor soul is dreaming.

Viewing a lawsuit as an investment clears away an element of fantasy that surrounds our legal system. Suing for what you think is owed you is neither good nor bad, or it is *both* good and bad, having all the same attributes and disadvantages of our capitalist economy that it so accurately mirrors. Our legal system, much like every other part of our national life, is based on property. Property is money, and it is the only currency that the law permits. In order for a plaintiff to set foot through the courthouse door, one of two requirements must be satisfied: The plaintiff must claim that he has already suffered damages that can be translated into dollars and cents; or he must ask the court to halt some activity that otherwise seems likely to cause such money damages.

Suing for money has been with us, root and branch, since the founding of the Republic. Our founding fathers were a litigious bunch; they would sue each other if one's stray horse ate another's clover. Controversies over land ownership were our earliest form of suits; everywhere new settlers went, lawyers were sure to go, straightening out (or perhaps confusing) farmland divisions. Early on, we grew accustomed to fighting among ourselves, almost liking it. Property has always been king in America. A widely used legal textbook on property law, written during the Cold War's McCarthy period, went to great lengths to equate private property with Americanism. Our belief in private property, the text said, was what separated us from the Communists. It was certainly seen as worth fighting over, either in court or out.

Despite our long-standing tradition of suing for money, this is one kind of suit that doesn't quite have full public approval. In researching this book, I told people I was exploring the reasons why people sue. "Money," was the immediate and unanimous sneering response. "People are greedy," one woman said in a typical comment. "They think of suing as a way to make a quick buck." The assumption is that people who sue for money are seeking something for nothing, and that they are unworthy of what they get. My unscientific poll reflects the low prestige of litigation as merely another type of get-rich-quick scheme.

To its credit, suing for money is certainly an advance over less-civilized means of exacting one's due, such as lynchings and blood feuds, extortion and blackmail. Debtors' prisons are now outlawed, and we have progressed beyond that primitive level where a person could be locked up merely because he was behind in payments on a television set.

Still, the pursuit of the dollar in court brings us up against some difficult ethical and perhaps even moral dilemmas which are otherwise hidden in our culture. Substituting money for every conceivable kind of loss, as we routinely do, seems to degrade the human spirit, as if we really could measure one person's worth against another's. After an airline crash, we typically discover the revised-for-inflation scale of human existence: An "average" mother of five is worth $200,000; an attorney is worth more than $1 million; a student only $50,000 because her life is just beginning. On an entirely different scale, the family of an arsonist shot and killed by police near the scene of his crime gets $330,000—not because the arsonist is worth more, but to punish the police for using unnecessary force. This cold-blooded equating of life and money strikes many as grotesque, but it is very much in keeping with the economic system that dominates our lives.

The counterpart of the money-equals-life principle is "money equals rights." Native Americans have discovered that their claims against the federal government for thousands of acres of land are frequently "bought off," and that the money doesn't quite satisfy.[1] The 360-member Cayuga Nation of upstate New York filed a claim for 62,000 acres of its former reservation. That claim eventually was settled for $8 million and 5400 acres of state and federal land.[2] In another case, the Temoak Bands, a small Nevada tribe of western Shoshones, were angered when the United States offered them $26 million in exchange for 24 million acres taken in 1872. Indians claim accepting money for land is against their religion. "If we give up our land, we are giving up ourselves as a tribe," says one Indian leader.[3] But the courts are not equipped to reconstruct Indian nations in the wake of broken treaties. When land is unavailable, money is the only medium of exchange.

The pain and sadness that many plaintiffs bring with them into court frequently blinds them to the limitations of suing. Indians, perhaps like any other litigants, cannot be expected to view their claims dispassionately. Still, without evaluating the legitimacy of their plea for land, it is possible and perhaps even helpful to view these Indian lawsuits as commercial transactions. At the risk of oversimplification, Indians may be viewed as attempting to sell broken treaties at some high price. They come into court because only the court has the power to force the federal government to recognize the validity of their treaties and, consequently, to enter into negotiations. That Indians, and any other plaintiffs, may not like the terms offered is one of the risks of litigation.

The fact that suing for money is held in low esteem does not stop people from doing it. We fight about money illspent, money defrauded, money still owed, and money yet to be accounted for. It's an old business, and an ugly one, filled with dashed hopes, petty disappointments, and never-ending proof of mankind's greed.

Most suits for money sound rather routine, but Joseph Beaudette, a twenty-three-year-old elevator operator, thought of a new angle. According to a wire service report of his case, Beaudette sued a bartender to recover a tip. Beaudette had given the bartender, Clifford J. Bice, a New York State base-ball-lottery ticket as a tip for service. Bice didn't know what to make of the ticket, but other patrons told him to hold on to it and see what happened. Sure enough, Bice won the grand-slam prize of $10,000—thereupon Beaudette sued, saying that the money belonged to him. A judge held the booty in an interest-bearing account, and the two men waited for trial. Tired of waiting, Beaudette suggested a compromise: He agreed to give the bartender half the winnings ($5000 still isn't bad for a tip). Bice said fine, as long as he got to keep the interest, too. Forthwith, the case was dropped.

Since all lawsuits speak of money, it becomes difficult to perceive which suits are really serious about it, and which want something else entirely. The multibillion-dollar suit against OPEC by the machinists' union (described earlier as a protest case) was really an outraged call to the Carter administration, and anyone else with sufficient clout, to take a more decisive role against the oil cartel. And the Karen Silkwood suit for several million in damages was actually another way of continuing the nuclear-safety goals for which the young woman died. The law, it seems, forces everyone who sues to appear at least slightly mercenary.

Clearly, there is money to be made by suing. Elias Howe, known to generations of schoolchildren as the inventor of the sewing machine, made no money at all from his invention, but made millions from his lawsuits charging others with violating his patent.

Howe was a poverty-stricken machinist who had lived hand-to-mouth for more than a decade working on his invention. Finally, in 1845, he developed his design for a machine that could form a stitch using two threads. He received a patent the next year. He was not the only one at work in this field, and in fact the machine had probably been invented three times before. But his was the only patent, a factor which was irrelevant for the next five years since no one wanted to buy Howe's product. Having dedicated at least a decade of life to his sewing machine, Howe was still down on his luck.

But in 1850, Howe discovered that his rival inventors—especially Isaac Merritt Singer—were cornering the market. Singer was a natural huckster; he made money where the woebegone Howe could not. In 1851 Howe visited Singer, demanding $2000 for the exclusive rights to his patent. Singer claimed he didn't have the money. Two years later, Howe demanded $25,000. Again Singer declined. Howe determined to sue. But lacking money, he couldn't proceed. Finally, a wealthy benefactor, George W. Bliss, agreed to advance money for the suit in exchange for a half-interest in the patent. And thus began the so-called Sewing Machine Wars, involving scores of suits and threats of suits in Massachusetts, New York, and New Jersey.

The suits, well reported in local papers and scientific journals, made stars of many of the participants. Howe won. A reporter for *Galaxy* magazine wrote at the time that "Howe litigated his way to fortune and fame." At one time, Howe had close to twenty-five lawsuits pending. George Bliss made back his "seed" money for the suit, and then some. When the dust settled in 1856, Howe got a $25 royalty on every machine sold, not just by Singer but by a host of new competitors. By the time Howe's patent license expired in 1867, his earnings were about $2 million.*

The Sewing Machine Wars began an American tradition of litigating patent rights, a tradition that survives today. In 1980 the U.S. Supreme Court decided that scientists can even patent life they create in test tubes.

In today's high-yield litigation market, the smart investor

---

* The Singer story is told in Ruth Brandon, *A Capitalist Romance*.

may be able to parlay a relatively small lawsuit into a multi-million-dollar award. In 1979, Peter Roberts won $44 million from Sears. But this was hardly his first verdict against the company. Roberts had been an eighteen-year-old sales-clerk at a Sears store in Massachusetts when, in 1963, he invented a new wrench with a handy improvement: It allowed a socket to be removed and released from a ratchet with one hand. Roberts submitted his invention to Sears in response to a company request for employee suggestions. Sears told him the wrench had little commercial future, but they might be interested. They gave him $10,000 for the patent rights and sent him on his way.[4]

Over the next fourteen years, Sears made nearly $60 million from the sales of that elegant one-hand wrench.

Roberts complained, and Sears offered him $250,000 more. He rejected the offer, retained an attorney (a few lawyers reportedly turned him down), and sued. A court awarded him $1 million. Roberts thought that was still too little. He appealed the verdict, insisting that he was entitled to a share of Sears's profits from his invention. A higher court agreed. The case was returned to a trial court to determine how much was owed the now-thirty-five-year-old Roberts, who worked in a delicatessen in Chattanooga. A jury decided on the $44 million after finding that Roberts had been the victim of fraud and that Sears had taken advantage of him.

Peter Roberts's perseverance and eventual victory over Sears is precisely the type of tale that adds luster to the money-lawsuit mythology. It supports whatever theory about these suits you choose to hold: Either "justice" was done, by which view Roberts played David to Sears's Goliath; or it was a case of greed, pure and simple, in which case Roberts should have settled for (a) $10,000, (b) $250,000, or (c) $1 million, but was aided and abetted by a runaway emotional jury.

Money lawsuits inflame our Puritan dislike for those who strike it rich. Hearing of these victories, we don't know whether to respect the winner or blame him. In the end, we fault the legal system for allowing these confounding situations to arise in the first place.

Perhaps because of the low repute of these money suits, attorneys have fashioned a series of legends to enshrine their task of litigation in grandeur and glamour.

There's the Income-Redistribution Legend, for example, based on the notion that million-dollar jury verdicts, taken over the decades, will rechannel money from the rich to the poor. In this legend, lawyers and litigants star in a peaceful economic revolution, a courthouse version of the War on Poverty. They play Robin Hood.

Then there's the Consumer-Advocate Legend, which says that large jury verdicts exact such a toll on product manufacturers, doctors, and other groups being sued, that these groups quickly shape up their act, raise standards, and increase quality control.

Lastly, there's the Political-Message Legend, in which lawsuits are a means for disenfranchised jurors and litigants to send a message to the heads of Firestone Rubber, the American Medical Association, and other faceless corporate entities, warning that the citizenry is angry and won't stand much longer for high prices and low quality of care.

These legends are low on substance and high on wishful thinking. The *National Law Journal* reports that in the last decade not quite 300 people won $1 million or more from accident trials.[5] This tiny group (which insurance companies nevertheless consider too large) is the primary basis of the Income-Redistribution legend. But if these people comprise a revolution, it's minuscule. In fact, it can be calculated that only .0001 of all the money earned in this nation actually gets shuffled around from million-dollar cases.*

---

* This figure is calculated as follows: The total annual income of all American households is about $1 trillion. (Source: 1978 U.S. Census.) Over ten years, that's $10 trillion. In the last ten years, 300 people were awarded $1 million or more in accident trials, for an estimated total of $1 billion from all verdicts. $\dfrac{\$1,000,000,000}{\$10,000,000,000,000} = .0001$

The poor should not be holding their breath waiting for accident cases to make them rich.

Obviously, too, plaintiffs don't get all the money they are awarded: Attorneys typically take about a third, and some take more. The legal system, then, did not create 300 new millionaires in the last ten years, though it did make successful attorneys even wealthier.

The whole question of who gets a million-dollar verdict bears some examining. These verdicts typically go to accident victims who are either partly or totally paralyzed, or brain-damaged, or have suffered the loss of limbs. These litigants will never work again, and will need round-the-clock care. Verdicts such as these, therefore, represent the total of an injured person's lifetime earnings, plus compensation for "pain and suffering"—with the latter figure frequently left to the discretion of the jury. All verdicts, then, must be measured against the average, noninjured person's lifetime income, which can be estimated at $375,000 (using the 1978 median income of $15,000 over twenty-five years). Of course, this "average worker" continues to enjoy the use of all his limbs and senses. The loss of these prerequisites to a normal life indeed might be worth another $625,000 (the difference between $375,000 and the $1-million award) over a full lifetime.

Since these huge verdicts are the focus of a great deal of fantasy and debate about the value of litigation, it's worth taking a closer look at them. Assuming a verdict of $1 million, $333,000 (one-third, the typical attorney contingency fee) comes right off the top. This does not include the other costs of litigation—transcripts, expert witnesses, jury fees, and the like—which may total as much as $50,000. But even assuming no trial costs (for the sake of simplicity), how does a person spend $666,000, which is his, tax-free? If he puts it in a high-yield account, he can earn more than $50,000 annually, but this figure is then income, and subject to taxation. Moreover, since the victim needs round-the-clock care, a nurse can cost $15,000 a year, or $375,000 over twenty-five years. (Additional surgery over the years, of course, must be paid for, too, unless it's covered by outside insurance.) That leaves $35,000 a year as an annual income, but what good is $35,000 to a person paralyzed, or without limbs, or burned over most of his body? The only thing one can say is, it's better than nothing—but not much better.

As for the Consumer-Advocate and Political-Message legends, while it is true there is great emotionalism in some jury verdicts, and various untapped civic concerns are being vented as the jury foreman announces the vote, it is by no means certain that those messages are heard and, if heard, respected. There is no indication, for example, that the outsize verdicts against Ford Motor Company, for building cars that can burst into flames upon collision, have affected its philosophy toward auto safety. The only thing that *is* clear is that, having suffered several whopping defeats, Ford is now settling cases rather than going to trial.

Huge jury verdicts do create bad publicity, but bad publicity and even loss of sales don't necessarily mean that a corporation will do anything concrete to correct the problem. Ford claims to have redesigned the Pinto's gas tank so it doesn't explode, but it is not provable that the trials themselves prompted Ford's action.

The "political message" attendant to high medical-malpractice awards is also difficult to trace. The medical establishment responded to high verdicts by lobbying for protective legislation limiting recovery in suits. Any attempt to upgrade the profession appears to be merely coincidental.

While these three legends have propaganda value in enhancing the way the public at large views litigation, they do nothing at all for the individual suing for his damages. A young man severely burned in a car crash cares neither about income redistribution, consumer advocacy, nor sending a political message. If he cares about anything, it's insuring that his hospital bills get paid, and that the auto manufacturer suffers in direct proportion to how he is suffering. And this last is the great downfall of money lawsuits, the great loophole that dooms so many plaintiffs to disappointment: The corporation will hardly feel a thing.

Certainly lawsuits are a nuisance, demanding the search of files, the testimony of executives, some unfortunate publicity. But corporations just don't feel their losses in the same ways as human beings. Their insurance companies handle the entire case, whittling down those million-dollar demands and judgments to some reasonable settlement figure. A victim's injury is just another business expense, deductible at tax time.

The legends of income redistribution, consumer advocacy, and political communication help justify litigation to the American tapayer, who must continue footing the bill for the running of the courts. But the litigant should have no need for such justification. If his claim is legitimate—that is, the person he's suing has actually done him some harm—then he should have no trouble sleeping as his lawsuit proceeds. And if he views his lawsuit as the investment it is, he will be better able to accept the inevitable disappointments he will face in trying to get his claim satisfied.

The plaintiff will confront the necessity for compromise at every stage of the proceedings. Doris Day, the actress, was awarded $23 million after a lengthy trial in which she accused her former attorney of mishandling her funds. After the trial, the attorney's insurance company persuaded her to settle for $6 million, distributed over the next decades. She agreed to the settlement to avoid the risk of the insurance company's appeal to a higher court.

A California man suffered massive brain injury in a car crash, which rendered him unemployable. At the time the accident occurred, he was a passenger in a car in which the driver was drunk. Total damages were estimated at more than half a million dollars, but in order to get any money at all, the young man (who purportedly was drunk, too) had to sue the host of the party they had just left, asserting that the man should not have served them so many drinks. Many years of litigation later, the California Supreme

Court ruled that one could indeed sue one's host on those grounds, and granted the young man the right to trial. No trial would ever occur. The man's attorney, recognizing jury indifference to the plight of drunks, accepted a settlement offer by the defendant's insurance company for $150,-000.

The entire litigation process—from the filing of suit to appeal in the highest court—must thus be regarded as a single piece, the goal being to get the other side to make a reasonable offer.

Sometimes a plaintiff's bargaining power is dramatically benefited or damaged by the resolution of a similar case or cases before his is tried. In one instance, the fate of more than 1000 individuals, adversely affected by disease suffered after contact with asbestos, hinged on the outcome of the Los Angeles trial of Richard J. Hogard in 1980. Hogard was a former shipyard worker who charged that asbestos manufacturers should have warned him of the health hazards of their product. He claimed to have contracted a lung disease, asbestosis, as a result of their failure to do so. A jury awarded him $1.2 million in damages, but the trial judge two months later lowered that verdict to $250,000.

By the time Hogard's latest verdict was reassessed, however, insurance companies for the asbestos manufacturers had already begun the negotiation process. The next eleven suits scheduled for trial were settled for a total $1.5 million, an average of only $136,000.[6]

Although suing is not easy, the modern plaintiff has several things going for him that earlier Americans lacked. Attorneys today (who are also prone to seeing these suits as financial ventures) are more available than ever before to help plaintiffs get into court. And, thanks to judicial activism over the past sixty years, the variety of claims being litigated has begun to truly represent the needs of all classes and types of American citizens. Lawsuits have always been an investment, but today there are opportunities for almost everyone.

It is satisfying to see how far we've come. On October 30, 1837, Nicholas Farwell, working as an engineer on the Boston & Worcester Railroad, was running his usual route between those two cities when a switchman named Whitcomb, whom Farwell apparently knew well, misplaced the short switch, running Farwell off the track at Newton. Farwell was thrown in front of the train, and a car passed over his hand, "crushing and destroying same," according to the court record of the case.

Farwell sued the Boston & Worcester line in one of the first cases of its type on record,* and in 1842 the case came before the Massachusetts Supreme Court under Chief Justice Lemuel Shaw. Shaw wrote 2200 decisions during his thirty years on the bench (1830–60) and was then the leading jurist in the land. (He gave us the concepts of "public utility" and "eminent domain," which granted state and federal governments the power to seize and control land for the building of railroads and canals.)

The question before Shaw and his colleagues was whether the railroad was responsible to Farwell for injuries caused by its employee, Whitcomb. Lemuel Shaw said no. He ruled that Farwell knew the job was dangerous, that such an accident was predictable, and that the risk of accident was part of his rate of pay (at that time, $2 per day). He also suggested that if workers wanted safety on the job, they should exert pressure on each other to do their jobs well.

The Farwell decision was soon copied by courts across the land, and the so-called fellow-servant rule was born.† This rule meant that employees could not sue their boss for accidents caused by fellow workers.

The Farwell decision is regarded as one of the great legal signposts of the Industrial Era, which continued into post–

---

* *Farwell* v. *Boston & Worcester Railroad,* 45 Mass. 49 (1842) .
† For the impact of *Farwell,* see Lawrence M. Friedman, *A History of American Law,* pp. 261–64.

Civil War reconstruction. During that era, the law reflected the way gentlemen did business: face-to-face, by negotiated contract. Simply stated, workers had no right to negotiate, and so the courts were closed to workers' business.

In our Postindustrial Era, the major problem has become devising standards of conduct between strangers. The courts have demonstrated great interest in this problem, formulating an entirely new body of law, called "tort" law, to untangle who owes what to whom under what circumstances. The fellow-servant rule is gone (replaced by workmen's compensation), and reliance upon written contract has been replaced by a concept called "duty of care." Automobile-accident and air-crash cases, malpractice, product liability—all are based on "torts" in which drivers, pilots, doctors and manufacturers are charged with breaching their (largely unwritten) duty to insure that innocent parties don't get hurt. Tort law reflects the danger we all face in an industrialized world. If there are problems in the relationships between strangers, the court wants to hear about them.

What Nicholas Farwell was to the Industrial Era, Donald MacPherson is to our present age. MacPherson, a stonecutter who sold gravestones in upstate New York, bought a new twenty-two-horsepower Buick, complete with rumble seat, in May 1911. A few months later, while driving a friend to the hospital, the Buick went out of control and swerved into a tree. MacPherson had been driving at about fifteen miles per hour at the time and couldn't figure out what went wrong. Looking behind him after the car stopped, he saw the left rear wheel lying on the ground, the shattered spokes strewn about.

MacPherson's lawyer told him that legally his only recourse was to sue the salesman who sold him the car, because only the salesman had made any promises that the car was in good shape. The lawyer suggested, however, that MacPherson bring a test case against Buick.*

---

* *MacPherson* v. *Buick Motor Co.,* 217 N.Y. 381 (1916). For background of the case, see David W. Peck, *Decision at Law,* pp. 33–69.

They won the case at trial, a jury awarding MacPherson $5000. Buick immediately appealed, and a large part of the young automobile industry was watching when MacPherson's case came before the New York Court of Appeals in 1916. Up until that time, warranty for any product had been limited to the relationship between buyer and seller. But Justice Benjamin Cardozo, as influential in his day as Lemuel Shaw was fifty years earlier, recognized that the seller in this case had no control over the quality of merchandise he sold. Under prevailing law at that time, manufacturers were only liable if the articles they made were inherently dangerous, such as poisons and firearms. Cardozo overturned that rule, stating that MacPherson could sue the manufacturer, who had a duty of final inspection before it put the goods out on the market.

With decisions like this, writes legal historian Grant Gilmore, Cardozo "turn[ed] the law of New York upside down."[7] Indeed, the MacPherson case, like the earlier Farwell decision, had enormous influence not just in New York but throughout the nation.[8] (Cardozo would have even greater impact when, in 1932, he joined the U.S. Supreme Court.) From the modern litigant's standpoint, the MacPherson case probably did more than any other to secure the right of Americans to voice their consumer complaints in court. MacPherson opened the field of product-liability law.

As the scope of litigation has broadened over the past decades, the investment possibilities for lawsuits have multiplied. "Legal duty of care," the concept Cardozo was exploring, is essentially a democratic notion, one that allows scores of new types of plaintiffs into court, asserting that some total stranger has, without knowing it, caused them pain. Obviously, in this interconnected world, any number of strangers at this very moment are acting negligently (without the proper degree of care) and may cause any one of us pain in the near future. Thus, the number of lawsuits zooms. A person may have no money of his own, but his rights—to his arms, legs, emotional well-being, a good night's sleep, even his sexual relations—once violated by another individual, may be translatable into money. He can bring all manner and style of injury into court for barter, claiming that, whatever these items may mean to others, they are worth a definite price to him.

There are an endless and unpredictable number of variables that affect the chances of success in a money suit. Depending on these variables, you can win on a small scale, or hit the jackpot—or come up with nothing at all.

Luck has a lot to do with it. Let's assume that, for most of us, the "jackpot" is the goal. In calculating the odds of making the million-dollar case, or being awarded some other enviably large figure you think will place you on Easy Street, consider that you must have, at the very least, a *real and believable injury; a strong motivation to sue; a wealthy party* to blame for the injury; *an unattractive opponent* whose actions will irritate a jury; and, finally, *a gambling attorney.*

The chances of every one of these five variables being present simultaneously are small indeed. That's why most cases, especially where money is the prime motivation, end in some small but reasonable settlement short of trial. But many others of us are gamblers at heart, and even a reasonable settlement offer doesn't entirely satisfy that urge for the big win. In one case involving a defective machine, lawyers for the defense offered $5000 less than the plaintiff wanted. A trial was held, and the injured person was awarded nothing. In lawsuits, those are the breaks.

A lawsuit will go nowhere unless the person suing has suffered a real and believable injury. "Real" and "believable" are, of course, two distinct matters. Sometimes a person may have suffered—and still be suffering—greatly, but no one believes him. Conversely, a good actor can sometimes fake a nonexistent injury with rare verisimilitude.

Georgia Hall has both real and believable injuries. She

also has a life that few would envy. Hall was a cabdriver in Washington, D.C., until a 1975 car crash left her totally paralyzed. A faulty universal joint in her car, manufactured by General Motors, was determined to be the cause of the accident. The question for the jury, which heard her case in 1979, was: How much money should General Motors pay to make life bearable for this once-active woman? Her life had become a living hell. She could do nothing for herself; she had to be hoisted in a net like a piece of freight into her wheelchair; she had to be bathed, have her teeth brushed, her bladder catheter and leg bag changed. Georgia's husband, Edward, quit his job to care for her. The jury, seeing all of this in a "home movie" shown during the trial, had no doubt that this tragedy was the real thing. They gave her $5 million, and awarded $1.5 million to Edward for loss of her comfort and sexual relations.[9]

Other cases are not so clear-cut. A man we'll call Fred was falsely arrested by house detectives in a posh Los Angeles hotel, and charged with trespassing and disturbing the peace. He had to pay for his own attorney in the resulting criminal trial, which he won. Once acquitted, he promptly sued the hotel for $25,000, citing the mental and emotional distress and legal fees resulting from the criminal case. But while there was no question that Fred suffered, no attorney would agree to take his case against the hotel as far as trial. Fred was nearing seventy, losing his hearing and his memory. His story changed in subtle details from day to day. Thus, though his injuries were real, they were not believable. No jury was likely to award him a penny. He was advised to take a $7500 settlement from the hotel's insurance company, and run.

James M. Kilpatrick's injuries, on the other hand, were believable but apparently not believed. Kilpatrick, a high-school student, was walking with a friend on the shoulder of a Florida highway when he was hit from behind by either the extended mirror or the antenna of a passing car. The young man was knocked unconscious and thrown to the ground. It looked like a pretty solid case: Medical testimony from three experts showed he suffered a bruise to his brain, aggravation of an old back injury, and psychological trauma as a result of the mishap. He sued the driver of the car, James Keener, Jr., and asked for recovery of medical bills totaling about $10,000. But his sure win collapsed during trial. A private investigator, hired by Keener's insurance company, had been following Kilpatrick since the accident. He testified to the jury that he saw the lad and some buddies pushing a 400-pound steel safe out the back door of a bakery. (Why they were doing that wasn't explained.) The jury could have given him nothing, but they were kind. The award: $1200.*

Even the most obvious and dramatic injuries are sometimes hostage to unpredictable forces. Rosalia Lococo, a forty-seven-year-old mother of five, was killed in the 1978 crash of a Pacific Southwest Airlines jet in San Diego. It was one of the nation's worst air disasters: 135 people died in the crash. The Lococo family, led by husband Frank, a commercial fisherman, sued PSA for wrongful death. (The cause of the accident was laid to pilot error.) Their attorney, Marshall Foreman, asked the jury for $1 million; less than this would be an insult to the family, he said. Foreman, who himself had once been injured in a plane crash, brought in wedding pictures, diplomas, photos from picnics and other Lococo family gatherings. Each of the five children took the witness stand to say how fine a mom she had been and how much they missed her.

The jury, however, thought this was overkill. After only two hours of deliberation, they awarded the family $200,000 —only $50,000 more than PSA's lawyers had offered originally.[10] A jury member later explained that although the family had suffered, they didn't believe Rosalia Lococo to be any more than a normally loving wife and mom. Her family's loss was real, but the jury did not believe that its extent was exceptional.

* *Kilpatrick v. Keener,* Fla App 1364, So. 2d 20, Oct. 16, 1978.

* * *

Our concept of injury changes with the times. Sexual impairment, for example, is an injury whose time has come only in the last decade. Until the 1970s, victims suffered their sexual traumas in silence. Although impotence is certainly as real and painful as a broken arm or leg, few people were willing to make that particular loss public. Those who did sue on sexual grounds were considered oddballs, and their cases were luridly treated in the press.

Gloria Sykes claimed she became a nymphomaniac—or, as her attorney explained, "a woman with an endless desire to be held by men"—as the result of an accident she suffered in a San Francisco cable car. Sykes had been a rush-hour passenger on the cable car when it screeched to a sudden halt, throwing her into a pole.

When she filed suit against the cable-car company, the press—both national and local—had a field day with the story, dubbing it "the Streetcar Named Desire case." The jury gave her $50,000, an amount that just about equaled the expense of mounting the trial. Her attorney Marvin Lewis, who pioneered these sex cases, insisted this was a stingy judgment that reflected the hang-ups of the public, circa 1971.

Certainly we've loosened up since the "Streetcar" days, and the cases coming into court reflect this unbuttoning. Now we routinely see suits about botched transsexual surgeries and other damage to sexual organs. Loss of normal sex relations (called "consortium") is almost an automatic part of accident cases. A lawsuit in Atlanta for loss of consortium once brought an $800,000 award. In California, a bungled spinal tap left a man with a permanent erection: The jury gave him $200,000. More-liberal sexual attitudes mean a host of new types of suits: Landlords are now being blamed when rapes (and other crimes) occur in their unlit parking lots; doctors and psychiatrists are sued for having sex with their patients; bosses who use their higher rank to demand sexual favors from employees are surprised to find themselves hauled into court, charged with harassment.

But the fact that victims are now willing to speak out doesn't mean they automatically will be rewarded. In 1977, three young female students sued Yale University. They charged that officials looked away while male professors propositioned and sexually harassed female undergraduates. All three cases were dismissed as unfounded, even though one of them was heard by a female judge. Said an attorney for the defeated students: "Sexual-harassment cases have been shoved in the closet for so long that any judge confronting it for the first time is going to have problems."[11]

Three years later, a Los Angeles woman had better luck. A (male) federal judge ordered the president of a glass-manufacturing company to stop sexually harassing a female receptionist.[12] The judge also said the company had to pay her back salary from the time she quit up to the date of judgment. While not a jackpot win, it was certainly a step in the right direction.

Even if "real" and "believable" injuries are sustained, the decision to sue still demands great motivation. Businessmen, for example, try to look at litigation dispassionately, on a cost-effectiveness basis. Debtors may try to provoke suits, considering them a worthwhile investment. During the inflationary period of the late 1970s, encouraging creditor suits made particularly good sense. Bank loans carried interest rates of nearly 20 percent, while the *legal* interest rate—that is, the fee added to any lawsuit verdict if the award went unpaid—was set at 7 percent. This meant that people who didn't pay their debts actually got loans at a 13-percent profit, assuming that their creditors bothered to sue them in the first place. From the creditor's viewpoint, suing didn't make much sense at all: Why pay $30,000 in legal fees or loss of employee work time merely to pursue an unpaid bill of $10,000? So they just forgot about it, writing it off as a loss.

Other times, however, a lawsuit can be good business policy even if it's a deficit operation. United Features Syndicate, which owns licensing rights to Snoopy, Charlie Brown, and the rest of the Peanuts gang, spares no expense to keep imitators out of the market. Three full-time attorneys and fifty investigators snoop for illegal Snoopys all over the world, a practice that doesn't begin to be self-supporting. Those who are caught with fake Lucy cards and Linus decals are sued for copyright infringement, which entitles United Features to recover all the imitator's profits plus damages. But though one counterfeiter gave them $75,000, most of the rest are small-time outfits offering only pennies. Still, United Features thinks of this as preventive litigation, protecting its copyright and alerting all potential violators to leave Charlie Brown alone.

Thus, the decision to sue is frequently based not so much on past injuries as on the prevention of future ones. That was also the motivation when Walt Disney Productions and MCA-Universal Studios sued the Sony Corporation in an attempt to outlaw the Betamax home video recorder. The suit was filed in 1976, just as the home-video market was getting off the ground.* The entire motion-picture and television industry was concerned about the incursion of these cassette recorders, fearing that any movies shown on television could be copied without charge. Lew Wasserman, head of MCA, said that if Betamax and its competitors were used without restriction, commercial television would be destroyed. He was worried about his company's rights to *Jaws* and *American Graffiti,* for example, two films that might lose their valuable re-release profits in movie houses if they could be copied off the air by home viewers. For its part, Disney already had refused to sell *Mary Poppins* and *Jungle Boy* to television because of this fear of copying. The refusal to sell cost Disney about $2 million in revenue.

Disney and Universal thus considered themselves to be carrying the banner for the entire entertainment community when they brought their suit. They didn't expect to win a fortune from Sony itself, but they did hope that a judge

* *Universal City Studios* v. *Sony Corp.,* 76-3520 WMB (U.S. Dist. Ct. L.A.) .

would order Sony's cassette copier off the market until the federal government devised a licensing-fee system to protect a show's copyright.

Film owners, writers, and stars were interested in this case, too. They had contracts guaranteeing them a continued financial interest in their movie work, an interest that would be jeopardized if home viewers could copy films for free.

The lawsuit was a gamble, but one that Disney and Universal thought they had to take. The record industry had taken no action when tape recorders first became popular, and they had suffered massive financial losses. In the face of a brand-new technology, songwriters, singers, and record producers had sat mum, and had lost out on all the royalties rightfully due them from copies made at home on blank tapes. The Betamax lawsuit was intended to prevent the movie industry from suffering the nightmare that had since beset the record industry; its goal was to keep the movie industry solvent.

Their gamble did not pay off. "I'm not sitting here for the purpose of changing the whole television industry, making it better, making it worse," said Judge Warren Ferguson in Los Angeles.[13] In October 1979 he ruled in favor of Sony: The Betamax home recorder could continue to be sold, he ruled, and anyone who bought one could tape commercial television programs for their own use. His ruling meant that if Disney and Universal meant to save the commercial movie market, they would have to appeal to Congress directly.

Since a jackpot payoff isn't always possible, the object in some suits is simply to get the best business deal you can.

Luis Valdez based his play *Zoot Suit* on the celebrated "Sleepy Lagoon" murder trial, involving the possible frame-up of seven Chicanos in Los Angeles during World War II. The play ran to critical acclaim in Los Angeles at the tiny Mark Taper Forum, then flopped on Broadway, and finally returned to Los Angeles for a successful eight-month run at

a larger theater, the Aquarius. Several of the real-life principals had been the playwright's guests at performances of the
show, and everything was copacetic. After the play had been
running about two years, however, the zoot-suiters filed suit
against Valdez and the Aquarius for invasion of privacy, saying that the play had embarrassed them and caused renewed
family concern about their roles in the "Sleepy Lagoon"
case.[14]

Valdez expressed shock, and one person close to him called
the suit "penny-ante stuff." But the zoot-suiters appear to
have known what they were doing: protecting their legal
and financial rights. Valdez was negotiating a movie deal,
and although he had already promised them a piece of the
action should a film production emerge, they apparently
weren't taking any chances.

Certain industries consider it beneath their dignity to sue.
Las Vegas casinos consider it bad manners to sue a guest who
doesn't pay his gambling debt; they write the loss off as
"image promotion." Books, at least until recently, have
been a "gentleman's trade," dominated by an unofficial but
nevertheless binding code of honor. Going to court was considered demeaning, like begging for money. And besides, it
looked terrible—a big bad corporation suing a struggling
artist. In 1975, therefore, thirty-seven publishers wrote off
advances totaling $3.35 million (or about 1 percent of net
sales) on books that had never been written.[15]

But as conglomerates buy up book companies, there are
indications that the "gentleman's code" is dying. Recently,
some publishers have demanded the return of advances on
books that had never been written, and in one celebrated
case they actually sued a writer for legal fees incurred when
both writer and publisher were successfully sued for libel.

It would seem obvious that in a lawsuit for money, a
wealthy defendant is a major necessity. Technically, the law
is blind to whether the parties are rich or poor: A bankrupt

who causes an accident will surely be found liable, and a heavy penalty assessed against him. But just as you can't get blood from a stone, the bankrupt or otherwise destitute person is what attorneys call "judgment-proof." His house (assuming he has one) and his paycheck (assuming he's employed) may be attached, but otherwise, you're out of luck. A modern-day nightmare for many drivers is that they should be involved in an automobile accident in which the culpable driver carries no insurance and owns only the shirt on his back. A lawsuit can do nothing for the victim in a case like this. He's at the mercy of his own insurance policy.

Since the affluence of the culpable party so directly affects the outcome of an accident case, the major goal of money suits is to identify the wealthiest person or persons among a whole cast of characters who might be to blame. Attorneys call this the search for the "Deep Pocket." Finding that Deep Pocket is a tricky business, not at all a simple matter of finding out who really or obviously caused a mishap.

It was almost 6:00 A.M. on April 9, 1968, when James O. and Earl D. drove away from the Buckhorn Lodge, a roadhouse in the resort town of Mount Baldy, California. They'd spent the whole evening at the Buckhorn, drinking and talking since 10:00 P.M. Now they left in the early dawn, long past the 2:00 A.M. closing time, wending their way along a steep, winding country road, one lane each direction.

They didn't get far. Almost immediately, James swerved into the lane of oncoming traffic, and collided with a vehicle driven by Miles A. Vesely, a carpenter in his late fifties. Vesely suffered a broken leg. A police report was issued. Everyone gave addresses and went home.

But when Vesely attempted to sue James, he couldn't be found.* Earl, the car owner, didn't have insurance. But the bartender, William Sager, whom Vesely would charge with unlawfully serving drinks to one already intoxicated, not only had insurance but owned the Buckhorn Lodge, too.

---

* *Vesely* v. *Sager*, 5 C 3d 153, 486 P. 2d 151 (1971).

Here was Vesely's Deep Pocket. Five years later, after several appeals and legal maneuverings, Sager's insurance company settled with Vesely for $15,000, of which he received two-thirds (the attorney got the rest).

The Deep Pocket is the bane of insurance companies and defense lawyers, who generally assert that their clients would never have been sued if they weren't wealthy. But lawyers and social scientists of a more humanistic bent justify it on the grounds that the "legal duty of care" defined by tort law is violated in every stratum of American life, and that suing is the only way of making the wealthy responsible for their negligence. Laura Nader, the anthropologist (she's the sister of consumer advocate Ralph), is from the no-man-is-an-island school of thought. Prescription-drug manufacturers, she contends, are indirectly responsible for the narcotic addiction of today's youth since they implicitly condone drug dependency in their advertising. Consequently, they should contribute toward paying for the damages that such addiction causes.

Melvin Belli, the well-known attorney, has been trying for years to get to trial on the question of whether cigarette companies that seductively advertise their product should be liable in part for the medical care of cancer victims. Behind Belli's suit is a philosophy which holds that the individual, however much free will he might have, is still at the mercy of large corporate forces that make profits off him without bearing their portion of the burden for the harm they cause.

Product manufacturers predictably take a narrower view. They believe in the old common law, that he who had the last clear chance to avoid the accident is the most responsible. This means that only the cigarette smoker himself bears liability when cancer develops, since he presumably knew about the potential danger each time he took a puff.

All three of these views—Nader's, Belli's, and the product manufacturers'—are valid responses to the question of responsibility in a complex world. Whichever view one holds will dictate how far to go in the search for the Deep Pocket, how far to extend liability beyond the actual actors who crash at the crossroads.

On the way to devising a satisfactory philosophy of liability, the Deep Pocket approach also contributes its share of sordid legal maneuverings. Among the worst are the so-called Mary Carter deals, named for the Mary Carter Paint Company in Florida, one of the first to use the technique. A deal is struck between a victim and one of the defendants in a scheduled trial, a deal forged so that the wealthiest defendant will get stuck for the lion's share of the jury award, regardless of that defendant's relative share of responsibility.

George Lahocki's case illustrates the maneuver well. Lahocki was driving a General Motors van in 1975 when he sideswiped some unlit highway barriers outside of College Park, Maryland. He broke his back in the accident, and sued both General Motors and Contee Sand & Gravel Company, which had erected the barriers on the highway. Since General Motors would be the Deep Pocket in the forthcoming trial, Lahocki's attorney approached Contee: If Contee, hoping the blame would be focused on General Motors, would cooperate with Lahocki during trial, then Lahocki would promise to demand from Contee no more than $250,000 in damages. The deal was agreed to by Contee, General Motors remaining ignorant of it.[16]

The trial proceeded, and Contee proved such a good friend of the injured Lahocki that a judge reportedly scolded the gravel company's attorney for presenting his opponent's side of the case. General Motors indeed was ruled to be the villain in the accident, and a jury returned a $1.2-million verdict against it, while Contee got off free. General Motors appealed, and the verdict was upset when the early deal was brought to light. But this questionable practice was given approval by another court in Arizona when a similar pact was made in another case.

*   *   *

Merely identifying the Deep Pocket and launching suit still does not guarantee that bonanza verdicts will be forthcoming. The outcome often hangs on subtle emotional issues, such as whether the jury likes the victim more than the defendant.

Paul Bindrim, a Los Angeles psychologist, sued author Gwen Davis for libel, disliking the way he'd been portrayed in her book, *Touching*.* Davis said her book was fiction, and insisted Bindrim didn't figure in the novel at all. Davis was certain she would prevail, for fiction is generally protected against suit by the First Amendment guarantee of free speech. But when trial started, it was not so much Davis's book that was at issue but Davis herself. Her former best friend took the stand against her, having also sued because she, too, recognized herself in *Touching* and didn't like the way she'd been portrayed.

Then it was revealed that Davis had signed an agreement with Bindrim not to write in nonfiction format about one of his nude marathon workshops she'd attended. Although Davis's whole defense was based on her having written fiction, not fact, a transcript of a tape recording made during that marathon bore astonishing similarity to a marathon portrayed in her book. And, under cross-examination, the nervous, emotional writer admitted she really didn't like Bindrim. Her dislike seems only to have reinforced the sense that Bindrim was indeed the subject of *Touching*. The jury gave a $75,000 verdict against Davis and her publisher, Doubleday.

Accident cases, too, hinge on the emotional response of the jury. Most accident cases merely ask for the jury's sympathy. If an injury is verifiably serious, and the accident appears logically to have been the fault of another and not the victim's own doing, then that sympathy will be forthcoming. But if it is possible to make the defendant appear not only negligent but truly evil, so much the better; for the jury may get really angry and announce a verdict large enough to truly

* *Bindrim* v. *Mitchell,* 92 C. 3d 61, 155 Cal. Rptr. 29 (1979).

punish the defendant. So-called punitive damages, where allowed by law, may be three times the victim's computed out-of-pocket or "actual" damages, and constitute a real prize.

Richard Grimshaw's case against Fort Motor Company gave an Orange County, California, jury ample opportunity to vent their fury. Grimshaw was a 13-year-old passenger in a 1972 Pinto that burst into flames when struck from the rear. He had all the requisites of a large, but not outrageous, jury award: real and believable injuries—burns over 90 percent of his body; a strong motivation to sue in that he had already undergone fifty operations at a cost of $125,000 and needed about twenty more, having lost four fingers, his nose, and left ear; and a Deep Pocket in the Ford Motor Company. But all of these elements taken together still do not justify the $128.5-million verdict the jury reached in February 1978. *That* big a verdict comes only when a jury is incensed and outraged at the actions of the defendant. That outrage was elicited by a Ford memo discovered by an investigator for Grimshaw's attorneys. It was called the "let 'em burn" letter, an internal-company document in which Ford appeared to acknowledge that the Pinto had a tendency to burst into flames upon rear-end impact because of a gas tank defect. Yet, according to testimony, the company opted against improving the gas-tank design, at a cost of $11 per car, because each year only 180 people would die, and another 180 burn, as a result of the imperfection. Ford appeared to calculate it could afford to pay whatever costs resulted from these accidents.[17] And so the jury, at the judge's instruction, calculated eleven dollars times the number of Pintos Ford built, and then, also as the judge instructed it might do if it was deemed appropriate, doubled that amount so that Ford would truly be punished and think twice before it chose such a cost/benefit approach again. Ford appealed, charging a runaway jury had made the award on emotional rather than legal grounds. The judge cut the verdict to $6.3 million. Still, the Grimshaw jury contributed to Ford's decision to avoid, if at all possible, ever again taking a case like this to court.

The Pinto controversy cost the nation's number-two automaker more than $50 million, and a senior lawyer for the company was quoted as saying that the reputation of the Pinto might have an effect on accident trials regarding other Ford cars.[18] Thus, Minnie Mae Green of San Diego got a $10 million pretrial settlement from Ford in 1980, for example. Her body was badly mutilated when her 1971 Mercury Marquis Brougham exploded in a Pintolike rear ender. Published reports indicated that the company settled rather than endure potentially damaging publicity. In this case, corporate documents had been discovered suggesting that the company opted not to remedy potential fire hazards in the Brougham in order to save $102 million in costs.[19]

The dramatic injury, the motivation to sue, the Deep Pocket, the unattractive opponent—these are the elements that get an attorney interested in a case. And an attorney's interest is crucial if a case is ever to come to court. Attorneys are gatekeepers to the court, a fact that critics of the legal system frequently mention as its number-one abuse. Laura Nader is fond of telling the story of a woman who bought a faulty stove. The woman wrote letters of complaint, but got no response. She went to attorneys, but the case was small potatoes—no money in it—and so no one would file suit. Finally, the stove started a fire and her house burned down. *Now* she had a case!

Lawyers are not opposed to taking cases for nothing, but generally they are cases with some romantic appeal. Protest cases, political-reform suits—these have appeal for attorneys who want to paint on a broad canvas. Frequently, a lawyer will also take a suit out of sympathy for a client. Don McGrath agreed to represent the Martinezes for both reasons after their daughter was raped and murdered. McGrath says he knew the suit against the state of California was like tilting at windmills, but George Martinez needed help. So McGrath spent $6000 of his law firm's money on the Martinezes's behalf, taking the case all the way to the U.S. Supreme Court, where, as predicted, it died. But McGrath liked the idea behind this suit: that the state be held responsible for the acts of its employees (in this case the parole board that freed a disturbed man). There was glamour in this case for him, in addition to sympathy, so he went with it.

When it comes to an $800 stove, however, the thrill just isn't there, for McGrath or for most other lawyers. Consequently, the major achievement of the consumer movement may be the passage of laws forcing the manufacturer of a shoddy item to pay the attorneys' fees of the complaining customer who wins his case. Attorneys' fees whet the appetite for even the most humdrum cases.

A Los Angeles man hired Sears to fix his roof one summer. The next winter saw horrible rainstorms; the roof leaked and the man's living room was flooded. But Sears would not make good. The damage was only $2500, and under normal circumstances no attorney would have touched it, since it would cost at least that amount in legal time to get the money back. However, California had a new consumer-frauds act granting attorneys' fees to the prevailing consumer. The homeowner soon found an attorney willing to take the risk, knowing that although the stakes were not high, at least if he won his work would not be for nothing.

There are several ways to get attorneys interested in a jackpot case. The easiest is to pay the legal fees up front. When the New York–based Smith Corona Marchant Corporation (SCM) started an antitrust suit against Xerox, it paid the Wall Street firm of Proskauer, Rose, Goetz & Mendelsohn about $1 million per year in fees.[20] In the first of several trials, SCM won a $37-million jury award. When that award was overturned, SCM went to another firm, and started paying legal fees anew. Corporate law firms generally dislike contingency-fee arrangements where they must wait until the end for a percentage of the take. For one thing, their overhead is too high to live off contingencies. Several of these large firms have as many as 100 lawyers, paying the newest employees

$30,000 right out of law school. Senior partners can make $400,000 a year.

Nevertheless, if the booty looks big enough, even the bigger firms will litigate first, get fees later. The New York firm of Breed, Abbott & Morgan fought for five years in a case involving the estate of artist Mark Rothko. The rights to Rothko's work were being disputed by commercial galleries and nonprofit foundations. Breed, Abbott represented the foundations, which eventually prevailed. The firm had hopes of getting 15 percent of the $50-million recovery, and asked the trial judge for $7.5 million in legal fees when the probate matter ended. But the trial judge wouldn't hear of it; he lowered the fee to $2.6 million, or about 5 percent of the estate—far less than they had dreamed of, but still $500,000 a year.[21]

Some cases represent pie in the sky for attorneys. They'll proceed on a hunch that they'll win, but nothing more. Harold Rhoden, a Los Angeles lawyer, labored more than two years trying to prove that Melvin Dummar actually was a rightful heir to Howard Hughes's estate. Rhoden gave up his entire practice and $500,000 to prove that the will naming Dummar was not forged. He thought he knew what he was doing, for at the end of this rainbow was millions in attorneys' fees. When the Mormon will on which he based his case was termed a fraud and Melvin Dummar was written out of the Hughes affair, Rhoden's hopes and his practice were crushed. It took him years to recover.

In accident cases, getting the "right" attorney to take the gamble can mean the difference between a minimal insurance settlement and a jackpot verdict. An eighteen-year-old boy jumped off a diving board at a Washington, D.C., hotel swimming pool, hitting his head on the bottom. He was paralyzed. As far as most people could see, it was his own fault. Enter Rex Carr, an attorney from East Saint Louis, Illinois. He sued the Sheraton Hotel where the accident occurred, and then began his research. He discovered that the diving board was a high-performance Olympic model; that the pool was the only one of its kind in the city and was built too shallow for the board; and, most important, that the pool manager knew of other instances when divers had hit the bottom. All of which added up to a solid case of hotel negligence. The jury awarded the boy $7 million. Carr's share: $1.7 million.*

While many attorneys will work for a percentage of the reward, not all of them can afford to go for the jackpot. Winning a big case means spending money—on investigation, on medical experts, on attorney time learning the jargon of whatever special field will be involved in the case. If it's a construction accident, the attorney needs to know about building materials, the movements of a crane or cement truck, the standard heights of ladders, procedures for erecting scaffolding, etc. One estimate is that for each million-dollar case, a law firm invests $70,000 and five years of its time. Obviously, few but the biggest firms can float that kind of loan. And sometimes it doesn't even pay off.

Sometimes, however, a case can pay off in other ways for the attorney. Marvin Lewis, a flamboyant, high-profile "gambling" attorney from San Francisco, won $50,000 for Gloria Sykes in the previously mentioned "Streetcar Named Desire" lawsuit. While he'd already invested that amount in preparation time, the case was probably worth another $50,000 for its publicity value alone. Such a case can be what marketing experts call a "loss leader": an attractive, high-publicity case that brings in new clients, who may have smaller cases, but who otherwise pay the bills.

The loss-leader concept may have finally been what encouraged Lewis to take another famous case, involving the NBC television show "Born Innocent." In the show, Linda Blair portrayed a runaway girl who was gang-raped with a bathroom plunger in a girls' reform school. Four days later, on September 14, 1974, nine-year-old Olivia Niemi was raped on Bakers Beach in San Francisco, not far from her home, by

---

* *Hooks* v. *Washington Sheraton Corp.,* 578 F 2d 313 (1977). The case was discussed in the *National Law Journal,* 16 August 1979, p. 14.

three girls and a boy, ages nine to fifteen, who shoved a bottle coated with sand up her vagina. When her assailants were caught by police, one witness reportedly said she heard one of the alleged assailants talking about the television show.

Olivia Niemi's mother went to several attorneys and expressed her desire to sue someone—though she may not have known exactly whom. (As it happened she had caught a glimpse of the TV show when it first aired. She later asserted that she immediately recognized the similarity between the fictional crime and the attack on her daughter.) But only Marvin Lewis was willing to take the risk. He had what he thought to be a landmark case: He believed NBC television to have negligently broadcast a violent program, the kind of program that, when viewed by adolescents, might give them big ideas. What better proof did he need? Olivia Niemi raped with a bottle so soon after Linda Blair was raped with a bathroom plunger. He sued NBC for $11 million and prepared for trial.

As a "gambling" attorney, Marvin Lewis wasn't looking for a sure winner. He had two prerequisites for victory: a little girl with an injury, and a mother who was motivated to sue. On the other elements he was willing to take a chance, for he saw signs that the public—including perhaps even some judges—was ready to make television networks more accountable for what they aired. The National Parent Teacher Association was then monitoring sex and violence on the tube, blaming the media for a generation of kids prone to violence. And as the case went on, the grass-roots movement for public control over television programming seemed to be growing. Television's responsibility for crime, for example, was the chief defense in Ronny Zamora's 1977 murder trial in Florida. Zamora said television brainwashed him so he didn't know right from wrong, and that's why he killed an old lady. The jury hadn't bought Zamora's excuse—but then, he had been the assailant not the victim. Olivia Niemi was innocent, she was the victim, and a victim, claimed Marvin Lewis, as he prepared for trial in 1978, of television violence. If he could establish a link between a crime on a beach and a television show, NBC would be his Deep Pocket. If his jury felt—like the PTA—that television violence led to crime in the streets, television could also be his "unattractive opponent."

For four years Lewis kept the case afloat purely on the strength of his own never-say-die interest in it. Early on, Olivia's mother was offered a small settlement by NBC to offset the girl's treatment by a psychologist. But she rejected it, vowing to fight on for an end to television violence. Lewis invested another $50,000 or more of his own firm's money in research and experts, but his case was repeatedly thrown out of court. One judge after another said that television was protected by the First Amendment and could not be sued for a program like "Born Innocent"; unless a show exhorted viewers to violence, it was safe from liability. Still, Lewis found loophole after loophole, always returning for one more hearing. In 1978, he called it a day. The courts weren't ready for such extended liability. The jury, he felt certain, would have been with him, but the court was not. He had gambled, and Olivia Niemi had lost.

Whether Marvin Lewis himself had lost is another question. For several months, it had seemed nearly certain that he would make it to a jury with his "Born Innocent" suit, and his name and his cause became a national issue. Newspapers and magazines had sent reporters to interview him. When he appeared in court, the halls were filled with television cameras. NBC counsel, who had previously thought the whole suit ludicrous, now paid him the honor of taking his ideas seriously, and talked about him with renewed respect.

For Marvin Lewis the Niemi case was a loss, but perhaps not a total loss.

In money lawsuits, there's no guarantee that the "best" or "better" side will win. "Right" does not always come out on top, at least not the simplistic "right" we've come to think of as "justice." If it did, then why would Fred and Martha Ann Grunwald,* a sad old farming couple from Granger, Minnesota, (population 1000), have to sell their farmhouse just to satisfy a judgment?

Fred and Martha Ann's story begins on July 16, 1967, when Karl Manlow, a twenty-seven-year-old gas station attendant, and his friend Peter, broke into the Grunwalds' deserted farmhouse, situated on an eighty-acre farm in Simpson County, Minnesota. It was 9:30 in the evening, and Manlow and Peter knew just where they were going, having cased the house on several occasions. They'd broken in a month earlier, taking some old bottles and fruit jars they thought to be antiques. Now they were coming back for the rest of the treasure.

Manlow left Peter in the kitchen and went alone toward the bedroom. Just as he opened the north bedroom door, a shotgun went off, blasting a hole through his right leg above the anklebone. The gun had been preset to ward off any intruders. Much of Manlow's leg was blown away. Peter helped him out of the house. Manlow crawled to his car, and his friend drove him to a hospital.

No doubt, Martha and Fred thought the young man got what was coming to him. This was sacred property they had invaded, part of Martha's inheritance. Her grandparents and her parents had lived there before her. When she married Fred, Martha Ann moved to his 108-acre farm some miles away, and after her parents died in 1957, no one had ever lived in the old place again. But she did her best to keep it up. Admittedly, her best was none too good—the house was covered with weeds. Still, she and Fred were incensed by the vandalism that plagued them. Over the past ten years, broken windows, housebreaking, and stealing on the old homestead had become part of their lives. They posted a "No Trespass" sign about thirty-five feet from the house, but to no avail. Finally, that June, after the last burglary, they had had

* All names of people and places in this account are fictitious.

enough. They set a twenty-gauge spring shotgun at the foot of the bed. "I was mad and tired of being tormented," Fred Grunwald said.

So far it seems that fair is fair—and what was there to fight over? But Karl Manlow had a father-in-law who believed in him. Manlow's father-in-law, who lived in a nearby town, didn't like it that Karl had spent forty days in the hospital, almost having his leg amputated, suffering permanent loss of tissue and one leg shorter than the other, because of what he considered to be a little mischief. Even the court had made light of the escapade; Karl had pleaded guilty to petty larceny and received only a thirty-day suspended sentence and a $100 fine.

He hired Karl an attorney to see what could be done. The attorney recommended suing to recover Karl's medical expenses. The Grunwalds might have wanted to scare off intruders, the attorney said, but they didn't have to use such extreme force.

The decision to file suit is the beginning of a terrible, long, emotional process. All the hatred and ill feelings are set in motion at the start and can't be stilled. The lines of battle are drawn. And whatever the truth of the original situation, it no longer matters, for a lawsuit creates a truth of its own. A lot of people in Karl Manlow's place might have been too embarrassed to sue. They might have felt that, having trespassed on the Grunwalds' property and broken into their house, hoping to take their belongings, they got what was coming to them. Of course, the Grunwalds had taken extraordinary measures in setting up that shotgun, but what was he doing at the farmhouse in the first place? The old gentleman's code of honor, which dictates just who should sue whom and who should not, might have told him that, whatever the Grunwalds had done, trespassing was nothing to be proud of, and certainly nothing for the guilty party to sue over.

Karl Manlow obviously didn't see things that way. And with his decision to sue, four of the five elements so necessary for a money win were called into play. He had almost everything: a "real" and "believable" injury to his leg, a strong desire to make up financially for forty days in the hospital, a Deep Pocket in the Grunwalds' farmland, an attorney who didn't have to gamble because he was being paid by Manlow's father-in-law. The only problem—it was a big one—was how to make the Grunwalds look worse than he did. His attorney would have to take care of that.

Stewart Turner, who had done the Grunwalds' tax returns for years, now was called on to represent them in court. From the day the suit was filed, Fred and Martha suffered. They couldn't get a loan for their plantings, so the corn and soybeans and cattle had to be supported out of whatever cash they had on hand or could borrow. But things would get even worse with the trial.

Turner explains how Fred and Martha Ann—Martha Ann in particular—came to be the bad guys in this soap opera. When the Grunwalds got on the witness stand in 1969, they were forced to explain step by step how it was that the trap was set into place: They told how they had gone out to the farmhouse on June 11, about a month before Manlow and Peter made their nocturnal visit. Fred had cleaned and oiled his twenty-gauge shotgun, which he knew quite well had deadly force, and together they had tied it to the old iron bed with the barrel pointing toward the bedroom door. Then they'd taken some wire and rigged the gun so that the doorknob would activate the trigger if the door was opened.

This information in itself probably was quite edifying to the jury. Even in Granger people were no longer in the habit of setting shotguns to protect their homes (though it was rarely an illegal act anywhere and was accepted country practice in the southern states). Though the Grunwalds had committed no crime in setting the shotgun, they had used extreme force, which civil law said was only justified if a trespasser like Manlow was committing a serious crime of violence, preferably one punishable by death. Karl Manlow had only meant to take a few old jars, a petty crime.

Manlow's attorney then asked the Grunwalds to tell the

jury how they decided where to aim the gun. They explained that Fred had first aimed it so that an intruder would be hit in the stomach. This hadn't seemed quite right to Martha Ann—she said the gun should be aimed to hit the legs. Fred went along with that, because, even though he was angry, he didn't really want to hurt anyone. Then he placed a loaded shell in the shotgun and put tin over the window so the gun could not be seen from outside. Then they left. On July 16, Karl Manlow had his leg blown to bits.

With this enlightening testimony, the case changed. Manlow was portrayed as a young man who had made a mistake. The entry into the deserted Grunwald farmhouse had resulted in only his first conviction, and he certainly hadn't meant anyone any harm. But the Grunwalds were something else again. They had plotted together, discussed the various angles of the gun. Says Stewart Turner: "I don't think the [all-female] jury liked the idea of a woman setting a shotgun. Each one of them could envision their son being shot up that way. They wanted to punish Mrs. Grunwald."

Turner tried to counter by pointing out that the Grunwalds were poor people; surely they were entitled to protect their property. If they had been rich, Turner told the jury, they could have afforded burglar alarms, or a guard. But they weren't. So they used the only protection at their disposal. He asked the jury to vote in favor of economic justice, and let the Grunwalds be.

Two years after Manlow's conviction for petty larceny, the jury went out on his civil case. And this time he was the winner: The jury awarded him a total of $30,000—$10,000 of it as special punitive damages for the couple's use of excess force.

That verdict, however, was by no means the end of the story. Fred and Martha Ann had no money to pay off the judgment. Granger came to their rescue, but in a way that only made matters worse. There was an auction of the eighty acres Martha Ann received from her parents, plus another thirty-five acres she owned. But because the town was so incensed that Manlow had won, few people turned out to bid. Martha Ann says no one wanted to help Manlow get his money, so the land only brought a total of $13,500, about a third of what it should have been worth. The eighty acres finally were bought by a committee of three local farmers. They, too, tried to do the right thing, letting Fred rent the land from them in exchange for taxes and bank interest. But friendship will only go so far. Minnesota land appreciated in value, and the committee in 1975 decided they could get a good deal by selling it. They offered it to Fred, but he couldn't afford it. Besides, by this time Fred had had a heart attack, followed by open-heart surgery. He could barely farm his own 180 acres, and had to give up cattle farming entirely. So the committee had to kick him off the land.

Thus began several years of suit and countersuit. Grunwald sued the committee to stop the sale of the eighty acres. The sale went through anyway, whereupon Manlow sued the committee for a share of the money they'd made off the sale. Then Grunwald sued Manlow for the antique jars he'd stolen. Grunwald won $1800, which Manlow refused to pay.

The final outcome: Fred and Martha Ann lost a total of 115 acres; Karl Manlow got approximately half of his total $30,000 judgment; the committee sold the land for $35,000, and today at least one of its members won't talk to Fred and Martha Ann.

"We'll speak to them if they'll speak to us," says Martha Ann, who bears no one ill will. "I hope no one else ever has to go through anything like this."

CHAPTER 6

Vindication

Of all the various goals of suing, vindication is the most subjective, the least definable, and consequently the most difficult to achieve. A person initiates a suit feeling he's been wronged: His reputation has been maligned, or he's been the victim of some humiliating fraud or even of his own ignorance, or he otherwise feels himself to be an outcast in some way. Psychologically, he feels rejected. He comes to the vindication suit with a tall order to fill: the reestablishment of his self-respect. More than a lawsuit, this is an emotional battle for pride, ego, and identity. And so he pursues his case, not stopping until he feels better, at whatever point that occurs. Some people are satisfied merely by starting suit; others need a jury verdict or a respectable settlement; while still others must appeal and appeal in a never-ending battle for approval and consolation.

A Las Vegas nightclub owner found his name on a list of underworld chieftains published by California's attorney general. The showman immediately sued for $51 million, charging that the official had libeled him. Anyone could see that the money was irrelevant to the case; the nightclub owner was seeking to publicly clear his name, and suing was the most effective means at his disposal. Of course, if he'd thought about it, he did have alternatives: He could place a newspaper ad or buy television time to tell his story; he could complain about it endlessly to his friends; or he could change his identity and move to another town. But of all his options, suing alone let him fight back, letting him clear his name with the public, through media exposure of his suit, and simultaneously get even with and attempt to bludgeon the person who had attacked him. It let him feel he was really doing something.

Nevertheless, a few months after filing his suit, the Las Vegas showman precipitously dropped it. "Too expensive," he asserted. But once again, money was not the point. (Certainly it would have been worth spending $10,000 or more for a reasonable shot at a $51-million judgment.) The showman had been seeking vindication, not money, and was apparently one of those who are satisfied with merely recording their outrage.

Fighting for one's reputation is difficult. John Henry Faulk had no choice but to sue: A Red-baiting group called AWARE, Inc., spread the rumor that he had Communist sympathies. Faulk was a popular radio announcer during the 1950s, but the false rumors about his character made sponsors withdraw from his shows. He sued AWARE, Inc., to save his livelihood, he explains in his portrait of the case, *Fear on Trial*. But the very act of suing created such tremendous publicity that no one would hire Faulk until the case was resolved, six years later.

The announcer's friends tried to dissuade him from his course, citing the disastrous story of Alger Hiss. In 1948 Hiss, a U.S. State Department employee, sued Whittaker Chambers, an editor at *Time* magazine, for calling him a Communist. Chambers produced "proof" of his charges (since then, somewhat discredited) in the form of microfiche which had been hidden in some pumpkins (and hence were called the "pumpkin papers"). Hiss was tried for perjury and served four years in prison. To Faulk's friends, Hiss's lawsuit amply demonstrated that suing can be a form of self-punishment.[1]

Faulk could not be dissuaded. He did have one job offer in those six years, but it involved moving to San Francisco and he couldn't leave New York while the suit was pending.

In 1957, a jury awarded Faulk $3.5 million (later lowered to $550,000) .[2] Faulk was justifiably thrilled that his risk paid off.

The yearning to defend oneself can be like a fever, and sometimes we proceed against all common sense. The most notorious example of this fever is, of course, Oscar Wilde. The noted British writer and bon vivant virtually destroyed his life by pressing charges against the Marquis of Queensberry, the father of Wilde's lover, Lord Alfred Douglas. Queensberry accused Wilde of sodomy. Though Wilde had never hidden his homosexuality, this charge so inflamed him that he apparently could not keep himself from taking action. During the trial, the sodomy charges were found to be true and Queensberry was acquitted. Thereupon Wilde was tried for gross indecency, convicted and served time in jail from 1895 to 1897.

In many vindication suits, the stakes are not quite so high as they were for Faulk, Hiss, and Wilde. And yet people bring their wrongs and injuries into court and pursue them with the same degree of fervor as if they'd been accused of Communist conspiracy or sodomy. The problem with vindication suits is that they are so personal. There is simply no objective standard for measuring which slights or insults are serious and which ones should be laughed off. A restaurant owner threatened suit against the *New York Times* critic who wrote in a published review that the restaurateur served bad food.[3] Blind citizens of Los Angeles have sued to be permitted on juries, insisting that their four good senses are sufficient for them to mete out justice. Anything that threatens an individual's sense of identity can be the subject of a lawsuit, but these threats can be so precious and personal in definition that frequently no one else takes them seriously. In varying degrees, all lawsuits are subject to misinterpretation, but few types more than vindication cases. The most farfetched of these look like simple greed, a disgruntled person looking for a payoff.

Courts are an imperfect mechanism for resurrecting self-respect or a damaged reputation. Daniel Webster, the great orator and statesman, discovered this fact when he sued an old friend for libel. Webster's biographer sees "Black Dan's" lawsuit against Theodore Lyman, Jr., as a "desperate attempt to create a new public image."[4] His old image was that of an elitist, and a former member of the Federalist party, some of whom had been implicated in a plot to dissolve the Union in 1808. During the acrimonious presidential election of 1828, in which Andrew Jackson defeated the incumbent John Quincy Adams, Webster's past federalism was once again an issue, and treason attached to his name. Theodore Lyman, Jr., himself a former Federalist, was now working for Andrew Jackson. Lyman wrote an editorial in which he implied that Adams might have been involved in the 1808 plot, basing that implication on Adams's friendship with Webster.

Two weeks later, Webster had Lyman sued on charges of criminal libel. (This type of lawsuit, calling for indictment by the grand jury or public prosecutor, no longer exists in the United States.) Webster's entire career was placed before the jury, including his reputation, his actions in 1808, some pamphlets he had written. In the end it was all for naught: The jury deadlocked and the case was dismissed. Writes Webster's biographer: "Even if he had won his case in court, he could not have won it in the American mind in 1828. It was still not possible to reconstruct a positive image of the Federalists that a majority of Americans would accept."[5]

The dream of the vindication suit is the "unringing of the bell"—bringing life back to how it was before the unpardonable act was committed. This would be "perfect justice." But perfect justice comes only by erasing memories, burning transcripts and newspaper clippings, and giving the victim back his lost time, often years. Vindication is thus nearly impossible to achieve. The victim has three very specific needs—apology, approval, and revenge—and no court has the power to wholly satisfy these needs. A judge can write a decision clearing a person's name or siding with him on some issue, and he can slap the opponent with a heavy damage verdict. But he cannot wipe the slate clean, nor force the opponent to issue a sincere apology. And even vengeance may be beyond the court: Sometimes money isn't punishment enough.

A Sacramento doctor was accused in scores of lawsuits of performing unnecessary and dangerous spinal surgery, leaving some of his patients paralyzed as a result. The plaintiffs all won their cases and got huge judgments, but many of these went up in smoke since the doctor carried insufficient malpractice insurance. A truer revenge came when the doctor was denied his license to practice, but this took years to accomplish. And as satisfying as license revocation might have been, it was short-lived—for the doctor surfaced later in New York, where he undertook training as a medical assistant!

Of course, the court is not to blame for its inability to bestow the covert victories like sincere apology and approval: Our legal system compensates all injuries, however personal, with money. There are, however, areas where the court could be of help, but doesn't choose to. During the late 1970s, for example, doctors fought back against an onslaught of malpractice cases by countersuing lawyers for bringing "frivolous" suits. These doctors were seeking vindication of their reputation, angered at having been named in actions that were baseless from the start. It was not an effective tactic. In several key test cases where doctors won jury verdicts, those verdicts were overturned on appeal. Some higher courts said outright that allowing these countersuits based on a theory of "malicious prosecution" would tend to discourage the valid medical malpractice cases. The message from the courts is clear: Vindication of this type is not a proper use of the legal system.

Despite the limited ability of courts to give plaintiffs what they seek, victims continue to pursue their goals of vindication by way of lawsuit. They often know the goal is impossible, and still they proceed—for, as is the case in so many other types of suits, suing is better than doing nothing.

Not only is it better than doing nothing, suing for vindication has therapeutic value of the same variety found in "grief" lawsuits, discussed in chapter 3. This view may offend some, but, without this healing component, many of these suits make no sense at all. Taken at face value, the shame or humiliation of which a victim complains is not, one would think, abated by further publicity in a lawsuit. Suits for "invasion of privacy" seem particularly suspect, since, if a person is sincere about protecting his anonymity, it would seem logical to cut his losses and do nothing to call further attention to himself, least of all bring a suit. But faced with the choice between sitting on one's anger or appearing somewhat hypocritical by filing suit, the victim may chance appearing hypocritical, because suing at least makes him feel better.

This question of hypocrisy in suing was raised soon after World War II in regard to the movie *They Were Expendable*. The film, starring John Wayne, depicted the bravery of a U.S. torpedo-boat squadron stationed in the Philippines. Wayne's character, Rusty Ryan, was based on a certain Lieutenant Robert Bolling Kelly, a war hero who had received a Purple Heart. But Hollywood moviemakers took literary license with Kelly's character, endowing Rusty Ryan with a robust temper, a love affair with a nurse, and a temptation to disobey orders (though the movie made sure he never gave in to that temptation). Kelly, the real-life hero, had given the producers of *They Were Expendable* licensing rights to his character only upon the express personal urging of the U.S. secretary of the navy, who said a film of Kelly's exploits would be good for the navy's image. But when Kelly saw how he appeared on the screen, he sued.

A federal judge in Boston, Charles Wyzanski, heard the case in 1948.* Kelly testified he'd been embarrassed by the picture: The concocted romance with the nurse had hurt and embarrassed his new wife, friends laughed at him, and fellow soldiers who saw the movie looked at him strangely. The filmmakers countered by questioning Kelly's sensitivity: If he'd been so afraid of publicity, why did he bring suit? they asked.

It was a serious question, which Judge Wyzanski met

---

* *Kelly v. Loew's, Inc.,* 76 F. Supp 473 (Dist. Ct. Mass. 1948).

head-on, acknowledging that suing is not the usual way of
dealing with criticism. "To be sure," Wyzanski wrote, "many
men of dignity, particularly professional men, are accustomed
to face with a stiff upper lip public minor misunderstanding
of their work." But Kelly apparently wasn't one of them, the
judge went on, and he should not be penalized. "A man of the
highest character and sensitivity may . . . come into court
and ask a large recovery for libel" just so the word gets out
far and wide that he was vindicated, Wyzanski ruled.

Lieutenant Kelly (by that time Commander Kelly) got
$3000 for his pain. (He had suffered, but not too much.)
However, a larger point was made: that men and women of
"sensitivity," in Judge Wyzanski's words, may use the courts
in ways that less sensitive individuals may regard as unnecessary.

In the years since Wyzanski's opinion was issued, sensitive
Americans of all stripes and professions have attempted to
use the courts to relieve their psychic pain. Meyer Levin, the
author of more than twenty books, tried to litigate away his
shame at having a play he wrote rejected. The play was *Anne
Frank,* based on the world-famous diary of a young Jewish
girl killed by the Nazis. Levin's inability to get a stage production of his drama became, in his own words, "an obsession."

As a correspondent during World War II, Levin had met
Otto Frank, Anne's father, and helped arrange the English-
language publication of the diary. He refused to accept any
money for his agenting of the book, but asked only for the
"privilege" of writing the script. Levin considered it beneath
his dignity and a show of bad faith to Frank to consult an
attorney. Thus, he began his adaptation without a contract.
His understanding was that if the play was good enough, he
would get dramatist's royalties.

In due course Levin completed his version. Several producers liked it. But Lillian Hellman apparently did not.
Levin says Hellman told Otto Frank, through intermediaries,

that the play was not "dramatic." Levin's play was out. Frances and Albert Hackett adapted the diary and subsequently won a Pulitzer Prize for their work. In 1955 the Broadway production opened. It ran eighty-six weeks.

Levin was heartsick. He felt he had been blackballed, the victim of a literary cabal, not just by Hellman but by a certain faction of the New York intelligentsia. For the next two years he protested to whoever would listen: It wasn't the money he cared about, he insisted, but that his version was deemed to be inferior. He wanted a tryout, he begged for a performance. He insisted his *Anne Frank* was truest to the spirit of the diary. But, lacking a contract, the producers ignored him.

Finally, in 1957, he sued. But his lawsuit did not actually attack the question of a cabal or any other form of censorship of his work. Levin sued producer Kermit Bloomgarden and Otto Frank for breach of contract, suggesting they had no right to reject his vision of the diary, and that they in fact had used parts of his work in the show that was eventually produced. Two years later, scraping for funds, Levin agreed to an out-of-court settlement of $15,000.

Levin apparently believed the settlement meant his play could be mounted. Anne Frank's father thought differently. Anywhere Levin's play opened, Frank got a court order shutting it down. Levin went through three different analysts trying to expel the demon of the diary, and finally considered suing again.

"I would go back to court, I would at last make a big scandal of the whole thing," he writes in his book *Obsession,* his story of the Anne Frank case. "I would succeed this time in bringing out the political side of the suppression. . . ."[6]

But Levin was worried about his reputation. People already considered him litigious, or so he thought. His attorney, Ephraim London, told him not to go near lawsuits for seven years so people would have time to forget. Since Levin was sued by Nathan Leopold, a murderer upon whom Levin had based a character in his novel *Compulsion,* he could hardly avoid the courts. But about *Anne Frank* he would do nothing more.

In 1967, Meyer Levin finally saw his own *Anne Frank.* It was performed in Israel. Otto Frank would immediately protest and demand that the play close, but not before the Israeli press had a chance to review it. They told Levin just what he wanted to hear: The Jerusalem *Post,* for one, said it was "closer to the original" diary than the Broadway version.

For a moment, Levin considered going to court to insist that his play get extended showing. But after a decade of fighting, he could go no further. At this point, no one would touch the play, fearing trouble.

"I had proved myself in court, my work had proved itself on stage, nothing more could be done," Levin writes.[7] His play would perhaps never be seen again, but he knew that now he had to let go.

While there have been notable vindication suits throughout American history, the recent mass-media explosion has made this technique particularly relevant to the modern age. A faulty news story is instantaneously broadcast to countless millions of people. Correcting an erroneous message can take a lifetime.

Jean Seberg, an American actress, apparently never recovered from false rumors planted about her by the FBI.[8] Those rumors, circulated at the time she was pregnant, suggested that the father of the child she was carrying was an unnamed Black Panther. The story was published in *Newsweek* and reprinted in several foreign publications in the fall of 1970.

A year later, Seberg and her husband, Romain Gary, the author and diplomat, filed libel lawsuits against the offending journals. She was awarded $8333 in damages; Gary, $2777 from *Newsweek.* But Seberg's baby had died at birth. She blamed it on the "physical and moral shock" of reading the *Newsweek* article, which she claimed "caused a premature birth," according to wire-service reports on the lawsuit. Each year on the anniversary of the child's death, Seberg attempted suicide. In 1979 she succeeded. She may have won her lawsuit, but one could say that Jean Seberg was never adequately vindicated.

It's not only the pervasiveness of the media that makes the vindication suit so much of our own day. The concern with personal "identity," with advertising oneself and escaping anonymity, has a post-Vietnam character to it. Suing is a self-conscious act, undertaken by persons who think they truly count. In today's America, where Andy Warhol's prediction that everyone will be famous for fifteen minutes has just about come true, it's the rare person who doesn't think he has something to sue about.

Contrast today's self-consciousness with the so-called alienated society of the 1950s. The "alienated man" and the beatnik used to worry philosophers and social commentators because they supposedly cared about nothing. They didn't care about their world and, worse yet, they didn't care about themselves. "In his own experience [the Beatnik] does not count," wrote Frederick A. Weiss, an analyst and writer on alienation. "He does not exist as an individual on his own." The person needing vindication is everything the alienated person is not. He cares passionately about himself. If anything, he is too sensitive to every one of life's little aches and pains.

After her husband, Marty Melcher, died in 1968, Doris Day was surprised to find herself in a precarious financial condition.[9] She had trusted everything to Marty and her business manager/lawyer Jerome B. Rosenthal. Marty had promised her she would never have to work again. But after he died, his investments were revealed to be less lucrative than predicted, and many of them were failures or marginal ventures. Day sued manager/lawyer Rosenthal. After a ninety-nine-day trial, a Los Angeles judge bitterly denounced Rosenthal's dealings with the actress, calling his conduct "outrageous, fraudulent and malicious." Day was awarded $23 million.[10]

But Rosenthal would not accept the verdict. He vowed to

appeal. This became impossible because the insurance company had already settled with the actress for $6 million, to be disbursed in twenty-three annual installments. Rosenthal yelled "Foul." He was fighting for his professional life: His law and business practice was in a shambles, his health had deteriorated. So he sued the insurance company, saying it had settled the case behind his back. Then he sued Doris Day, for libeling him by discussing the case in her autobiography. He even sued *New Yorker* magazine writer John Updike for his comments while reviewing her book. In all, thirteen suits and countersuits were filed between the actress and the attorney. Rosenthal sought $20 million, saying she owed him that amount for his management of her business affairs over a period of twenty years. "I insist I am totally innocent," Rosenthal said eleven years after Melcher's death. "I am not a person of recrimination. Recrimination is destructive."[11]

Recrimination, no. But vindication, yes. He vowed to fight until his name was cleared, however many decades it would take. The case is still in the courts. Rosenthal insists his fight is about money, but if that were so, there would be room for compromise. What Rosenthal cannot compromise on, it appears, is the vindication of his reputation. And though it seems clear that no court can force Doris Day to apologize, nor can it erase the scathing denunciation the attorney suffered from the judge, nevertheless Rosenthal insists upon trying.

Regarded as a litmus test of social status, the vindication suit suggests which groups and individuals are feeling good enough to fight back and which are beginning to worry. After decades of sitting in silence, for example, a group of concerned black parents filed suit against their local school board, insisting that racial discrimination on the part of school personnel was a major reason why more black students than nonblacks were kicked out.

"We expect the [school] district to say that black kids act worse and require more discipline," an attorney for the parents' group told the *Los Angeles Times* in 1980. "Our clients will tell you that's crazy. The problem is the school's insensitivity to cultural differences."[12]

Whatever the lawsuit itself might accomplish (the case is still in the courts), the willingness of parents to bring their views out in the open marks a major step on the road to vindication.

On the other hand, it is interesting that Senator Barry Goldwater not only sued, but pursued through the trial stage his libel lawsuits against the little-read *Fact* magazine. During the 1964 presidential campaign, *Fact* (now demised) ran a spurious "psychological" profile of the Republican candidate entitled "1,189 Psychiatrists Say Goldwater is Psychologically Unfit to Be President."[13] Goldwater sued *Fact,* its provocative publisher Ralph Ginzburg, and writer Warren Boroson for $1 million in actual damages and another $1 million in punitive damages. It was a case that Stanley Arkin, New York defense attorney for Boroson, said was worth "a pail of sand." (That the "survey" itself was hardly a scholarly piece of research is beside the point.)

Four years later, when the case came to jury trial,* Goldwater took the stand and tried to explain his suit as one of principle: "I don't want to see [articles like] this permitted in American politics," he said. "I don't want to see Hubert Humphrey or Dick Nixon be confronted with something like this. . . . I think it is a filthy thing."

But as a primary motive for his suit, the broad principle of protecting American candidates from psychological profiles quickly fell apart during trial. Goldwater was exposed to the jury as a man concerned about possible misinterpretations of his own past, and nervous about what the American public would think of him. He didn't think they were ready to know

---

* *Goldwater* v. *Ginzburg,* 65 Civ 2676 (U.S. Dist. Ct., Southern District of New York) .

about some alleged health problems, or about his fiery temper, or that he was reportedly something of a practical joker. The man who was the Republican standard-bearer in 1964 and a figure of nationwide respect for more than two decades seemed to believe that his entire public image could be tarnished by a few nasty allegations made in a minor-league magazine.

He testified: "I feel it will be absolutely necessary for me to do this [sue]. I think unless I did this, I would be foolish to attempt any excursion into further political life."

To clear away the stain of the article, Goldwater was willing to endure even further personal hardship. His wife was questioned at length on the witness stand; the Goldwater courtship was relived: Why had he given her two parakeets? Was she more in love with him, or was it the other way around? Goldwater's doctor was interrogated at length in his Arizona offices, and the senator's medications and illnesses were all noted for the public record.

But when it was all over, the jury was not terribly impressed. Boroson was exonerated from any liability, though he paid half of the $1 in actual damages the jury assessed against publisher Ginzburg. (The jury was sufficiently outraged by the "poll" that it fined Ginzburg and *Fact* a total of $75,000 in punitive damages, perhaps hoping they would never do a similar job again.)

Goldwater retained his seat in the United States Senate and over the ensuing decade his quotient of respect as an American statesman rose. His lawsuit, parenthetically, did nothing to stop the spate of psychohistories and investigations into presidential character. In the book *The Running of Richard Nixon,* Leonard Lurie reprints a short story written by young Richard, age ten. The future president wrote the story as a letter to his mother, opening with "My Dear Master" and signing it "Your good dog Richard."[14] The letter was reprinted in the *Los Angeles Times* during the Watergate scandal. And when Ted Kennedy entered the race for the presidency in 1980, magazines ran stories on his "off-duty" relationships with women.[15] Neither man filed suits.

Since a vindication suit begins with a "victim" who wants to demonstrate that he "counts," this type of lawsuit forces people to defend themselves, to talk braver and act tougher than they might otherwise feel. Suing is a means of proving to oneself that "I've got the stuff."

A young Los Angeles woman, for example, whom we'll call Mary Green, recognized herself as a character in a book about a therapy encounter group. She didn't like the portrait, and sued the author. But when asked to describe the reasons behind her suit, the book was only a part of it. Said Mary: "I once had a botched operation and I never sued the surgeon. I decided it didn't matter and tried to forget the whole thing. But by letting him get away with it, I couldn't forget it at all. I had nightmares for months, but it was too late to do anything. And so I decided, the next person who takes advantage of me is going to suffer."

The mere decision to begin suit is itself a grand assertive gesture, transforming self-pity into anger. Carol Burnett, the comedian, describes how she decided to sue the *National Enquirer*.[16] In 1976 the tabloid published a gossip item claiming Burnett had a drunken row with Henry Kissinger, former secretary of state, in a Washington, D.C., restaurant. Burnett's parents were alcoholics, so she didn't take the accusation lightly.

As she was walking across 57th Street in New York, on her way to rehearse a television special with Beverly Sills, a cab-driver shouted to her, "Hey, I hear you let Henry Kissinger have it." "I was so mortified, I remember I started to cry," she later told a reporter. She knew what the cabdriver was referring to because a friend had called her with the news of the story a night before. "When I got to work, Beverly [Sills] asked me what was the matter. I was absolutely at sixes and

sevens. . . . I said, 'I'm going to sue. That's all there is
to it.' "[17]

Once the decision was made, she stuck to it vehemently.
"If this sucker goes on for fifty years," Burnett said in 1980,
when the suit was still a long way from resolution, "I'm going
to be there in a rocking chair facing the jury. I want this to
go to trial."[18]

Having chosen to fight back rather than hide, the person
who decides to sue begins to see himself in a new, heroic light.
Those close to him may admire his courage, too. Quentin
Reynolds, a respected writer and journalist, was viciously
maligned by J. Westbrook Pegler, a notorious newspaper
columnist. When in 1950 Reynolds told his wife he intended
to file suit, she is said to have responded: "I'd have divorced
you if you didn't. I thought you'd never get angry."[19] (Reynolds was awarded $175,000.)

With the help of counsel, the wounded litigant also gains
a new appreciation of the strengths and weaknesses of his
enemy, who no longer looms as large. He can see where the
"other side" has problems, when only a short time ago they
looked invincible.

A Los Angeles attorney, whom we'll call Jim Smith, ran
for judge during an election held in 1975. There were several
candidates in the race. To assist voters, the highly political
Los Angeles County Bar Association began evaluating candidates for the judgeships, and Smith was rated "not qualified"
in results published with great fanfare just before the polls
opened.

Smith was humiliated by his evaluation, and it made him
feel even worse to discover that an opponent with even less
trial experience but more political clout had been rated "well
qualified." After the primary (in which Smith got 43 percent
of the vote, but not the 50 percent necessary for election),
Smith faced a difficult decision: He could attack the bar's
evaluation program as being undemocratic, thus reawaken-
ing the charges against him, or he could keep quiet. He de-

cided to attack, suing the bar for conducting unfair and unauthorized procedures.*

"This is a case of the big law firms running the county bar and trying to run the judiciary," Smith argued. Although he was a member of the Bar Association, there was no way he could influence the policies of the organization but by filing. Little guys like Smith just can't make an impact by going through normal channels, he complained. "I feel strongly there's no way they can keep politics out of it."

The lawsuit failed, but Smith insists he did the right thing by suing. And for the subjective purposes of a vindication suit, it's possible he accomplished most of what he wanted: The formerly isolated attorney almost immediately got response from his colleagues concerning the case, many of them applauding his action, making him feel he was not alone and that his principle was right.

Crossing the threshold into the lawsuit "arena" can be the highlight of the victim's case. He'll frequently tell his lawyer he feels "much better already," as if he's recuperating from an illness.

John Henry Faulk described the euphoria he felt on deciding to sue AWARE, Inc., and its leader, Vincent Hartnett. After leaving Louis Nizer's office, Faulk writes in *Fear on Trial,* "I went home, lighthearted and excited. I began flexing my muscles and fancying myself a dangerous foe indeed to all wrongdoers, especially AWARE. Now my union foes would tremble! And up and down Madison Avenue, word would go out that John Henry Faulk had Louis Nizer fighting his case. . . . I was almost manic with joy."[20]

Psychiatrists explain that this elevated sense of well-being, described by Faulk, comes after months of worry, obsession, and inactivity in which a victim is too afraid to do anything at all on his own behalf.

"The worrying person," writes F. S. Perls, the "father" of

---

* *(Jim Smith)* v. *Los Angeles County Bar Association,* Los Angeles Superior Court #C31147.

the Gestalt psychology movement, in *Ego, Hunger and Aggression,* "does not take full action, his aggression is partly repressed and returns as nagging and worrying."[21] Suing puts an end to all this. If nothing else, it's a concrete action, an assertive, affirmative exercise. The determination to sue announces, if only to the victim, that he is prepared to deal with the demons that plague him and finally put them to rest.

As a form of therapy, suing does more than permit a wounded person to talk out his hurt. Suing gives him specific tasks to perform that may make him feel like a winner even if the court finally rules against him. These tasks closely resemble the work involved in running a political campaign. Remember that the very basis of this lawsuit is the winning of public approval, not only from the judge, but from the world at large. Thus, from the moment the lawsuit is filed, and in many cases even before, the litigant will be attempting to stockpile endorsements from whatever influencers are at hand. He does this in much the same way that a political candidate attempts to appeal to labor unions, chambers of commerce, and other key pressure groups. Campaigning might exhaust and irritate other types of litigants, but it's precisely what the vindicating plaintiff needs.

It's possible to analyze a lawsuit by the type of endorsement the "candidate" seeks: He may shoot for the little endorsement (a jury verdict), the big endorsement (a United States Supreme Court decision), or stop at any point along the way. In some vindication suits, the wounded litigant gets all the support he needs without ever setting foot inside the courtroom; the mere announcing of the suit is sufficient for all manner of supporters to step forward.

When Lillian Hellman, the playwright, filed a $1.75-million libel suit against Mary McCarthy, the novelist, a large part of the New York literary world took sides in the ensuing campaign. The suit was sparked in January 1980, when Mary McCarthy went on television's "Dick Cavett Show" and told the host that Hellman was "a bad writer and dishonest writer," then added: "I said in some interview that every word she writes is a lie, including 'and' and 'the.' "

Behind the rush to suit, as countless national newspaper articles were breathless to explain, lay a long-standing feud between the grandest dames (although they had barely been formally introduced), dating back to positions the women had taken on the leadership of Joseph Stalin and the Moscow show trials of 1936. McCarthy was reputedly a confirmed anti-Stalinist; Hellman reputedly remained sympathetic to the Russian leader.

The "mental pain and torture" that Hellman claimed in her suit to have suffered at the hands of the author of *The Group* might have been soothed by the spectacle of so many old friends running to her defense. By 1980, Hellman was in her late seventies and stricken with emphysema. But if she felt out of the swim, finished, the response to her suit may have demonstrated to her that she did in fact still "count." "It's not just two old ladies engaged in a catfight," said Irving Howe, a well-respected intellectual and the editor of *Dissent* magazine. "The question involved—of one's attitude toward communism—is probably the central political-cultural-intellectual problem of the twentieth century."[22]

Scores of other comrades responded in similar context, siding with one writer or the other. The two women's careers as writers were compared, their respective critical and commercial successes contrasted.[23] The defenders of both completely forgot—if indeed they ever believed—that a libel suit about Hellman's use of "and" and "the" was all that was at stake. In an essay in *The New York Times Book Review,* Norman Mailer begged Hellman to drop the suit, which he compared to a duel for honor. Lawsuits, Mailer wrote in his public plea for peace between the two women, are a "disaster." (He knew from personal experience.) "Men used to kill each other in duels," he said, "now women try. . . . Lillian is an honorable and much-damaged warrior who could not raise a pistol since she can no longer see."[24]

The prospects of Hellman living to see the final judgment of her case—or to spend the proceeds—were dim indeed. But the campaign that she inaugurated with the filing of her lawsuit gave her a good run for her money.

While a jury's confirmation of one's "rightness" is not absolutely necessary for vindication, inevitably people who file suits do look for a favorable verdict. A plaintiff may insist he couldn't care less if he wins or loses, "just so long as I hear the verdict straight from a jury of my peers." This appeal to the jury is a populist tactic, much like the strategy of American presidents who try to sell their policies directly to the American public if they can't get them through Congress. The jury is the "common man"—a guy just like him, who is sure to understand his problems and approve of him. Transparently, the victim cares passionately about winning, though he professes to the contrary, and the jury represents his grassroots support.

Achieving "the little endorsement" from the jury was the goal of several lawsuits stemming from the shootings at Kent State University. On May 4, 1970, Ohio National Guard troops, ordered onto the campus by Governor James Rhodes in an effort to disperse and contain an antiwar rally, shot and killed four students and wounded nine others. The question of excessive force and perhaps even criminal intent on the part of the National Guard was raised immediately. The sense of moral outrage and grief extended far beyond the parents and relatives of the dead and wounded; the shootings became a symbol of the still-seething war in Southeast Asia, evidence, as the protesters would claim, that the real war was being fought at home. The extraordinary grief and anger that the parents of the dead students brought to the trial may, in this writer's opinion, more appropriately be classified as a "Why me?" response (see chapter 3). Herein, the discussion will focus on the litigation of the wounded.

The nine students—acting first independently, but ultimately as a group of litigants along with the parents of the four dead—filed suit against a total of forty-four National Guardsmen, charging that their civil rights were violated by the use of excessive force and that they had been deprived of their right to peaceful assembly. The background to the confrontation bears repeating:

Antiwar protests began on the Kent State campus on May 1. Random incidents of violence erupted almost immediately. Kent mayor LeRoy M. Satrom requested the National Guard on May 2. By 8:30 P.M. that day, the campus Reserve Officers Training Corps building was set on fire. Satrom declared a state of emergency. Governor Rhodes arrived on campus the morning of May 3 and vowed to use all force necessary to keep the campus open. The National Guard arrived at 4:00 P.M. Kent State students were ordered to disperse, and all demonstrations and rallies were banned. At 11:40 A.M. the next day, students and guardsmen confronted each other on the Commons. Some rocks were thrown. At 12:24 P.M., sixty-seven shots were fired at the students, killing four, wounding nine.

Among the merely wounded was Dean Kahler, a freshman who was paralyzed as a result of the shooting. Others suffered less serious injuries, including broken ribs and a knee fracture. But regardless of where they were hit, they regarded the prospect of a trial as a way to make the state of Ohio accountable for its actions. They each had sued Governor Rhodes personally, the head of the National Guard unit, and the individually named guardsmen.

It took a while to get the case to the jury. The period from 1971 through 1973 was filled with appeals on the question of whether the governor of Ohio and the guardsmen could be sued without permission of the legislature. "A lot of judges seemed to think there was something subversive in suing a governor for damages resulting from an executive decision," writes Joseph Kelner, chief trial counsel in the case, in his book *The Kent State Coverup*.[25] The personal liability of the governor was the issue before the United States Supreme Court in December 1973. In April 1974, it was decided in favor of the students. The case was set for trial the next year.

This desire to get to the jury is particularly ironic for two of the students, who, since the shootings, had declared themselves to be political "radicals." Logically, a radical would abjure a civil suit altogether. Suing is essentially a "conservative" political activity, a testimony of faith in the system, not cynicism. Those who truly believe there is no hope would probably regard a trial as a waste of time and effort, and find some other way of getting their message across. Thus, however much students Alan Canfora, wounded in the hand, or Robbie Stamps, shot in the back, might remark the trial was futile, their decision to file suit speaks for itself.

"This isn't an accident case where someone has been run over by a car," Robbie told Joseph Kelner. "We've been run over by the governor and the whole state of Ohio. Any jury we get is going to think of themselves as protecting Ohio against a bunch of Communist hippies."[26]

Canfora put up a fuss, too. He refused to cut his hair to make himself more "presentable." Instead, he tied it in a ponytail and put on a wig.[27]

But however they felt, they never pulled out of the case. Apparently they did have faith. A trial would offer the nine victims their only public opportunity to tell the "truth" of the May 4 shootings as they saw it. The Establishment point of view, to their minds, was one of neglect and cover-up. The National Guard had promoted many of the soldiers who did duty at Kent, rather than reprimanding them. Though President Nixon immediately sent in 100 FBI officers to investigate, no grand jury would investigate the charges of illegal Guard activity until 1974, three and a half years after the event. Meanwhile, law-enforcement spokesmen, including Attorney General John Mitchell, attempted to create a public image of the Guard as "young boys" incapable of murder, while the students were portrayed as "radicals." And finally, salt was thrown on the wounds of grief when, in October 1970, the Ohio grand jury indicted, not the soldiers, but twenty-four students and one professor for inciting a riot. (Most charges were dropped for lack of evidence.)

In short, the student "victims" had a choice of the jury trial or nothing. And so they hoped for the jury.

As the students took the stand in the spring of 1975 to tell the world what happened at Kent State, they were surprised to find they had little opportunity to vindicate anything. The National Guard was hardly apologetic. Either the passing of five years had made little impact on their sensibilities or they had sufficiently rationalized their actions to feel little personal guilt. In any event, the students found they were going through the Vietnam War all over again. The "protesters" once again were asked their political beliefs. What did they think of Jerry Rubin, a "yippie" leader who appeared on campus shortly before May 4? Attorney Kelner objected: He insisted politics was irrelevant; the only issue was the civil rights of the students. But the judge overruled him.

Robbie Stamps was asked: "Have you ever made any statement about the police being pigs and having also beaten you?"

"Yes, I have," he answered.

When Stamps got off the stand, he complained to Kelner of having been "treated like a goddamn guilty party or defendant."[28] Stamps left Ohio for California before hearing the jury verdict.[29]

It was just as well. After a fifteen-week trial, the jury sided with the Guard and the governor. Not one penny was awarded for any of the thirteen plaintiffs. The shock registered immediately.

"Murderers!" shouted Tom Grace, Sr., father of wounded student Thomas Mark.[30]

"This is an outrage!" Alan Canfora exclaimed. "There is no justice."

Despite their disappointment, they hoped to try again. In 1977, a federal appeals court found error in the record and ordered a new trial. But they could not take advantage of this limited victory, for their funds ran out. They asked the American Civil Liberties Union for help, and got a new lawyer. But he was pessimistic and urged them to settle. Joseph Kelner thought they could win at a new trial, but he was no longer on the case. In 1979, the Kent State victims refused the first offer of settlement—slightly more than $300,000. But they accepted the second offer, $675,000 (of which more than half went to the paralyzed Dean Kahler), because it was accompanied by a statement the victims interpreted as "I'm sorry."

The statement, signed by Governor Rhodes and twenty-six of the remaining Guard defendants, said noncommittally that "In retrospect, the tragedy of May 4, 1970, should not have occurred. . . . We devoutly wish that a means had been found to avoid the May 4 events. . . . We are . . . profoundly saddened by the deaths of four students and wounding of nine others which resulted. . . ."

They accepted this as an apology, and told themselves that, in a small way, they'd won vindication.

A favorable jury verdict is certainly a major step on the road to victory. (If your opponent doesn't appeal, it can actually be the real thing—victory itself.) But the jury casts a small shadow in many respects compared to what might be called "The Big Endorsement"—a decision in your favor by the United States Supreme Court. This is the Mount Everest of victories, the highest of the highs of vindication. No one else has understood you: Your peers think your battle is crazy, the jury has ignored your claims. But now, at the Supreme Court, you will finally be appreciated—or so you hope.

Those who signal their intention to seek The Big Endorsement by announcing, "This case will go all the way to the Supreme Court," are either bluffing to impress the other side they're serious about their suit, or they're on a psychological "long march," hoping to build a bandwagon along the way to the nation's capital.

Lonn Berney, who masterminded the lawsuit against H. R. Haldeman over proceeds from *The Ends of Power* (see chapter 2) , may have been out for vindication when he first began his fight. He insisted to the *New Yorker* that his lawsuit involved such a novel theory of constitutional principles (that is, the question of whether former public officials can keep profits from books written about their criminal escapades) that nothing less than a U.S. Supreme Court decision would put the matter to rest. But after the first months of pursuing his action, Berney never again mentioned the U.S. Supreme Court or the specific legal doctrine he was raising. Obviously he was more interested in the "protest" aspect of the case.

On the other hand, once Webster Bivens filed his lawsuit,* the campaign for his case grew so strong that achieving The Big Endorsement became almost inevitable.

Bivens's case began in Brooklyn, New York, at approximately 6:30 A.M. on the morning of November 25, 1965. There was a knock at his door, and six agents of the Federal Bureau of Narcotics forced their way into his home. They suspected him of selling dope, and though they came without a search warrant, they apparently felt righteous in their pursuit. While Bivens's wife and young children looked on, the thirty-five-year-old black man was handcuffed and all their belongings thrown into the middle of the living room. The family was threatened with arrest if they, too, didn't cooperate. The narcotics officers searched the house and took Bivens away to police headquarters, where they stripped him, fingerprinted him, and booked him.

According to his attorney, Stephen Grant, Bivens thinks he knows what they were after: information about someone who perhaps was supplying him with his "merchandise." They never found it. But a year or so later, after Bivens had

---

* *Bivens* v. *Six Unknown Named Agents of the Federal Bureau of Narcotics,* 403 U.S. 390, 91 S Ct. 1999 (1971) .

been convicted on a separate and unrelated charge, and sent
to an Atlanta prison, he was still fuming about that morning
raid. Many of the prisoners had nothing to do but sit around
discussing their cases, and one of them directed Bivens to a
New York statute permitting lawsuits against state police
officers who act unlawfully. Bivens followed it up. Even
though his case involved federal and not state police officers,
he handwrote his petition for a lawsuit against "Six Unknown Named Agents of the Federal Bureau of Narcotics."
He asked $15,000 from each of the six.

Bivens's lawsuit found its way before Federal Judge
Henry J. Friendly, who promptly rejected it. The prisoner's
papers were drawn up all wrong: He was using a state law
in federal court, and suing Federal Bureau of Narcotics officials under a statute meant only for New York State police
officers. Still, Friendly thought Bivens had a valid point: If
the search was illegal, perhaps Bivens was owed some money
in compensation. Friendly appointed a lawyer for the prisoner, requesting that the issue be researched on appeal.

Without the interest of Judge Friendly and appointed
counsel, Stephen A. Grant, Bivens's campaign for vindication
might have stopped at the courthouse door. The magic moment in a vindication suit occurs when a private party with
a desperate need to clear his own name, or otherwise end
some personal injustice, meets up with a lawyer who is in
love with the "principle" of the case. Stephen A. Grant, then
thirty years old, worked for the prestigious New York law
firm of Sullivan & Cromwell. Over the next eight years, Sullivan & Cromwell would spend $50,000 in Grant's time on
Webster Bivens. "I didn't take the case because I wanted
Webster to get the money," says Grant, who generally practices corporate law. "I took the case because of what it could
mean to 200 million Americans."

The principle Grant advanced was that the police cannot
violate the sanctity of the American home without a search
warrant; but that if they do, it's better to allow the officers
themselves to be personally sued for their misconduct than

to throw out any of the "tainted" evidence gained from the illegal search.

Grant tried out his idea on the federal appellate court, where it failed. Generally, lawsuits against government agents are prohibited unless specifically authorized by law. There being no such statute for narcotics agents, they were deemed immune from suit.

But finally, Webster Bivens got lucky. The controversy over illegal police searches was a hot one in 1971, the year Stephen Grant asked the U.S. Supreme Court for a hearing. The idea that the victim of an illegal search could sue for damages was still quite new and the High Court had never ruled on it. In 1971, however, Webster Bivens got The Big Endorsement. The U.S. Supreme Court ruled, five to three, that civil suits for money damages were indeed in order after illegal searches and seizures. Where constitutional rights are violated, the justices said, no specific statutory authority for suing is required. A year later, the low court went a step further and ruled that agents of the federal government do not have total immunity. Bivens had won the right to go to trial.

But then what? Having won his case twice, he now had to face a jury to see whether in fact the illegal raid on his house in front of his wife and children was worth $15,000 from each offending agent. But as the trial date neared, Stephen A. Grant came to believe that the likelihood of getting that "little endorsement" was small indeed. He told Bivens that the jury would not feel sympathetic toward him, a black exconvict, no matter what the police had done. He told Bivens that they should quit while ahead.

In 1974, Grant approached the narcotics men and offered to settle the case before trial. The "Six Unknown Named Agents of the Federal Bureau of Narcotics" dug into their own pockets and came up with something less than $100 each. Thus Webster Bivens got two Big Endorsements and $500 cash as a total settlement. Bivens was vindicated. And Stephen Grant thinks the rights of all of us were reinforced.

CHAPTER 7

Harassment

There are lots of ways to irritate an enemy. Place phone calls at 3:00 A.M. Spread rumors about him in the community. Tell his creditors he's gone bankrupt. But for long-lasting, costly, never-to-be-forgotten harassment, few techniques beat the lawsuit. Here is troublemaking raised to an art form—a stylized, basically civilized way to fight dirty, yet keep your hands clean.

From the standpoint of the defendant (the person being sued), *all* lawsuits are harassing, whether or not the plaintiff intends it that way. The entire labyrinthine process is excruciating, and even if the defendant wins his case, the headaches incurred along the way rob him of most of the joy in his victory. Lawsuits spell trouble, and that's why some plaintiffs love them.

The craving to punish is often ignored or forgotten by court critics. Firmly believing in the inherent goodwill of the American public, they blame the rules and procedures of our legal system rather than the litigants themselves for the irritation of suing. Anne Strick, for example, wants our adversary system entirely discarded because she finds it both "antisocial" and unnecessarily brutalizing. In her book *Injustice for All,* Strick says that because each side of a conflict must hire an attorney, representing his interests alone rather than the interests of justice, the end result is that the truth gets hidden, not revealed.[1] Like Shakespeare, Strick would reform the law by getting rid of all lawyers. She promises that this act alone will simplify matters immediately.

No one who has ever participated in or witnessed a court in session can avoid the conclusion that the process does punish both sides. Still, the fact remains that these same harassing qualities are what attract some people to the system. And it may always be so, however our courts are reformed. The desire for retribution is an inextricable (if unappealing) part of the need to litigate.

A Sacramento man recognized the harassment possibilities of suing when he named his chief business competitors in a lawsuit. The competitors had joined hands against him, capitalizing on a state investigation of his business practices. Now it was his turn to respond, and the best mechanism at his disposal was the courthouse. He charged the confederates with conspiring to interfere with his business relationships, a complaint that is difficult to prove. Maybe the case wouldn't even get to trial, the businessman acknowledged, but at least these unscrupulous fellows would have to pay an attorney to respond to all his legal papers. He felt warmed merely at the thought of the bills that would be coming their way.

The harassment lawsuit is among the best examples of what psychiatrist Eric Berne might call "the games people play with lawsuits." People act in court precisely as they do in the "real world." Some of us like to fight, and bring our arguments before a judge merely as a way to raise the ante.

That each side wanted to fight at least as much as they wanted "justice" is a possible reading that emerges from newspaper accounts of the case of the San Diego woman who welshed on a baby-sitter.[2, 3] When Michele Dressin refused to pay a $52 baby-sitting bill to Sharon Russell, the irate sitter first responded by taking hostage the favorite doll of Michele's eight-year-old daughter, Stephanie. Sharon vowed that the eighteen-inch plastic windup doll, called Sandy, would not be returned until the debt was cleared. But the debt remained unpaid despite the capture, so Sharon took Michele to small-claims court (where neither side needed an attorney).

When the case came up for hearing, both women played it to the hilt. Michele dragged Stephanie to court to watch the proceedings. The story became front-page news nationally— one newspaper running Stephanie's photo, a teary-eyed little girl who only wanted her dolly back.

The small-claims judge ruled that Michele did owe Sharon the money, and he ordered her to pay both the debt and $8 in court costs.

Michele still refused to comply. For ten months there was a stalemate, and the doll stayed locked up in the babysitter's closet. Then the judge ordered Sharon to pay Michele $11.87, the fair market value of the doll. Now it was Sharon's turn to refuse a court order. Stymied by such resistance, the judge ordered her to bring the doll into court, where it would remain in the safety of his chambers until this tempest was cleared up.

And the matter did get resolved, no thanks to either of the two participants. Harvey Massey, the father of a nine-year-old girl in Ripley, Ohio, finally saved the day. He had read in his local newspaper about the plight of the little girl who wanted her doll, and he sent a check for $52 to the San Diego court. The judge, Ronald A. Mayo, paid the court costs out of his own pocket. The case settled, Stephanie and the doll went home and had tea.

The harassment suit thrives on procedural overload—the more complex the rules of the system, the better. Exploiting those rules is the name of the game; for in the harassment type of case, the process is itself the punishment. Consequently, it flourishes in the American courthouse like the canopy of moss in a rain forest. The enterprising litigant finds ingenious complexity everywhere: The rules of court change from one jurisdiction to another, from state court to federal. What creative opportunities exist here for torture by due process!

A Los Angeles woman was pregnant and wanted her boy friend to help her support the child. But he wouldn't hear of it, and in fact denied that the baby was his. Angry, she sued him to establish paternity and for child support. Years later she would say she regretted the action because the judge awarded her only a small monthly payment. Yet, in reminiscing, she laughed at the memorable little ways she used her lawsuit for "poetic justice." Among the high points of the suit: She initiated the action and had him served with the papers on Father's Day, just to underscore that the child was his; and, since he was a teacher, she made sure that legal papers pertaining to a forthcoming hearing on the case would arrive at his home on the first day of the new school year, just to crush his optimistic mood. "I wanted to bug him," she admits.

He apparently wanted to bug her, too. After she sued him, he countersued her for fraud. Specifically, he charged that she had told him she was using birth control, and, relying on her statement, he had agreed to have intercourse. The child, he therefore argued, was not his responsibility even if he *was* the father.

This argument got nowhere in court, but the young man insisted he would pursue the case through many appeals. He had good reason: The judge in the paternity case had hinted he might reconsider upping the father's child-support payments once the fraud case was finally determined.

Savvy litigants can sometimes gain a crucial alvantage in their lawsuit during the so-called race to the courthouse. When two people are fighting and it's only a matter of time before one of them sues, the party who files suit first is believed to have a certain psychological advantage. This advantage probably stems from the fact that the person who sues appears to be asking the court to make peace between the two

camps, and consequently is regarded by the judge with somewhat more sympathy than his opponent, who in comparison
may be cast in the role of agitator. The party who comes in
second in the race to the courthouse may be left only with the
option to file what is called a "countersuit." In it, he tells his
own sad story based on the same set of facts, but he may feel
at least slightly burdened by the stigma of having to be heard
last.

In some states, the initiation of a lawsuit is not complete
unless the defendant named in the suit is personally served
with notice that a lawsuit is pending. Sometimes an individual who knows a lawsuit is being filed will leave his home or
office so the process server can't find him. Since he has not
been served with notice, this case is not official, so he runs to
the courthouse and files his own suit against the same party.
If that party hasn't been warned in time to flee, he is forced
to accept service, and thus, frustratingly, his lawsuit must
take second place.

But creative thinking about harassment lawsuits only
begins with the race to the courthouse. A Colorado rancher,
Wallace Dunlap, filed suit against a judge who had made
an adverse ruling in Dunlap's child-support case. The very
filing of the lawsuit meant that the judge had to remove himself from hearing any further cases in which the rancher was
involved. This apparently was fine with Dunlap, who already
was scheduled to have another child-support hearing. But the
judge whom Dunlap sued did not take the matter lightly. He
filed a suit against Dunlap, accusing him of defamation.

"I've had it up to my ears," the judge, Robert Sanderson,
told a reporter. "It's damaging to your reputation, no matter
how frivolous it may seem."[4]

Still another inventive example of lawsuit harassment
comes from a little-known common-law loophole that permits
irate taxpayers in some midwestern states to place liens on
the private property of governors, judges, and other officials
with whom they disagree. A lawsuit is filed in which the plaintiff asks several million dollars in damages from a public

official after accusing him or her or some unlawful act. Then a notice of pending litigation (called a *lis pendens*) is placed on the property of the person sued, putting title under a legal cloud until the (probable) dismissal of the suit. These cases can be irritating. One Nebraska official was subjected to title harassment while he was attempting to sell his home, and the cloud on the title slowed its sale considerably.[5]

The harassing litigant need not do anything particularly innovative, since the system when working normally is unpleasant enough. As has been stated, most defendants are predisposed to hate the entire process, and may wish only to get the whole thing over with as soon as possible. Some plaintiffs rely on this, hoping to reap some advantage.

In early 1969, a black woman whom we'll call Charlene Lyons was hired as a typist in the federal Office of Equal Opportunity in Washington, D.C. Though she had taken a few advanced courses, she had no college degree. Still, for each of the next two years, Lyons was promoted, first to secretary-typist and then to administrative assistant. When she advanced no further, Lyons began to file complaints against her supervisor, making various allegations.

In 1975, as a result of her complaints, she was promoted to program assistant, retroactive to 1973, and then to program specialist, effective 1975. The director of personnel apparently concluded at that point that Lyons had climbed as high up the General Services personnel ladder as she was destined to go, according to a judicial summary of the case.

Still, Lyons aimed higher. When she was denied another advance, she complained to the Equal Employment Opportunities Commission, charging her supervisor with race and sex discrimination. (The record indicates she made a total of nine complaints against him.) These latest claims seemed patently ridiculous, since the office throughout these years was 80 percent black, and females outnumbered males two to one. Nevertheless, when her appeal was rejected, Lyons filed suit in federal court.

A full hearing was held, and Lyons was permitted to display whatever evidence she had of race and sex bias where she worked. The judge was not impressed: He termed Lyons's witnesses "incredible." In ruling against her, the judge concluded that Lyons had engaged in a personal vendetta against her supervisors. "This civil action is an integral part of the . . . vendetta," he wrote, "it is the culmination of a long series of intentionally vindictive and abusive actions taken to harass her supervisors."

So concerned was the judge by what he termed the "baseless and frivolous" charges in Lyons's suit, that he took the unprecedented step of making her pay for the federal government's attorneys fees—about $4000—for having to defend the supervisor. More than likely, Lyons hadn't thought it would come to this. She probably was relying on the government to hate lawsuits, and to give in.

Recent technological advances, having absolutely nothing to do with the court's own rules, have updated the lawsuit as a modern weapon of retribution. The computer typewriter, which stores and organizes material and then types automatically at the press of a button, has increased tenfold the number and variety of questions a lawyer can direct at the opposition in the form of "written interrogatories"—a procedure intended for the gathering of relevant evidence before trial.

Two California corporations were engaged in a legal battle over the rights to a mine. The plaintiff's attorney had just bought a computer-memory typewriter. He threatened the defendant's lawyer: "I'll paper your client to death if you don't settle." When the defendant refused to give in, the president of the company received a 240-page list of questions, with the hint that other corporate officers and directors would receive the same.

Recognizing what it was up against, the defendant corporation did the appropriate thing: It hired a new attorney, one who had his *own* computer typewriter. Two can play the same game. Within a short time, the once-cocky plaintiff corporation began to receive its own 240-page lists of questions. This was truly justice, albeit of a strange sort.

From a personal psychological perspective, the individual who undertakes a harassment case does not perceive himself as engaged in an antisocial act. He comes to his suit with a perhaps surprising degree of self-assurance. Like the plaintiff in our "vindication" lawsuit, whom he may resemble, he feels that he has rights which have been trampled upon. But unlike his vindicating fellow litigant, our wounded party has no doubts about his standing in the community. This person or group now going to court does so in the firm conviction that, as people of standing and dignity, they should not be messed with. They have no need for a bandwagon telling them that it's all right to get even. They're totally convinced that they have that right, even without public support. Hence, theirs is an act of aggression in which the adversary is regarded either as an equal or an inferior.

Pillsbury Baking Company, for example, was hardly the shy violet in defending the sanctity of its Doughboy and Doughgirl trademarks against the allegedly obscene use of the figures by *Screw* magazine. In February 1978, Pillsbury corporate executives learned that *Screw,* which bills itself as an adult magazine of satire, had run a photograph of Pillsbury's animated baking dolls, Poppin' Fresh and Poppie Fresh, enjoying each other's sexual favors. Across the photo ran the Pillsbury slogan "Nothing Says Lovin' Like Something from the Oven, and Pillsbury Says it Best."

Screw publisher Al Goldstein insisted that the photograph was a spoof, an "obvious, good-natured parody." But Pillsbury didn't get the joke. For reasons that remain unclear, the corporation waited until April to take any action. But when it did, it acted fast and mean. Although corporate headquarters are in Minnesota, Pillsbury sent its attorneys on a rush mission down to Atlanta, Georgia, where no more than 500 copies of *Screw* had been delivered each month, and filed their lawsuit for $1.5 million.* Ken Norwick, attorney for *Screw*, received notice on Friday at 4:30 P.M. that a hearing would be held the following Monday morning in Atlanta, for a court order barring the publication from reprinting the photo.

Pillsbury won the court order, and prepared for a trial on damages it had suffered from the printing.

While Pillsbury certainly had a legitimate trademark-infringement complaint (the unauthorized use of a symbol or logo is considered a violation of the owner's property rights), the manner in which they went about fighting back was noteworthy in its severity. For one thing, even their decision to initiate litigation may be seen as punitive. Ken Norwick says he found that when Pillsbury had suffered trademark infringements in the past, it had generally handled them with a warning letter. If lawsuits were filed, they were quickly disposed of with an agreement by the offending party never to do it again.

But *Screw* represented a more severe case. The baking company insisted that the photograph was an "advertisement," and the very idea that Pillsbury would place an ad in a publication like *Screw* was appalling. Photos of Poppin' Fresh and Poppie Fresh in such "sordid" association "tortuously soil and demean" the company, Pillsbury's attorneys insisted. *Screw* was the "antithesis of wholesomeness and decency," which Pillsbury claimed to represent.

"I had no malice against the Doughboy. He's never hurt me," insisted Al Goldstein. But when Pillsbury began to take the hard line, Goldstein fought back. He bought stock in the company, and published the "welcome stockholder" letter he received in an issue of *Screw*, along with the hint that one of Pillsbury's executives had a venereal disease.

As it became clear that Pillsbury intended to get even with *Screw*, indicating what some might call a lack of corporate good humor, the lawsuit itself became the subject of scorn

---

* *Pillsbury* v. *Milky Way Productions*, Civil Case #C78-679A.

and ridicule within the advertising community. Fred Danzig, a respected columnist for *Advertising Age,* wrote: "To my mind, the legal document in this case is what is sordid and obscene. I wonder how much this inane, dumb, etc., example of legalistic overkill is costing Pillsbury and its stockholders."[6]

Goldstein was no stranger to the untoward effects of his type of satire. During the 1960s, he'd published a photograph of the head of New York City mayor John Lindsay superimposed on the torso of a well-endowed nude male body. Goldstein had been cited by police within twenty-four hours.

When he was deposed by Pillsbury attorneys, Goldstein was not about to act contrite. He taunted the attorneys with facts about the corporation that contradicted its image of "wholesomeness." He quesioned Pillsbury's ownership of Steak & Ale restaurants, which sell alcoholic beverages, and further noted that the company had been investigated by the Federal Trade Commission and otherwise been charged with antitrust violations. "Surely it must be possible to poke a little fun at such a major corporate conglomerate without being subjected to such a sweeping federal court censorship," Goldstein complained.

But still Pillsbury pressed on. Attorney Norwick says he made settlement overtures on behalf of the magazine: *Screw* was willing to agree never to publish the offending photo again (*Screw* had already used it three times), and even to admit that it had done wrong in using "Nothing Says Lovin' " and the two doughy dolls. But Pillsbury attorneys insisted that *Screw* pay the corporation's legal fees for the more than one year of litigation that had already transpired. The estimate: $43,000.

Norwick said nothing doing. And he insisted that the record in the case reflect that the only reason the litigation was continuing was that "Pillsbury wants the money. . . ."

Screw, never in robust financial health, could better afford (and psychologically, Goldstein preferred) to fight Pillsbury in court rather than pay such a high ransom for its freedom. The legal games continued.

Of all the tactics used against Goldstein, the decision to file the case in Georgia was the most harassing. Why Georgia? he asked. The choice of a court so far away from the corporate headquarters of both sides of the case had, he estimated, already dragged out the case by many months.

But Pillsbury, as initiator of the case, was able to choose any court in the land as long as Pillsbury products were sold in that jurisdiction. When *Screw* attorneys made a motion to change the venue of the case to New York (where several Pillsbury cases had been tried in the past), Pillsbury argued vehemently that Georgia was where it would have the greatest tactical advantage. Pillsbury clearly thought of Georgia as Doughboy country: They cited statistics showing that Georgians ate nearly twice as many biscuits as the national average; New Yorkers, by contrast, ate about one-third fewer biscuits than the norm. "New Yorkers," Pillsbury said, "tend to breakfast upon such alien foods as danish, croissants, and bagels."

It was a war between bagels and biscuits, and biscuits won. The judge refused to remove the case. And while Pillsbury held on, several volumes of "evidence" were compiled, corporate leaders on both sides were endlessly questioned, and the papier-mâché images of Poppin' Fresh and Poppie Fresh (used in making the offending photo) were fought over in court. (*Screw* got custody.)

Perhaps one day a compromise will be reached. But as of this writing, two years of litigation have already gone by, and the case is still in court.

Figuring out which cases seek vindication and which basically want to make trouble can become a problem. It is often impossible to isolate the two aims: They are inseparable —opposite sides of the same coin. In most lawsuits we want *both:* to be right, and to punish the opponent. The American style of litigating caters to both of these needs, and in fact encourages us to get it all.

The vindication lawsuit, as we have seen, tends to transform the meek, the outsider, the socially insecure, into a person with a belief in himself. Mary Green, the woman who never forgave herself for having failed to sue her doctor, finally sued a writer who had done her a small harm, basically to show she had the "stuff." And once you get the "stuff," it's only a small step to reach the self-righteousness required to go to court for vengeance. The vindictive litigant, generally a newcomer to the lawsuit game, relies on the standard institutions for his reward: the judge, the jury, the U.S. Supreme Court. By contrast, the harassing litigant, who may become a more frequent user of the courts as he finds himself more deeply fascinated by the inherent possibilities of suing, gets his revenge before any verdict is reached.

The first clue that vindication is not actually the major motivation of the suit (despite the plaintiff's insistence that this is what he craves) generally comes in examining what he or she hopes to gain. If these self-stated goals seem unlikely on the surface, it's probable that getting even is a predominant motive.

The *National Law Journal,* for example, reported that police officers across the nation were using lawsuits to "polish images tarnished by citizen complaints."

"We were getting tired of people making false accusations against police officers. We had to go to court," an official of the International Brotherhood of Police Officers said.[7]

And yet, it seems impossible. Lawsuits don't "polish" the image of a group, especially if only a handful of the membership are in court suing on their own behalf. These lawsuits do have the salutary effect of vindication cases in making the police officers feel like they're fighting back, and standing up for their cause. But beyond that, it seems more likely that the true function of these cases (and where they are truly the most effective) is in punishing the nonprofit groups that represent the poor, "getting even" with them by making them dig into their coffers for some high-priced legal representation. And while obviously it also costs the police to process their own cases, the deterrent value of such cases is frequently regarded as worth the price.

The *National Law Journal* reported that one officers' association had spent $70,000 on behalf of two San Diego sheriff's deputies who, it was charged, were "defamed" by would-be citizen investigators who said the deputies had killed a man. The officers sued the investigators, and the jury awarded each officer $2.

But if the awards to the deputies were a paltry return on the dollars invested, the cumulative effect on the opposition was regarded by some as a small bonanza. The NAACP was particularly hard hit; not only was its treasury drained by having to defend clients sued by police, but the organization itself was the target of several multimillion-dollar cases. As vindication, the "blue suits," as these are called, did not mean much. But as harassment, they served the required purpose by providing torture by process as well as making the adversary pay penance in the form of attorneys' fees. No wonder one police official could boast that the number of police-brutality complaints had dropped "sharply" because of these suits.

There are very good reasons why people don't admit they're in court to punish or vex each other. For one thing, it's bad manners. It doesn't reflect well on your cause to admit that your highest objective for being in court is to give the other guy a beating. On the other hand, asserting that you're "vindicating" some right or other seems to enhance the battle, and if you're really convincing, you'll even convince *yourself* that you have an all-important "right" at stake.

On the surface, Dustin Hoffman's lawsuit against First Artists Production Co. and its president, Philip Feldman, may appear to be an attempt to vindicate Hoffman's creative abilities as a producer. This $30-million battle pits Art (represented by Hoffman) against Money (Phil Feldman) in classic Hollywood style.

The two films in question are *Straight Time,* a film about

an incorrigible criminal, which Hoffman both directed and starred in, and *Agatha,* about the mystery writer Agatha Christie, which he produced and starred in, along with Vanessa Redgrave. The Academy Award–winning actor, with a reputation for being sensitive to the point of pain about his image, asked a jury to confirm that he, and not Feldman, knew what was best for the two films, which he says were callously taken away from him by the overweening (and misguided) company management.

As in the case where Pillsbury went to great lengths to defend Poppin' Fresh and Poppie Fresh, Hoffman's lawsuit enjoys the imprimatur of legal validity: He had a contract that he claims guaranteed him total artistic control and that he claims was broken. But as much as Hoffman might enjoy a jury endorsement of his two films, it's hard to believe that this is his major goal in the suit. The background of the case indicates that going to court was just another round in a five-year war between the two irreconcilable opponents. The $30-million case, rather than being a single-shot attempt to assert Hoffman's creative rights was, instead, part of what one reporter called "a game of suit and countersuit" in which both parties used the court as a sword to strike blows against the other.

Seen as part of a continuing battle, it appears likely that Hoffman pursued his case in order that Feldman might be punished—and silenced. And if that was his goal, he succeeded.

A little background will assist: First Artists began as a dream filmmaking company, owned by superstars Barbra Streisand, Steve McQueen, Paul Newman, and Sidney Poitier. The dream was that First Artists stars would control their own projects from start to finish, and reap a lion's share of the profits. Hoffman joined the company in 1972, First Artists' third year in business, forgoing his usual $1-million-a-picture salary so he could do the films he wanted.

"It is very rare for an actor to be given such creative control of a film and that right was something I wanted very much," Hoffman recalled in his legal papers.* "By doing this, I could establish myself not only as an actor, but also as a filmmaker." He said he hoped to be like Robert Redford, an actor who went on to produce *All the President's Men,* wielding considerable artistic power.

But by 1975, the year Phil Feldman took over the company, the dream had died. First Artists reported a $33,000 loss. Only two of about fifteen pictures made substantial profits. The stars picked bad projects, at least from a commercial standpoint, and bought scripts they never intended to film. Phil Feldman, a Harvard-trained lawyer and businessman, vowed to put an end to waste, and have the company make a profit.

Enter Dustin Hoffman. When Phil Feldman looked at the assets of First Artists, he noted that the actor, who had a contract for two pictures, had not yet even committed himself to his first film, which legally had been due several years before. Meanwhile, he'd made several lucrative pictures for others, including the blockbuster *President's Men* for Redford. Feldman wrote the star, asking him what's up? Hoffman ignored his letters.

Feldman feared a stockholder suit, a legal action that can be brought against corporate officers and directors for mismanagement of money and assets. Such a suit was possible, Feldman believed, because many shareholders bought First Artists (which was traded over the counter) relying on solid revenues from star-studded films. If Hoffman wasn't living up to his obligations, Feldman feared, he, as company president, would be held responsible.

And so Feldman threatened Hoffman: If he didn't start work fast on one of his required films for First Artists, Feldman would take him to court for breaking his contract. Getting no response, the legal papers were prepared. Hoffman now responded by saying he needed $4 million for *Straight Time,* a million more than his contract permitted. Feldman

---

* Dustin Hoffman's lawsuit is contained in the file *Sweetwall* v. *First Artists,* Los Angeles Superior Court Civil Case #C23061.

said no deal unless the actor agreed to complete both his films —and to work for no one else until he'd done so. Hoffman agreed, and shooting on *Straight Time* began in late 1975.

As might be guessed, their relationship only further deteriorated once filming began. Though Hoffman was nominally the director of *Straight Time,* differences of creative opinion arose. Feldman took Hoffman off the picture before final editing was complete. Later, in 1977, during the filming of *Agatha,* the businessman stood watching Hoffman's every move, and again assumed control. When Hoffman went to work on a new film, *Kramer vs. Kramer,* for another film company, and refused to do some additional dialogue that Feldman thought necessary for final production of *Agatha,* Feldman sued to get him back to the studio. The lawsuit failed. Hoffman now sued Feldman, to regain control of *Agatha,* complaining he hadn't been given enough time to make the film achieve his vision. That lawsuit failed as well.

Agatha was completed without Hoffman, and was released to dismal reviews in 1979.

Up to this point, Hoffman and Feldman had engaged in a game of lawsuit quid pro quo. But when Hoffman persisted in his litigation, insisting that he would go on to trial for damages, it signified he probably was out for blood. The mere filing of the suit had alarmed some stockholders and probably scared off some would-be investors. The legal documents, accumulating daily in the courthouse, made sexy news and magazine feature stories, which only confirmed what Wall Street analysts had thought all along: First Artists was a company in which management generals could not control the troops. Publicity about the Hoffman case reached a crescendo in fall 1979, just as the company's board of directors was considering whether to renew Feldman's contract. He didn't give them a chance. In October, he resigned.

With Feldman's resignation, it would seem, Dustin Hoffman had gotten his revenge. Yet, by spring 1980, Hoffman's lawyers still insisted the case would go to the jury, probably late the following year. Why was Hoffman continuing the battle? "He wants to vindicate his creative rights," insisted attorney Robert Marshall. "Plus, there's substantial dollars at stake. A lawsuit doesn't go away just because the film is completed."

The problem of acknowledging a lawsuit for the fistfight it can be is made even worse by the duplicity of some attorneys. Lawyers are forbidden by their Canons of Professional Ethics from bringing frivolous suits. Harassment implies, though it doesn't always mean, that the case has no legal merit. Violating the canons can mean a fine or loss of license to practice law. Consequently, the statements of attorneys regarding the high motives of their clients should not always be taken at face value. (In fact, some attorneys may not even know the *real* or *true* motives of their clients and regard it as none of their business.)

A Baptist couple once brought suit against their own daughter, attempting to get a court ruling that she was insane. The reason for suit: After leaving home, the daughter had gone to Las Vegas, where she earned enough money as a show girl to put herself through college. The Baptist parents figured that any daughter of theirs who could live the low life in "Sin City" had to be out of her mind. But when the case came to court, it was thrown out abruptly, and the attorney was held in contempt of court and fined $1000 for having agreed to bring the action.

Attorneys are usually more adept at covering their tracks, and most harassment cases have at least one legitimate issue of fact that allows the opposing sides to go after each other. As one attorney commented, "Any charlatan can find a fact." And once that fact is found, it seems the courts spare the rod in punishing either side for fighting too hard.

Dorothy and Eugene "Tex" Taliaferro were divorced in California in 1944, but continued taking each other to court on a yearly or biyearly basis until Dorothy died in 1978. According to Dorothy's attorney, Tex had gone to law school and wanted to become a lawyer. But court records show that during Prohibition he left his job as a government agent investigating the sale of booze and began selling it himself.* Caught redhanded by some of his former friends, he served some time and probably would have been unable to get a license to practice law. Tex nevertheless spent the rest of his life in court, litigating more than 100 cases, most of which he started himself, and the vast majority of them against his former wife, Dorothy. Although he nominally represented himself in all his cases, Tex did retain a licensed attorney to help him with his papers.

Tex complained that the original property-settlement agreement signed during the divorce was unfair.† Consequently, he refused to pay Dorothy most of the child support and alimony she was entitled to unless she sued him for it. Even then, he appealed every court order two or three times. Each time he lost, he'd sell some of the acreage he owned to pay her. Then the process would start over again. "Legalistic parthenogenesis," one appellate court judge called it,‡ as time and again virtually every line and paragraph of that old document was held up to judicial scrutiny.

When he wasn't naming Dorothy directly in a case, Tex included her in his actions against others.§ He once asked the local district attorney to file a criminal complaint against her for alleged perjury in the sale of some land. When the district attorney refused, Tex sued him for failing to do his job.

While the courts tried to discourage Tex from suing, denying almost every one of his lawsuits over thirty years, there was apparently little they could do to stop his legal tyranny. For a period of time, the court slapped him with a series of fines for bringing frivolous suits. The fines totaled $1000 over

---

* *Taliaferro v. United States,* 47 F 2d 699 (1931).
† *Taliaferro v. Taliaferro,* 125 CA 419 (1954).
‡ *Taliaferro v. Taliaferro,* 179 CA 2d 784, 4 Cal Rptr 689 (1960).
§ *Taliaferro v. Locke,* 182 CA 2d 752, 6 Cal Rptr 813 (1960); and *Taliaferro v. Hays,* 188 CA 2d 235, 10 Cal Rptr 429 (1961).

a decade, but had little impact, because the property he and Dorothy squabbled over was worth about $100,000. He could afford to keep on going.

Interestingly, while at first Dorothy was angry at Tex for the endless suing, eventually she got used to it. She was married to one of his employees for a short time, but after this marriage ended in divorce, almost her entire lifetime was spent in the courthouse battling Tex. She must have grown fond of the legal actions, because just before she died of emphysema she had him and their children and grandchildren over for Thanksgiving dinner. Tex was old. But even as he ate Dorothy's turkey, he had a lawsuit pending against her, relitigating the same old claim.

It's not that the courts want to inspire the use of litigation as a weapon in personal squabbles. It's merely that, much as you and I, judges have difficulty discerning the truly frivolous and vexatious case from the mere waste of time. Furthermore, judges are concerned that they might be punishing an attorney for doing what his stubborn client insists be done.

Not long ago, newspapers carried the story of Tom Hansen, the boy who sued his parents for $350,000, charging them with giving him a poor upbringing. Though Hansen's case was thrown out of every court, that was not the end of the family's legal battle. Tom's mother filed a $10,000 lawsuit against the psychiatrist who was said to have urged Hansen to sue rather than kill. She wanted the psychiatrist to reimburse her for attorneys' fees incurred in her son's case.[8]

Whatever the outcome of the suit (it remains in litigation), it clearly represents a continuation of the domestic battle, with the major purpose of punishing the psychiatrist. Some would call this case "frivolous," but a judge might have a hard time deciding that it was totally without justification— or, if it was indeed "frivolous," who was to blame.

Justice Cardozo articulated a belief shared by many jurists when, in 1914, he upheld the right of one William Morningstar to complain about the food at the Lafayette Hotel in New York. Morningstar lived at the hotel and apparently took his meals there on a bed-and-board plan. Dissatisfied with the fare, he bought some spareribs at the market and gave them to the chef to prepare for him. This the chef did, but presented him with a bill for $1 for the cooking. Morningstar refused to pay the bill, calling it exorbitant, and subsequently the hotel refused to serve him his meals. He sued for damages,* and the hotel presented evidence, which Cardozo deemed irrelevant, that other hoteliers had found Morningstar to be a chronic complainer.

The esteemed justice wrote: "It is no concern of ours that the controversy at the root of this lawsuit may seem to be trivial. . . . To enforce one's rights when they are violated is never a legal wrong, and may often be a moral duty." If Morningstar was wrongfully refused a meal, he was entitled to damages, his reputation notwithstanding, Cardozo wrote. (He apparently returned the case for a retrial, but whether Morningstar ever collected is unknown.)

Judges since Cardozo's day continue to fear that, in throwing out a lawsuit that appears specious, they may be unknowingly robbing an individual of the justice he deserves. In general, they believe that it's better to give a case a hearing and *then* dismiss it, rather than deem the case unworthy merely on the face of it. In recent decades, various states have passed laws barring "frivolous suits," and attempts have been made to hold plaintiffs' attorneys responsible for the defense's legal fees (a system much like the one that exists in England). But as beneficial as this reform might be, often attorneys find a loophole they can crawl through, and such inhibiting laws rarely are effective.

The problems involved in the malicious use of lawsuits frequently surface with regard to conservatorship matters. In August 1934, unbeknownst to Emil Hauser, his half sister, Augusta M. Bartow, had him declared incompetent to handle his own affairs. She was put in charge of Hauser's business and personal dealings and had him removed as an officer and director of a company in which they were both stockholders.

---

* *Morningstar* v. *Lafayette Hotel*, 211 N.Y. 465 (1914).

For reasons still obscure, it was not until March of 1935 that Hauser discovered what had taken place. A trial was held, and Hauser's sanity was affirmed. His half sister, however, as permitted by the court, billed him $2100 for services rendered to him over the past seven months.

Hauser sued her for "malicious prosecution"*—a legal catchall phrase meaning that litigation has been misused. But the New York appellate court said he had no case against Augusta. "Whatever may have been [her] motives, she used the process of the court for the purpose for which the law created it," Judge Hubbs decided. "She used it, she did not abuse it."

Chief Judge Crane, to his credit, dissented. "One who has been wrongfully declared insane without notice or hearing . . . must have some remedy for such injustice," he said. (Such hearings are now required in many states.)

Modern judges, more activist-minded than Judge Hubbs and his compatriots, are less restrictive in the face of abuse of the courts. When faced with particularly egregious examples of legal inequity, they are more prone to order an immediate reform, even if the process complained about is in technical compliance with the law.

One notorious case involved the Merchants Collections Association, which filed over 2000 lawsuits a year in the Oakland-Piedmont area just north of San Francisco. These 2000 cases represented almost 14 percent of all lawsuits filed annually in the area. The only trouble was that the debtors being sued lived everywhere in California *except* Oakland. This was entirely legal, since the collection agency was allowed by law to sue in the area in which it was located. But it was an obvious strategy, based on the expectation that poor people being filed on would be unable to represent themselves from so far away and would probably default.

When this ploy was challenged in the California trial courts, it was upheld, for it was indeed legal. But the California high court, which during the 1970s was the leading

* *Hauser* v. *Bartow,* 7 N.E. 2d. 268 (1937).

bench in the land (often predicting legal theories later adopted by the U.S. Supreme Court) , ordered it stopped.* In 1972, Justice Matthew Tobriner, writing for a unanimous court, cited evidence that this practice of encouraging default was widespread not only in California but throughout the nation. One collection agency had achieved 10,000 defaults in a single year by using this filing practice. Armed with a default, agencies can then attach property and sell it off for their own profit, having technically satisfied the legal requirement of giving debtors the opportunity for a hearing. If the court doesn't come to these debtors' aid, Tobriner considered, no other legal remedies are available. He thereby ordered the practice of long-distance filing to be stopped.

The genius of the harassment lawsuit is that it not only uses the inequities in the system to wreak havoc, but also creatively exploits the very advantages and benefits of our system that otherwise are considered as reforms, providing a living nightmare for social architects who see their work corrupted.

The libel laws offer a good example of how this works. Before a person can bring a lawsuit for libel against a newspaper or other publication, he must first make a written request for retraction of the offending article. This retraction policy permits newspapers and others to admit their mistakes and publicly apologize to the maligned party.

During the last decade, two "cult groups," Scientology and Synanon, became increasingly adept at using both lawsuits and the retraction policy as a way of silencing reporters and critics seeking to expose their operations. It may be said, in fact, that the use of lawsuits became a salient part of these cults' religious dogma. In an in-depth report on the litigation tactics of the Scientology group, the *Los Angeles Times* quoted a 1955 pamphlet written by church founder L. Ron

* *Barquis* v. *Merchants Collection Assn.,* 7 C 3d 94; 101 Cal Rptr 745, 496 P2d 817 (1972) .

Hubbard,[9] in which Hubbard said that the purpose of a law-suit against those revealing church materials "is to harass and discourage rather than to win."

"We do not want Scientology to be reported in the press anywhere else than in the religious pages of newspapers," quoted the Los Angeles paper. "Therefore, we should be very alert to sue for slander at the slightest chance so as to discourage the public presses from mentioning Scientology."

A *Los Angeles Times* investigation showed that the church had initiated 100 civil lawsuits in the past decade in the United States and Canada, against reporters and church critics. The paper cited alleged Scientology actions against former members who wrote books, against reporters on small newspapers who began examining church finances, and against assorted other enemies. Among the most dramatic stories, the paper cited the case of Gabriel Cazares, former mayor of Clearwater, Florida. While he was in office, Cazares apparently had objected to Scientology's purchase of the Clearwater Hotel in his city. The church sued him for $1 million, charging him with libel and slander, among other charges. The *Los Angeles Times* referred to documents seized by the FBI at church offices, which purportedly admitted that Scientologists staged a phony hit-and-run automobile accident involving a pedestrian and Cazares in order to discredit him. Cazares countersued, objecting to the rumors they were spreading about him, but he had to drop that effort when legal expenses in his own case alone topped $40,000. Cazares lost a congressional election and became a stockbroker.

Synanon, which began as an alcohol- and drug-abuse treatment program and later took on the trappings of a religion, has a legal department of sixty to sixty-five people. A major part of the law department's work involves reading items on Synanon that appear in the national press and immediately filing requests for retraction whenever a publication seems to misunderstand or otherwise criticize the program's inner workings.

While Synanon had only fifty-five lawsuits in that same

decade compared to Scientology's one hundred, it proved just as experienced and forceful in prosecuting its enemies. Some of that force derives from the ripple effect of two major settlements Synanon received in lawsuits against the Hearst corporation and *The San Francisco Examiner.* In 1976 and 1978, Hearst agreed to pay the group $600,000 in the first case and $2 million in the second to forestall trials in these matters.[10]

Although the dockets of the litigation have been sealed, it became known that a burglary of Synanon offices took place while the first suit was pending, and that sixty-nine confidential tapes belonging to Charles Dederich, Synanon's founder and leader, were reported missing. Dederich and Synanon charged that the Hearst corporation, in addition to causing the burglary, tried to scare off major contributors to the group (which calls itself a charitable enterprise) and otherwise interfered in Synanon's ability to earn income.

The publishing corporation was unwilling to go to a jury to defend itself against Synanon in light of these allegations. And it didn't help their case that the Hearst reporter who wrote two articles that displeased the group had claimed to have written some previous articles from mainland China when in fact they were written in Hong Kong.

These two settlements, with their bizarre subplots, have horrified editors and publishers across the nation. At least one small publication has determined not to mention the organization at all in print unless entirely necessary.

Meanwhile, armed with what can only be termed a victory in the Hearst cases, Synanon has continued suing and threatening to sue. It filed a $76.7-million lawsuit against *Time* magazine in January 1978 immediately following *Time*'s publication of an article headlined "Life at Synanon Is Swinging: A Once Respected Program Turns into a Kooky Cult."

Evidence offered in court included a declaration from Charles Dederich threatening that Synanon's friends might attempt to punish *Time.* Threats were purportedly made on the lives of *Time* editors, and hundreds of abusive letters were reportedly sent to the magazine, warning of plans to "destroy" or "kill" *Time*. The magazine's management considered the $76-million lawsuit to be merely another example of intimidation.

Two years after starting the suit, Synanon attorneys asked the court to dismiss its own action, claiming the law department was being overstrained by other lawsuits. In 1980, Synanon leaders were facing criminal charges in Los Angeles, stemming from the rattlesnake bite inflicted upon attorney Paul Morantz, who had just won a $300,000 judgment against the group.

Synanon's legal ventures are made possible through the in-house support of the organization's members, several of whom are lawyers or have legal training. Others provide unpaid paralegal assistance. But *Time* is not so fortunate. In the two years of litigation, the magazine reported it spent $1.25 million in preparing its defense, which it asked the court to order Synanon to pay. That motion is still pending.

Just as the case against *Time* was ending, however, United Press International, one of the two major wire services that feed news to most of the nation's newspapers and magazines, reported that it, too, had been threatened by Synanon. In a letter to the National News Council (a group of press leaders that attempts to mediate problems between citizens and the media), UPI complained that the group had made systematic efforts "to threaten UPI's reputation and relationships with subscribers and, generally, object to any news coverage which reflects unfavorably upon Synanon."

UPI asked the News Council to investigate. But the results of that inquiry, published in the *Columbia Journalism Review*, can hardly make the wire service feel more secure.

"It is clear that Synanon is using a law presumably passed to protect publishers and broadcasters . . . as a weapon for coercing the press into silence about Synanon and its affairs," the council wrote. "It is also clear that, as a result of this legal harassment, many editors and news directors . . . are refraining from publishing or broadcasting news they deem legitimate affecting Synanon." But, said the council, there was simply nothing that anyone could do to stop Synanon from taking such actions.

The advisory group pointed out that Synanon had a free-speech right of its own, and could use the courts in pursuing that right as it saw fit. The council could only take heart in the fact that those publications that did fight back against Synanon ultimately won their lawsuits—albeit at great financial cost. The answer "must lie in the press having the courage to stand up for its freedom," they concluded.[11]

The National News Council thus had come up against the conundrum of the harassment lawsuit: It uses the system to fight the system; it uses the same rules to play a different game. Those who would outlaw it, even with the best intentions, soon discover that any reform merely creates another loophole for agents of harassment to exploit.

CHAPTER 8

The Last Resort

Suing may be painful, but when an adversary absolutely refuses to be charmed, cajoled, implored, or threatened into changing his ways, there frequently is no peaceful alternative other than suffering in silence or going to court. All else has failed—irresistible force has met immovable object—so we sue as a last-gasp effort.

Some people and institutions practically beg to be sued. An automobile repairman botched a job of replacing a manual transmission in a BMW. Time after time the frustrated customer demanded satisfaction, and finally took the repairman to small-claims court. "Okay, you win," the repairman said when a judge finally ruled in the customer's favor. He handed over the check representing the cost of a new transmission, and congratulated his opponent on a battle well won. "You told the truth," he said, implying he knew that the verdict had never been in doubt. But until a judge ordered him to pay up, he had vehemently refused to do so.

This repairman manifests the all too common defense-mindedness that has arisen in the face of lawsuits. Taken to an extreme, it becomes a ploy, shielding those who do wrong from their moral and ethical (not to mention legal) responsibilities. The tendency to stake out and defend one's territory is a fact of modern life. In 1976, the federal government undertook an immunization program against a potential epidemic of swine flu. The shots caused more problems than the disease itself, resulting in some cases in permanent paralysis and sickness. At least 732 claims were filed against the government (the first step in initiating suit) , and in 1978 Joseph A. Califano, Jr., then secretary of health, education, and welfare, promised that the government would assist, rather than impede, settlement for those individuals most seriously hurt.[1] But it was not to be. Within a year of Califano's announcement, a judge denounced the pledge as a "public relations ploy." A *New York Times* investigation into the swine flu cases showed that the government was fighting each and every one, sometimes insisting that the victims had contributed to their own sickness.[2]

This defense mentality of denying everything is so common that anyone who admits he's at fault is regarded as suspect. In May 1979 an American Airlines DC-10 jet crashed, killing 275 persons. A lawyer representing several of the bereaved families filed papers accusing the airline's insurance company of admitting fault—as though such an admission were an act of turpitude.[3,4] In fact he had reason to be suspicious: Experienced plaintiff's attorneys thought they smelled a rat—an attempt by insurers to limit the airline's liability, thus keeping the ultimate payment to survivors at the lowest level possible.

Defendants and would-be defendants sometimes start their barricade building long before the plaintiff even has a lawsuit in mind: There's a come-and-get-me dare to their actions as they warm up for the battle. Some adversaries just love a good fight (and by going to court they often gain financial and strategic advantages that encourage a favorable settlement) ; others don't recognize a person is serious unless a lawsuit summons is in their hands. This tactic of barricading and defense building is tacit acknowledgment that, for the plaintiff, the courts are truly the last resort.

Cleo Kyriazi tried every maneuver she could think of before she went to court against her employer. Her case, reported in the *National Law Journal* and *Savvy* magazine,[5,6] began in 1965 when Kyriazi, at age thirty-two, joined the Western Electric Company, the manufacturing subsidiary of

American Telephone and Telegraph, at its Kearny, New Jersey, plant. A Greek immigrant, she had two degrees from Columbia University, in business and in engineering, and expected a swift rise up the company ladder. But soon she noticed that men with less experience and education were being promoted while she was going nowhere. Kyriazi complained of this to her superiors, trying to keep things polite. She got no response. Time went by and Cleo became more insistent. She confronted her bosses again, and this time the confrontations became bitter. She couldn't persuade them that she deserved better work.

Working conditions became so hostile that her bosses at Western Electric prepared to defend themselves against the sex-discrimination suit they apparently saw as inevitable. Rather than attempt to compromise, her supervisors, according to published reports based on the court file, apparently launched a campaign to force the young engineer into submission. They secretly began to tape-record her telephone conversations (hoping the transcript would serve to show that Kyriazi was mentally unstable), and enlisted the help of several of her coworkers to harass her still further. On one occasion they left an obscene and degrading cartoon of Kyriazi on her desk; then they chided her for being unmarried and questioned her virginity. The coworkers kept records of their "dirty tricks," which later would be subpoenaed in federal court. When Kyriazi complained, her boss said she should be flattered by the attention and told her bluntly that things like this happen every day in a working man's world.

Kyriazi hung in. She continued to be passed over for promotion, and continued to grumble about it. She was the victim of sex discrimination, she was certain, but her bosses kept denying it, choosing to characterize her complaints as paranoia. The setup became obvious when one supervisor warned her to get medical help or else she would be fired.

At this point, with her sanity in question, Cleo Kyriazi had finally had enough. She filed a complaint with the New Jersey Division of Equal Rights in August 1971. (Until 1972, most equal-opportunity complaints first were heard before state boards like this one in New Jersey. Today, the federal Equal Employment Opportunity Commission hears them directly.) Western Electric responded by summarily dismissing her for insubordination, though reprisals are illegal.

The New Jersey board and, later, the Equal Employment Commission both found that Kyriazi was right: She *had* been the victim of sex discrimination. But both agencies refused to sue on her behalf, using their prerogative to reject even fully justified cases for further suit. In 1973 she retained her own attorney and filed suit in federal court, seeking back pay for all the years of harassment and mistreatment. She was now forty.

Judge Herbert A. Sterns, who heard her case in 1979, said, "The court does not mean to suggest that Kyriazi was a paragon of virtue, nor that she was an easygoing person, nor one possessed of a pleasing personality. Far from it. . . . A weaker, more pleasant, less demanding person than Kyriazi might well have capitulated some principle, and survived at Western. But the law does not impose such a duty on anyone."[7]

But personality was not the issue, as had become clear in 1976 as Kyriazi's attorney prepared her case. While going through crates of personnel records that Western Electric had produced as part of the discovery process in the matter, her attorney's investigator discovered the first clues that more than one unhappy woman's career was at stake here: The investigator unearthed documents in which department heads at the telephone subsidiary specified the sex of the person to be hired for particular jobs. These documents, which the attorney later referred to as the "smoking gun," were marked in different color inks with M for Male, F for Female, and MF where it didn't matter. With this "smoking gun," a company-wide policy of systematic illegal discrimination against women would be proven. Sterns awarded Kyriazi $100,000 in damages for having been a victim of such unlawful policies.

But this was not the end of the story. Now that the policy of discrimination had been unearthed, 2000 female employees and unsuccessful job applicants all filed suit against the company. Cleo Kyriazi, who had spent almost a decade alone, the victim of a strategy that Judge Sterns found was intended to depict her as divisive, disruptive, and close to demented, now was leading a class-action suit with a cast of thousands.

Western Electric vowed to appeal each and every one of those 2000 suits separately, refusing to allow plaintiffs to come together as a class. But the company's legal fees by 1979 already totaled $1.28 million, and though company lawyers told reporters they could tough out the battle for five years, in July 1980 they decided otherwise. That month, Western Electric agreed to pay $7 million in back wages and compensation to the women at two of its plants, and another $1.5 million to women at nine other New Jersey facilities.[8] An affirmative-action program was instituted, and women who are denied promotions in the future will be told the reasons in writing. All of this arose because one woman had been pushed to the brink.

People like Cleo Kyriazi bring their problems to court as truly a last resort: There simply is no other institution capable or willing to hear their problems; whereas courts have no choice, they must give every case at least an initial hearing. But even as a last resort, suing is controversial. One young woman reported her father's sarcastic reaction on hearing that a class-action suit was aimed at her employer: "You got those Commies there, too?" he said. To the person fighting an injustice, however, a lawsuit may be the only tool his adversary respects. It is not sufficient that a law exists plainly declaring the injustice to be illegal. No laws are self-executing, and many are ignored until a lawsuit makes an opponent pay attention.

The 1964 and 1972 Civil Rights Acts barred employment discrimination on the basis of race, sex, national origin, and, eventually, age. Though these pioneering laws were something of a congressional miracle (having been introduced repeatedly for the previous two decades), the statutes themselves were weak, demanding very little substantive change in employment policies. Some have said the law, especially the 1964 version, was little more than a statement of principle. But by 1970, 52,000 people had filed complaints charging bias in employment. The sheer weight of public use of this law gave it strength, leading to continual congressional revision, until by 1980 both the law and the Equal Employment Opportunity Commission that enforces it had something approaching real clout.

During the decade of the 1970s, more than a quarter-million grievances concerning job bias were filed. Even in the face of tougher laws, many employers continue to exhibit an "I dare you" obstinacy, refusing to alter their ways or settle claims against them until the case is in court. It took the threat of sustained legal pressure and the possible loss of $36 million in federal contracts before Uniroyal, the tire company, agreed in November 1979 to a $5.2-million settlement of a lawsuit involving 750 women workers.[9] This pressure was only possible because the Department of Labor backed the suit. For those who sue on their own, such leverage is impossible. Still, they persevere. Suits have been aimed at all levels of enterprise, including city and state government, police and fire departments, Wall Street brokerage houses and law firms, and the coal industry. (One woman— Marilyn McCusker—died in a mine collapse soon after her legal victory gave her the right to work as a miner.) Few American institutions have escaped the charge of job bias, though employers have fought the inevitable every step of the way.

Even Congress has been sued for sex and racial bias. In 1974, Congressman Otto Passman fired his senior aide, Shirley Davis. He wrote her a goodbye letter saying, "I conclude that it was essential that the understudy to my administrative assistant be a man. I believe you will agree with this conclusion."[10]

Shirley Davis did not agree, and sued him in federal court for discrimination. Passman hid behind his congressional status, and for five years his lawyer insisted to various courts that Passman's congressional immunity meant Davis had no right to sue him. Finally, the U.S. Supreme Court disagreed, and returned Davis's case to a trial court for hearing.[11] At the very last minute, rather than face a full trial (which might prove a disastrous precedent for the other members of Congress), the seventy-eight-year-old Passman, who by this time was a congressman no longer, settled with her out of court for an undisclosed sum.

Just as some adversaries provoke lawsuits, they also mete out punishment and reprisals when litigation arises. The risks implicit in a lawsuit against an employer should be obvious. When four female law-school graduates sought to protest the allegedly discriminatory hiring practices of two of Dallas's largest firms, they were so fearful of retaliation that they refused to put their names on their suit.[12] When a federal judge ruled they must identify themselves in order that the case might proceed, they dropped out.[13]

These women are justified in their fears. While there are times when an employer immediately capitulates in the face of suit, offering a plaintiff almost everything she wants rather than going through the harrowing court process, such a response cannot be assumed. Federal law, as already stated, prohibits reprisals against those who sue for job rights. But as we've seen, this prohibition can be meaningless. Employers are savvy, they know how to show you the door—legally. It takes a hardy soul to undertake a lawsuit of this type and to stick with it. The attrition rate is high.

Tamila C. Jensen conducted a follow-up study of ninety women who filed sex-bias actions. Fifty-one women had left their jobs two years later, nine more intended to leave, and another seven were undecided. Only five women stayed until the litigation was completed. Reprisals, many of them overt, were common, and were reported by about 60 percent of the women queried. Women said they were excluded from staff meetings they had previously attended, received less desirable assignments, and in more than half the cases were criticized for their work more stringently than previously. Of those who remained on the job, only three thought employment conditions had improved; twenty others were staying because the job was convenient or they were too old to change companies. "I could never advance to the top after filing this complaint," one woman complained.[14]

In 1971, Pat Warren and nearly two dozen female co-workers at *Reader's Digest* began protesting the magazine's employment policies. Of 3500 workers, 75 percent were women, but few were in positions of power. Employees in the all-women departments—chiefly clerical—were watched on closed-circuit television and had to ask permission to go to the bathroom. Men suffered no such indignities.

Warren and colleagues requested a meeting with management, at which they voiced their complaints. For more than a year discussions continued between the two sides. The women offered suggestions for improving working conditions, and a "white paper" was presented in which the women detailed statistics and relevant data about sex bias at the company. They were optimistic that something would be done.

"We were very nice, and very quiet," Warren told interviewer Tamila C. Jensen later. "We didn't stage protests, we didn't burn our bras. And we presented them with the white paper and they proceeded to ignore it."

When it seemed to them that nothing was happening, the women filed a complaint against the company, which culminated in a lawsuit. Despite the nationwide visibility of the women's movement, which throughout 1971 was staging boycotts and parades and sit-ins in various offices of the media, *Digest* management, they felt, acted as if the whole thing would blow over. "They really didn't take us seriously until the moment at which they found out that we

were actually filing the complaint," said Warren. "And
then they were very disbelieving and very angry, and very
upset. And there was quite an uproar for the next few
weeks."

In 1977, six years after the first meetings with management, the *Digest* women won a $1.5-million settlement in
their case. Management agreed to back pay and immediate
salary increases for 2600 women employees.

Still, contemplating their suit and their victory, Pat
Warren stopped far short of recommending litigation as a
way of life. "It is very heavy business," she said. "When you
get into a large company with certain very set traditions and
certain very set ways of doing things which very much contrast with your view of it, it's not an easy thing."

It is not management alone that makes life difficult for
would-be reformers. In December 1971, even as Pat Warren
was moving against *Reader's Digest,* a similar protest was
brewing against the National Broadcasting Company's corporate headquarters in New York City. But by the time NBC
women finally filed suit charging the company with sex discrimination in employment, the women discovered they were
fighting for respect not only from their bosses but from their
coworkers as well.

The protest began as a rather benign affair. Marilyn
Schultz and Katherine Powers, two production assistants on
the nightly news show, refused to serve their bosses coffee.
They were fed up with being servants, and, fuming as they
huddled together in the file room, they vowed to change the
situation. It was difficult enough for women to rise from their
entry-level position of secretary, but what was the use of promotion if duties remained the same?

With that small protest, a core group of sixteen women
was formed, endeavoring to change network policy that they
felt constituted blatant sex bias. Two-thirds of the 900 women
at the New York national headquarters were secretaries.
Those few who rose to production assistant, like Schultz and
Powers, were treated as secretaries. Working life at NBC

seemed a prototype for *The Best of Everything*—the career-girl movie in which women either left their jobs to get married or else considered suicide. Though many of the women had been promised advancement or were induced to regard their low-level jobs as a "stepping-stone" to bigger dreams, the rule at NBC was much like that for women throughout the television and magazine world: Once a secretary, always a secretary. Even the pay scale appeared to be sex-biased: Secretaries got pay hikes as their bosses went up the corporate ladder; if he went nowhere, she went nowhere.

The women complained of all this to management. They also researched employment statistics and did a feasibility study of reforms management could make. If NBC incorporated their suggestions, the women told each other, the matter would end right there. The Steering Committee didn't know what to expect. Some women had wanted to sue the network immediately; others were too scared to do anything. The conservative contingent held sway, urging their coworkers to wait and see—perhaps negotiation was possible.

The feasibility study was presented to management. Immediately afterward a heavy depression settled over the women employees. Although management had promised to consider their report, the women had smelled condescension permeating the meeting room, and felt the paternal pat on the head as they were dismissed.

Some weeks later they were summoned to Julian Goodman's sixth-floor President's Council office. Management was ready with its answer. It was in the form of a slide show, much as salesmen offer to prospective customers, and it was nothing if not slick. Great care had gone into the slides, one for each and every one of the women's grievances and suggestions, with two boxes on each one for the possible responses "yes" or "no." A public-relations man read the slides aloud one at a time, and the women watched in horror as a large check mark appeared in the "no" box of every suggestion.

The women were crushed. Years later Marilyn Schultz would remember with fresh outrage how she had trusted management to deal in good faith and how disappointed she was with their pettiness. They turned down every idea, she complained, nitpicking even over the question of whether the women could hold their meetings in NBC offices, and whether they could put up notices in the ladies' room. Joan Ward, another Steering Committee member, remembered the shame she felt in her dealings with management. "They never took us seriously," she said. "They thought we were going to go away, they thought we were dumb."

The slide show was the last straw. With the President's Council's flip rejection of their suggestions (management eventually would concede the right to post notices in the ladies' room), the political composition of the Steering Committee altered radically. The militant faction, which had favored suing from the first, now ruled the day. Within months, they approached Janice Goodman and Nancy Stanley, New York lawyers who had started the nation's first feminist law firm, and the road to suit was begun. It was not a happy occasion for the women at NBC. None of them had ever before undertaken an act of such aggressiveness. But they felt abused by their employer, felt condescended to, as if they didn't count. To continue working for the company, they had to get management's respect. They saw a lawsuit as the only way to accomplish their goals.

The sixteen women on the Steering Committee believed they were fighting their battle on behalf of the 900 others who did not speak out, but they soon discovered that many of their women colleagues wanted no part of their fight. Though the plight of women at the network irritated and frustrated almost everyone, each woman had a separate idea of how to improve her lot. They were split a hundred ways, according to self-interest. The few professional women in the company had a snobbish disdain for secretaries and didn't want to associate themselves with their problems. For the female anchorpeople and other on-camera personalities, the issue was how to get better assignments; television writers wanted equal pay for equal work and a chance to work on better shows; programmers hoped to get supervisory positions.

A separate problem was posed by workers who openly sided with management. "We'd have meetings where women would tell us how good the company was," recalled one participant in the case. This group was playing into management's hands. Once, the vice-president of personnel met with the Steering Committee. He warned them that for every woman who left the network, there were 200 others willing to take her place at the same rate of pay. A sizable number of women feared his message and dared not rock the boat.

The Steering Committee found it difficult to placate so many competing interests. Since secretaries were in the majority, most policies had to please them, but this alienated the upper-level women, who had needs of their own. When management noted that the most influential women at the network had not joined in the demands, it concluded the suit was frivolous. The male management took advantage of the women's factionalism. They kept asking the committee, "What do you women want?" But because the committee sought to represent everyone, they wanted too many things, and their goals soon became unfocused. Even if management had truly been interested in compromise or negotiation, it was difficult to know where to begin.

It didn't help morale that seven of the Steering Committee quit the network while the suit was in progress. Or that, five years after suit had commenced, there were still women who didn't know or care about it. Those who knew would greet Steering Committee women with a casual "How's your suit going?" as if they had no stake in it. But when in 1977 the $1.6-million settlement was reached, including back pay and affirmative-action programs, it became "How's *our* suit?" If management had been cavalier about the women's demands, it must also be said that NBC employees didn't help each other too much, either.

Lawsuits are complex, and so it is difficult to speculate why some have better results than others. Still, the sex-bias case of women against *Newsweek* magazine offers an instance where management and employees learned to cooperate without going to court.

The *Newsweek* women filed their complaint in March 1970, challenging a magazine tradition by which women could rise to a position no higher than researcher. One woman leader recalls that at first the magazine's management reacted to the demands much like the chiefs at NBC and *Reader's Digest:* They were furious, and they denied any such discrimination existed. But by August 1970, only months after the women filed their complaint charging bias, peace was restored, management voluntarily agreed to guidelines for improved working conditions, and women started their upward climb on the editorial ladder.

A big difference between *Newsweek* and other sex-bias suits was the numbers. The NBC women could barely raise a quorum of supporters, and at *Reader's Digest* women had distributed a "loyalty" petition attesting that they were not participating in the suit. But at *Newsweek* forty-six out of fifty women employees were united for change. Organizing had been such an enormous success, management either attended to employees' grievances or risked a walkout. After due consideration, management issued a 1500-word pledge to promote women at a faster pace. The pledge coincided with the first (and apparently last) annual Women's Strike Day, which was also the fiftieth anniversary of women's suffrage. *The New York Times* ran the story of the *Newsweek* settlement right beneath the presidential proclamation honoring suffrage day and near a huge photo of jubilant women marching down Fifth Avenue in a solidarity parade. The layout made it appear that *Newsweek*'s board had been doubly magnanimous, acting in the interest not only of its own staff but of women everywhere.

Such enlightenment, however, is rare. As the NBC and *Reader's Digest* women discovered, corporations don't change policies just because new suggestions make sense. In fact, they frequently won't budge even if it can be demonstrated that the old ways are both unfair and costly. In the face of such resistance, suing may be the only way to grease the corporate wheels.*

The federal government's lawsuit against American Telephone & Telegraph demonstrates the intransigence of both corporate management and unions in the face of change.† By the time the Equal Employment Opportunity Commission became involved with AT&T, 2400 individuals had already filed separate job-bias claims against the nation's largest utility.[15] For various reasons, the company chose to fight, rather than negotiate, these potential suits.

The commission, hoping to make an example of AT&T to warn other corporations, did a study of the Bell telephone system and its nearly 1 million employees. The survey found racial and sex discrimination running through the corporate fabric. Men and women, the study found, were segregated in each of Bell's twenty-four companies, and only men could rise up to management rank. Although Bell hired thousands of blacks (about 10 percent of its work force), almost all of these were black women, thus compounding the discrimination problem.

Using this survey, the commission attempted to make equal employment look like good business sense for the utility: It tried to show that race-and-sex bias was costing AT&T many of its best and most productive workers, who quit because the salary was too low and there was no chance for advancement. But in all, the survey made little impact. From 1971 to 1973, AT&T stalled all attempts by the government to force it to change its ways. Then the commission got tough: Either AT&T changed its policies, the agency threatened, or it would be sued in federal court.

---

* Tamila C. Jensen interviewed the major plaintiffs in the *Reader's Digest,* NBC, and *Newsweek* cases for a study, *Title VII: The Costs, the Benefits* (videocassette copyright, Indian University Foundation, 1977).
† *EEOC* v. *AT&T,* 6 Fair Employment Practices Cases 645 (1973).

A lawsuit would keep AT&T in court for years, defending itself not only against the government but against all those other private suits as well. But although the threat of suit was great inducement to settle, the conglomerate kept hedging. There was no way to defend its employment policies, so it didn't even try. Finally, the commission had to take drastic steps: It challenged the telephone company's rate hikes in hearings before the Federal Communications Commission. Only then, with billions of dollars in potential revenue at stake, did the phone company's wheels start to turn. In 1973 a $35-million settlement was reached, adding thousands of new management jobs for women and initiating a major push to hire minority men.

But as soon as the phone company agreed to settle, the Communications Workers of America, the nation's largest union, threw a monkey wrench into the deal. Throughout the long years of negotiations with AT&T, the union—as collective-bargaining agent for most telephone workers—had boycotted all discussions, and no settlement with AT&T would be binding if the workers refused to comply. For two years, the CWA let the telephone company and the government wheel and deal about new roles for women and minorities. Then, two days before the crucial settlement was announced, the CWA filed suit in federal court saying it had been illegally denied a role in the negotiations and that consequently AT&T workers had been denied a voice.

This ploy was outrageous and it didn't work. Though purporting to represent all AT&T workers, the union was obviously concerned only with its white male members, who now would have to compete with minorities and females for job advancement. Judge Patrick Higginbotham, hearing the case, was livid. "For two years," he wrote, "CWA has been begged to enter the administrative arena to negotiate and litigate for the rights of those members who presumably endured deprivations by reason of their sex or race." Since the CWA had consistently refused to participate previously, the judge would not let the union hold up the settlement for as much as an hour. He chided the union on its behavior, and laid the blame for rampant discrimination at the union's door. The CWA, he asserted, had sanctioned and tolerated abuses throughout its years of negotiations with AT&T, agreeing to contracts that excluded minorities and women. If AT&T was guilty, the court reasoned, CWA was also guilty.

After Judge Higginbotham's ruling, the CWA found several minor procedural grounds for appeals to higher courts, but it never prevailed. The effect of the settlement was profound. The Conference Board, which tracks job conditions for women in business, reported that the AT&T settlement was primarily responsible for a 22-percent increase in the number of women managers nationwide.

One might assume that labor unions would have taken up the battle for employment equality for the minorities, women, and the aging in their membership. Not so. The attitude Judge Higginbotham discovered within the CWA was rampant in unions nationwide. Unions permitted all-male and all-female locals to coexist without protesting unequal salaries for women who did the same jobs as men. They ignored all-black locals, whose members were employed by the same factories as were members of all-white locals, but with grossly unfavorable contracts. Dissatisfied workers seeking to change these situations have frequently had no other recourse but to sue, either in court or before the National Labor Relations Board established to solve labor disputes.

But to be fair, it's not necessarily antifemale or antiminority bias that keeps organized labor from integrating its ranks. By the time integration became an issue for unions to consider, the seniority system was embedded in concrete, and white men had been promised certain rights which they were not about to relinquish voluntarily. Integrating with blacks and women—or any kind of new blood—meant white men lost what courts call their "vested interests," including higher pay and early retirement, which come with their rank. Faced with the frustrating task of reconciling two irreconcilable obligations—the necessity of obeying two conflicting laws— no wonder union leaders frequently prefer to leave the problem to the courts by letting disgruntled workers sue.

In early 1980, eighty-two black truck drivers won $2.74 million in back pay from a trucking company based in Oklahoma City. The Equal Employment Opportunity Commission convinced Lee Way Motor Freight, Inc., to settle a seven-year-old lawsuit by agreeing to that payment, which represented what the men might have earned had they been hired when they first applied to the company for a job. Five truckers each received $100,000 from the suit. Lee Way also agreed to hire more blacks and Hispanics, but, to make this part of the settlement stick, the commission needed agreement of the International Association of Machinists (IAM) and the Teamsters, both of which had contracts with the trucking concern. The IAM agreed, the Teamsters did not. It was not made clear how the settlement could proceed without Teamsters cooperation, or what the government might do to get it. That part of the case is still pending.

But even when a plaintiff wins his case—getting a court order for integration, back pay, or other favorable judgment—defendants don't always just fall in line. In one case, a female local of the glassblowers union in Illinois filed suit to force the male local to take them in. Even after the National Labor Relations Board ruled in favor of the women, ordering merger, the men still locked them out. The board had to take the glassblowers to court, at which time the male local agreed to yield.

Although unions may ultimately agree to accept new members, the grudging manner in which they do it often guarantees the matter goes back into court. In one case, a white local of a paperworkers' union in Bogalusa, Louisiana, had won greater benefits from collective bargaining with the Crown Zellerbach Corporation than those won by the black local of that same union at the same Crown Zellerbach plant. The black local sued for merger.* The white local agreed, but placed all black workers at the bottom of the white list, regardless of years the black workers had spent on the job.

Judge Wisdom, in ruling that this type of wedding was inadequate, had sympathy for both sides: The blacks were entitled to equal opportunity, he reasoned, but the whites had been given to expect seniority. The judge didn't want to reward white workers who had for years been profiting at the expense of their black brothers, and yet he could see that whites were entitled to what they had been promised years ago, before society changed.

In the judge's opinion, this conflict was one of the most perplexing issues facing the courts. And when it came time to rule, he favored the black worker. As long as blacks had the qualifications for the job, he said, black and white seniority must be the same as if they'd been working side by side all these years.

As with so much else in suing, deciding one has reached the point of last resort is quite a subjective matter. Some of us reach our limit of conflict at the drop of the proverbial hat; others never get there at all.

Marco De Funis, for example, was accepted by three northwestern law schools, but not his hometown school, the University of Washington in Seattle, where he hoped to practice law. He could have accepted his rejection as fate, as thousands of other law-school hopefuls do. Instead, he sued the university, insisting that its affirmative-action program, designed to help nonwhites become lawyers, was illegal.

De Funis won his case at the trial level, and was ordered admitted. The school complied, but appealed the decision. After a series of appeals, with varying results, Justice Wil-

* U.S. v. Local 189 United Papermakers and Paperworkers, 1 Fair Employment Practices Cases 877 (1969).

liam O. Douglas issued a stay of all proceedings until De Funis completed his course. De Funis was weeks away from his law degree when the U.S. Supreme Court heard oral arguments, in February 1974, on this first of the so-called reverse-discrimination cases. It raised a ruckus. Civil-liberties groups were split on the ideological question of whether quotas should exist; law schools from Harvard on down filed friend-of-the-court briefs defending their affirmative-action programs. But the court finally ruled, five to four, that the issue was moot: De Funis no longer had stake in the controversy, the justices ruled, so there was nothing to decide.

But the issue of reverse discrimination would not rest. Allan Bakke, a former engineer with the National Aeronautics and Space Administration, started applying to medical schools at age thirty-two. Two years later, he'd still had no luck. He'd been rejected by ten schools in all, several of them citing his age as a disadvantage. Bakke was placed on the waiting list at the University of California, Davis campus, but was never admitted. As an engineering student, Bakke had had excellent grades, and when he finally sued the California school, he would insist that if not for a special admissions program favorable to minorities, he would be on his way toward getting his medical degree. The trial-court judge disagreed, impressed by evidence that even more qualified whites than Bakke had been rejected.

"*Bakke* is a third-rate lawsuit," Ralph Smith, a black law professor active in civil rights, wrote in *Juris Doctor* magazine as the case headed for High Court decision. "A third-rate case shouldn't make hard law." Like many civil libertarians fearful that the Court would erode hard-won rights, Smith profoundly wished that the issue had never been raised in the first place. "The Supreme Court has no magic wand to dispel differences and still debates," wrote Smith. Society should struggle with this problem without Supreme Court help, he suggested.[16]

But to a surprising extent, Smith got what he wanted. In 1978, the U.S. Supreme Court handed down a decision that satisfied no one—and everyone: Race could be considered in minority admissions, the Court ruled, but not race alone. As legal scholars went home to ponder what the High Court meant, Allan Bakke was ordered into medical school, armed with a legal decision that seemed to benefit him alone.

Those who use the courts as a last resort rarely evaluate the long-term significance of their victories or defeats. They're generally so pleased that the court is open to them, they plow right ahead. Lawsuits are a form of self-help, and people who use them are not the type to take "no" for an answer. America's small businessmen during the late nineteenth century refused to wait for state legislatures or Congress to bust the evil big-business "trusts": American courts were full of lawsuits filed by those minor companies squeezed out by coal, oil, sugar, salt, and other industrial combines. Two decades before the Sherman Antitrust Act was passed in 1890, state court judges had already ruled that monopolies were illegal and in violation of public policy. While no one of these judicial decisions seems to have had the impact of the Sherman Act,[17] nevertheless the courts had done their job of providing succor where it otherwise did not exist.

But there are risks attendant to using the courts. Virginia Minor felt certain that the United States Constitution permitted her, as an American woman, to vote in all elections. In 1872, however, the laws of Missouri, where she lived with her lawyer husband, disagreed, and Minor was not allowed to register as a voter. She filed suit against the state Department of Elections and continued her suit to the U.S. Supreme Court. In 1874, the court ruled against her, saying that certain classes of citizens could be deprived of their rights. Voting guidelines, it said, were a state prerogative, and the federal government could not interfere.*

This was the same rationale that had deprived Dred Scott of his freedom some twenty years before, and, as far as women are concerned, its results were nearly as disastrous. The Minor decision was a setback that took forty-six years to

---

* *Minor* v. *Happersett*, 88 U.S. 162 (1875).

rectify, with the eventual passage in 1920 of the Nineteenth Amendment, guaranteeing women's suffrage.

The courts similarly were of no help to Myra Colby Bradwell during this same period in her attempt to become a member of the bar. Bradwell passed the examination to become a lawyer in Chicago, but state law precluded her from practice. When she appealed finally to the U.S. Supreme Court, the justices ruled against her, fearful that if women could become lawyers, they might, as one justice wrote, also "be made governors, judges and sheriffs. This we are not prepared to hold."*

Chances are, even if Virginia Minor and Myra Colby Bradwell had known they would lose, they would probably have pursued their lawsuits in any event. The beauty of the American legal system is that the courts must stay open and judges must listen. They need not always rule in your favor, and a judicial decision may be frustratingly inadequate to deal with a particular problem, but, in the vast majority of cases, they must grant a hearing. This opportunity to be heard is an almost irresistible magnet, one which sometimes misleads people into thinking that, merely as a result of being heard, their fondest wishes will be granted. It doesn't work that way, but still, as long as the chance for the hearing exists, few people turn it down.

* *Bradwell* v. *State,* 83 U.S., 16 Wall. 130 (1872).

CHAPTER 9

Lexiphobia

Nothing in the preceding chapters seems destined to relieve or tranquilize those who suffer from what might be called lexiphobia, or fear of lawsuits. Lexiphobia is a deeply felt terror that immobilizes the victim, making him envision lawsuits coming seemingly from out of the blue and transforming him from a relatively harmless, innocent individual into a target defendant, one whom all of his so-called "enemies," real and imagined, are "out to get." Fear of lawsuits has become a disease of the modern age, influencing the way we Americans do business and conduct our lives.

However bad the "lawsuit problem" may be, it is certainly not assisted by the outsized fear of being sued that so preoccupies American society. Typically, those who worry claim to have more than money on their minds: They *say* they are concerned about ethics, morality, proper behavior in polite society, the future of our civilization, and, of course, "justice." Certainly there are social and financial costs attached to our habit of suing for every reason—costs both to the individual defendant and to society as a whole. But one suspects that these statements of principle are frequently used to cloak a rather blind and uncontrollable fear of lawsuits as a form of witchcraft.

The old voodoo apparently still works: Litigation is a kind of devil's curse, evil and contagious. This voodoo does more than place the already mentioned "cloud" on the specific defendant facing suit; it also seems to damn everyone even remotely associated with him, causing them to fear for their safety and magnifying a particular legal problem beyond its rational scope. An outbreak of lexiphobia is very much like a fever, running a predictable course from day of contact, to paralysis or other form of incapacity, to eventual recovery. Rest assured, those afflicted do recover, though while they suffer they believe that the end of their world is at hand.

Fear of lawsuits reached epidemic proportions among doctors in the early 1970s. It was almost impossible to have a medical appointment with a dermatologist or family practitioner (two specialties with relatively low rates of claims against them) without getting treated to a lecture on the litigiousness of patients. Although these doctors had not themselves been sued, they had heard of a colleague who had been "taken for everything he was worth." Now these doctors lived in dread that the litigation disease, like smallpox, was "going around," and they would be hit next.

In retrospect, one can see how this frenzy got started. It began when doctors' insurance companies announced rate hikes of 200 to 400 percent. The underwriters justified their demands by citing an increased number of lawsuits against medical practitioners and a spate of higher jury verdicts. Though the companies never documented exactly how many more lawsuits had been filed (and were never made to account for their contentions before either the public or the government), doctors responded by panicking. The implication that *more* doctors were being sued was immediately taken to mean that most or *all* doctors were vulnerable. The dark cloud appeared, and the insurance companies seemed to be the only available shelter. Nerves were frayed. Doctors lived in a climate of anxiety.

It is no secret by now that some insurance companies used their premiums to offset their poor financial investments in the stock market and mutual funds. But this was unknown at the time. The question of control of the insurance companies, and the larger related problem described by columnist Max Lerner as "the prevailing belief that insurance solves every life problem,"[1] were totally obscured by the hysteria that reigned. In scores of articles (an insurance-industry clearinghouse sent out packets with reprints of fifty articles written in a four-month period during 1975), editorial writers ineptly attempted to solve the "malpractice crisis." They blamed doctors, lawyers, the patients themselves, juries, the quality of life in America. They reported interviews with unnamed doctors who were retiring early rather than live in fear of suit. They demanded legislative protection to save both the medical profession and the patient from the legal system. And they wrote of their nightmares of how it all would end: lawyers and doctors facing each other at gunpoint.

These commentaries fanned the emotional flames in the medical community, where doctors in some specialties were being asked to pay as much as $30,000 for annual basic insurance coverage.

The malpractice-insurance crisis was indeed complex, and the growing incidence of lawsuits against doctors could not be denied. Still, it is not often recognized how a manufactured climate of fear—created in equal parts by the media, the insurance companies, and the perceived helplessness of the doctors themselves—created a market desperate for insurance coverage at any price. Eventually, the crisis ended when doctors circumnavigated the traditional insurance structure and formed their own insurance companies, setting their own rates, making their own investments in the stock market, and controlling their own coverage.

Some people are so fearful of lawsuits that they immediately capitulate, giving in to the plaintiff without much of a fight. Fear of lawsuit appears to be the reason the Los Angeles school board agreed to demands that women fill 50 percent of all school administrative jobs. But while voluntary action is always commendable, and while as a matter of principle one applauds an increased role for women in all walks of life, one can nevertheless deplore the use of suit as a form of blackmail to force one's way. Women already filled 37 percent of the administrative posts in the school district, according to a report of the case in the *Los Angeles Times,* hardly "a flagrant case of discrimination against women," as one female school board member referred to the situation. And of 1000 lower-level jobs also covered in the settlement, the ratio between men and women was already one-to-one, the *Los Angeles Times* reported.[2]

Still, the school board consented to the demands, subjecting itself to hiring quotas for the next decade. The board said that the threatened suit might have resulted in a stringent court order requiring millions of dollars in back pay. At least as described in the Los Angeles paper, the case looked like an extortion attempt in which the school board was a cooperative victim.

In today's "legalistic" environment, it does take true grit and a strong sense of personal security to overcome the fear of being sued. The threat always seems to be in the air, aggravated by the publicity and notoriety that press coverage gives to litigants and their causes. Writers on legal affairs and lawyers have made a sport of raising novel legal problems which have not yet surfaced, under the guise of preventing future hassles.

Preventive law can be helpful to individuals about to embark on risky ventures (such as marriage, where prenuptial contracts have been of some assistance in promoting wedded bliss), but this crystal-ball gazing also often creates problems out of whole cloth, planting seeds of ideas for future lawsuits. Panels are already engaged in mock litigation arising from space exploration and interplanetary colonization. The Sunday *New York Times* magazine devoted almost a full page to the possible legal ramifications of scientific advances in human reproduction. The writer conjectured about lawsuits brought by sperm donors who want fatherhood privileges for the child they "sired," and also speculated on whether a woman who consented to carry a child for another woman who couldn't bear might later claim that the child was hers.[3] Such questions may seem farfetched now, but no doubt in time they will be raised in lawsuits. In the meantime, raising such questions is bound to make one wonder if it's safe to take any actions at all.

It's not just the law of the future that gives pause. The law of the present is plenty scary. Courts in New York State have convened panels of experts to decide whether certain terminally ill patients should be taken off artificial life-support systems. The clergy protests the legal invasion of life and death, but it is only through such court scrutiny that doctors can feel sure they will not be charged with criminal activity once the patient dies.

Even the most apparently cut-and-dried type of lawsuit may call forth a novel theory threatening to the rights of one interest group or another. Our national appellate courts are daily flooded with friend-of-the-court briefs by assorted associations claiming that their rights will be infringed and that an Orwellian future awaits if such and such a theory of law is endorsed in a pending case.

Despite this exaggerated diligence, life does go on almost precisely as before, regardless of what the courts say or do. Somehow we overcome our anxieties and go back to work, despite the possibility of suit, and even despite the results of suit. It may not be a uniquely American trait, but our citizens have a highly developed ability to separate and insulate themselves from the lawsuit effects they don't like. Kenneth Dolbeare, a political scientist, has noted, for example, a "halo effect" in regard to decisions by the U.S. Supreme Court. Such a "halo effect" apparently allows people to disregard or even openly flout the rulings of the high court (as occurred with the outlawing of prayer in the schools), while continuing to tell themselves they are obeying the law. Americans, Dolbeare suggests, refuse to see themselves as scofflaws, and therefore also refuse to change their ways unless there is a great inducement to do so.

The insulation process takes place over time. When psychologist Paul Bindrim won a $75,000 judgment against novelist Gwen Davis and her publisher, Doubleday, because of her unflattering portrait of him in *Touching* (see chapter 5), writers and members of the book-publishing community exhibited an almost phobic reaction to the news. It was one of the first successful libel lawsuits based on a work of fiction, and it caused a great deal of commotion and concern.

As word of Davis's defeat spread, attorneys knowledgeable in the field of libel law attempted to soothe the jangled nerves of writers throughout the country who feared that they, too, would be subjected to suit by any possible real-life models of their fictional characters. "*Bindrim* is a one-of-a-kind case," one constitutional lawyer kept repeating. An attorney in a New York publishing house told a reporter, "If no one paid attention to this case, it would just go away."

But phobias being the way they are, it was impossible that writers could ignore the Bindrim matter and the perceived threat it posed to their livelihood. In the beginning, they rallied to writer Gwen Davis's defense with wholehearted support.

"Libel Suits—Plot Thickens for Authors" was the headline of a page one story in the *Los Angeles Times* by reporter Bill Boyarsky in January 1978. In this first major piece on the case, Boyarsky painted a sympathetic portrait of Davis, and a surprisingly Machiavellian picture of Bindrim. Placed high up in the text and then repeated in greater detail later on were several inferences that Bindrim had changed both his appearance and his "identity" so as to more closely conform to "his" character in Davis's book, Simon Herford. Specifically, Boyarsky noted that by the time Bindrim appeared at his trial, he had "changed from the clean-shaven, short-haired man Davis had met in the Hollywood Hills [site of the nude marathon] to a man with a big hairy beard," much like the "Santa Clausy" Herford that Davis had drawn, and had also "earned" a doctorate in the interim from a correspondence "school without walls."

" 'I went to great pains to fictionalize,' " Davis was quoted as saying. " 'I took a hairless, close-cropped fringed man that I had some experience with and transmuted him into Santa Claus. How was I to know he would grow a beard?' "

For most of the next two years, gossip in the Los Angeles literary community was uniformly favorable to Gwen Davis. Concern among writers was focused on Paul Bindrim's beard, the alleged stupidity of the jury for failing to see through his "ruse," and the Kafkaesque legal system that permitted Bindrim even to get to trial. When the story moved East, Davis was portrayed as a champion of free speech. In the summer of 1979, Herbert Mitgang, a reporter who covers the publishing industry, wrote in *The New York Times*: "Gwen Davis to Appeal First-Amendment Libel Case." He suggested that the question posed was of utmost seriousness: "To what extent can an author create fictional characters and events out of real-life persons and situations?" In an interview for the United Press International, Davis claimed to be carrying the banner for novelists who "pass on information in fictional fashion."

And so the coverage went—until the day in December 1979 when the Supreme Court announced that it would not hear Davis's appeal. It may have been mere coincidence, but from that day Gwen Davis's image suffered a radical change. (The Supreme Court's refusal meant that the lower court order stood, and Davis was liable to Bindrim for the damages. However, the ruling had no national significance and its impact was, strictly speaking, limited to California.)

The Los Angeles Herald Examiner, which earlier had written sympathetically of Davis's problems, ran a major story the week after the Supreme Court announcement with "newly discovered facts" of Gwen Davis's past history. Davis, it seemed, had once filed a lawsuit of her own against author Ken Kesey on much the same grounds that Paul Bindrim used against her: She charged that Kesey had used her as a model for the character of a nurse in his book *One Flew Over the Cuckoo's Nest*. The story said that Davis had settled for $8000, and that the character was also removed as part of the settlement. "In addition," the article reported, "during Davis's career as a novelist, two people have sued her for portraying them unfairly, and Kesey threatened to sue her on the same principle."[4]

This new theme was picked up in stories in *The American Lawyer, New York* magazine, and the *Village Voice,* among others, and the relationship between Gwen Davis and the First Amendment was made to appear increasingly tenuous.

The release of this new information seems hardly coincidental. Bindrim's attorneys had known about the Kesey lawsuit for years (one of them had represented a client in an unrelated case against Kesey) and had told anyone about it who would listen. But in the days of Gwen Davis's martyrdom, few people were interested. Now that she had lost, the new "facts" gave writers just what they needed to reassure themselves that Davis's case was indeed, as their attorneys insisted, "one of a kind," and nothing for them to worry about. (They would rally to her defense, suffering a relapse of lexiphobia, when Doubleday took the extraordinary step of suing her for $140,000 in attorneys' fees they had incurred while defending themselves against Bindrim's charges.)

The coverage of the case in the press, then, seems to have been at least partially, if unconsciously, designed to soothe and calm reporters and writers. Eliot Fremont-Smith, writing in the *Village Voice,* noted the emphasis on personalities in the stories that had been published, and worried that this focus obscured the seriousness of the free-speech issue at stake.

"[The] importance of *Bindrim* is filtered [in the press] through the character and antics of Bindrim, Davis and Doubleday," he wrote, "which are not kept separate from the decision, but function to keep *us* separate from it and, because they're all somewhat grubby, feeling okay, even amused."[5]

But the point he misses is that this very separateness must be created to counterbalance what might otherwise be an intolerable environment of fear. In order to continue writing, authors had to convince themselves that their own work would pass legal muster, that they need not fear suits. At first, feeling themselves and their profession under attack by the jury verdict in favor of Bindrim, they rallied to Gwen Davis's defense. Then, recognizing that there would be no help from the U.S. Supreme Court, writers panicked. When the panic was no longer sustainable, they found ways of dealing with it—in this instance, by looking at the behavior of Davis, Bindrim, and Doubleday, making them human, finding the loopholes. The loopholes provided release, temporarily at least easing the sense of crisis.

This process of insulating oneself from the problems of others may be a significant defense mechanism in a litigious society. Doctors would refuse to practice or operate if they truly believed their every patient was plotting to get them into court. Instead, they act in the faith that they are immune or somehow protected. Most lawyers, if asked, say that *they* do not fear lawsuits, that it's the "other guys," the bad apples of the profession, who have to worry. When lawsuits strike so close to home, a natural response is, "It doesn't apply to me." In a sense, each one of us holds veto power over court decisions, deciding how much weight we want them to have in our lives.

"There's no such thing as justice," Clarence Darrow, this country's most famous trial lawyer, is said to have remarked. After examining the ways in which Americans use lawsuits, one can understand what Darrow meant. Justice is like a sixth sense, an unreachable itch, as much emotion as science. Those who think they've tasted of it say that, like chocolate, it's bittersweet and addictive.

Roscoe Pound, the great twentieth-century educator and legal scholar, came a bit closer when he described justice as "the ideal compromise between the activities of all in a crowded world." But if it is a compromise, it's one hammered out without the knowing or express cooperation of either side. Plaintiffs with their hidden agenda, defendants who both fear suit and encourage it, come to court expecting the miracle of perfect justice. That they are inevitably disappointed is not so much the fault of the courts, or the laws, or the lawyers (though of course none of these are blameless). The fault is with us, with the dreams we bring to court, the ill-fitting ways we insist upon using a man-made system.

Lawsuits are simply a tool, no better or worse than we are. We use this tool with extraordinary invention, and not always in ways that legal "authorities" would prefer. We use the courts blindly, with a child's faith that right will be done, somehow. We demand decisions from the courts which we promptly find ways of avoiding; and we want restrictions placed on the suing of others, but none upon ourselves. For all this, despite our basic ignorance of a legal system we nevertheless worship, the lawsuit remains *the* great populist tool, a weapon we can use without getting permission or approval from anyone. It is a tool of freedom, though it carries intimations of imprisonment. In the plenitude of its uses and its potential for good or ill, lawsuits mirror American life.

Notes

Chapter 1

1. Bohannan, p. xii.
2. *Los Angeles Times,* 31 October 1979, p. 4.
3. *Los Angeles Times,* 26 February 1980, p. 2.
4. Calvert D. Crary, "The Quagmire of *U.S.* v. *IBM,*" *National Law Journal,* 22 January 1979, p. 19.
5. Griffin B. Bell, "Proposed Amendments to the Federal Tort Claims Act," *Harvard Journal on Legislation,* Winter 1979, p. 6, fn 22.
6. Austin Sarat, "Alternatives in Dispute Processing: Litigation in a Small Claims Court," *Law and Society,* Spring 1976, pp. 339–75.
7. *ABA Journal,* January 1979, p. 25.
8. Huizinga, p. 79.
9. Frank K. Upham, "Litigation and Moral Consciousness in Japan: An Interpretive Analysis of Four Japanese Pollution Suits," *Law and Society,* Summer 1976, p. 587.
10. Donald P. Lay, "Why Rush to Judgment? Some Second Thoughts on the National Court of Appeals," *Judicature,* November 1975, p. 175.
11. *Los Angeles Times,* 22 June 1980, p. 3.
12. Mark R. Arnold, "The Good War That Might Have Been," *New York Times* magazine, 29 September, 1974, p. 73.
13. Knightley et al., pp. 251–53.
14. Craig Wanner, "The Public Ordering of Private Relations," Part 1, *Law and Society,* Spring 1974, p. 425.
15. Joel B. Grossman and Austin Sarat, "Litigation in the Federal Courts: A Comparative Perspective," *Law and Society,* Winter 1975, pp. 321–46.
16. Marc Galanter, "Why the 'Haves' Come Out Ahead: Speculations on the Limits of Legal Change," *Law and Society,* Fall 1975, pp. 103–46.
17. Craig Wanner, "The Public Ordering of Private Relations," Part 2, "Winning Civil Cases," *Law and Society,* Winter 1975, pp. 293–306.

18. Thomas L. Haskell, "Litigation and Social Status in Seventeenth Century New Haven," *Journal of Legal Studies,* 1978, p. 229.
19. Lawrence M. Friedman and Robert V. Percival, "A Tale of Two Courts: Litigation in Alameda and San Benito Counties," *Law and Society,* Winter 1976, p. 301.
20. Leopold Pospisil, "The Attributes of Law," in Bohannan, pp. 25–41.
21. *National Law Journal,* 30 April 1979, p. 6.
22. *Atlantic,* July 1979.
23. Reisman, p. 436.
24. Bowen, p. 134.
25. Ibid.
26. Boorstin, *The Colonial Experience,* p. 204.
27. Hughes, p. 7.

Chapter 2

1. *New York Times,* 29 November 1959, p. 51.
2. *Los Angeles Times,* 29 April 1980, p. 1.
3. Ibid., 26 April 1979, p. 1.
4. *Sacramento Bee,* 20 June 1979, p. 3.
5. *Los Angeles Times,* 20 June 1979, p. 17.
6. *New York Times,* 24 June 1979, p. 20 E.
7. Ronald K. L. Collins and Robert M. Myers, "The Public Interest Litigant in California: Observations on Taxpayers' Actions," *Loyola of Los Angeles Law Review,* 1977, p. 329.
8. "Plaintiff," *New Yorker,* 3 April 1978, p. 26.

Chapter 3

1. Staten's testimony is reprinted in Stern, p. 43.
2. Erikson, pp. 106–7.
3. Stern, p. 104.
4. Ibid., p. 302.
5. Erikson, pp. 248–49.
6. Jeanie Kasindorf, "Freddie Prinze's Last Laugh," *New West,* 14 March 1977, p. 35.
7. Pruetzel, p. 221.
8. Jonathan Kirsch and Jeanie Kasindorf, "Is Suicide the Doctors's Fault?" *New West,* 21 November 1977, p. 15.

Chapter 4

1. Dolbeare and Hammond, "Inertia in Midway: Supreme Court Decisions and Local Responses," *Journal of Legal Education,* 1970,

pp. 106–23. See also Weisbrod, Handler, and Komesar, *Public Interest Law.*

2. Sheingold, pp. 144–45.
3. *Los Angeles Times,* 1 March 1980, Part 2, p. 6.
4. *Los Angeles Daily Journal,* 4 June 1979, p. 1.
5. Cortner, p. 36.
6. Quoted from Kluger, p. 39.
7. *Los Angeles Times,* 10 May 1976, p. 1.
8. Howard Kohn, "Karen Silkwood v. Nuclear Power," *Rolling Stone,* 17 May 1979, p. 53.
9. Ciji Ware, "The Silkwood Coalition," *New West,* 18 June 1979, p. 25.
10. *New York Times,* 19 May 1979, p. 1.
11. Peter Matthiessen, "How to Kill a Valley," *New York Review of Books,* 7 February 1980, p. 31.
12. Kluger, p. 123.
13. D. Kelly Weisberg, "Barred from the Bar: Women and Legal Education in the United States 1870–1890," *Journal of Legal Education,* 1977, p. 485.
14. "The Karen Silkwood Trial," *Trial Diplomacy Journal* (promotional issue), p. 8.
15. *National Law Journal,* 21 May 1979, p. 15.
16. Weisbrod et al., p. 401, and Handler, *Social Movements and the Legal System,* pp. 48–57.
17. John Denvir, "Towards a Political Theory of Public Interest Litigation," *North Carolina Law Review,* 1976, p. 1137.
18. Harry Brill, "The Uses and Abuses of Legal Assistance," *The Public Interest,* Spring 1973, pp. 38–55.
19. *Los Angeles Times,* 29 October 1972, p. 1.

Chapter 5

1. *Los Angeles Times,* 5 November 1979, Part 2, p. 7.
2. *New York Times,* 2 September 1979, p. 6 E.
3. Jerry Mander, "This Land Is Whose Land?" *Village Voice,* 10 December 1979, p. 25. See also Howell Raines, "American Indians, Struggling for Power and Identity," *New York Times* magazine, pp. 48–50.
4. *National Law Journal,* 18 June 1979, p. 1.
5. Ibid.
6. *Los Angeles Times,* 22 July 1980, p. 1.
7. Gilmore, pp. 74–79.
8. Friedman, p. 589.
9. *National Law Journal,* 18 June 1979, p. 1.

10. *Los Angeles Times,* 23 March 1980, Part 2, p. 1.
11. *National Law Journal,* 8 October 1979, p. 1.
12. Ibid., 16 July 1979, p. 3.
13. Ibid., 12 March 1979, p. 3.
14. *Los Angeles Times,* 29 November 1979, Part 4, p. 3.
15. Judith Adler Hennessee, "Publishing's Dirty Little Secret," *More,* December 1976, p. 18.
16. *National Law Journal,* 3 March 1980, p. 1.
17. Mark Dowie, "Pinto Madness," *Mother Jones,* September 1977, pp. 18–32.
18. *New York Times,* 10 June 1979, p. 12.
19. *Los Angeles Herald Examiner,* 7 March 1980, p. A16.
20. *American Lawyer,* February 1979, p. 3.
21. Ibid., April 1979, p. 3.

Chapter 6

1. Faulk, p. 51.
2. *National Law Journal,* 18 June 1979, pp. 12–13.
3. *New York,* 18 February 1980, p. 46.
4. Bartlett, pp. 112–13.
5. Ibid. See also Wiltse, pp. 382–83.
6. Levin, p. 11.
7. Ibid., p. 272.
8. Lee Grant, "Jean Seberg: Did Gossip Kill Her?" *Los Angeles Times* (Calendar section), 23 September 1979, p. 5.
9. A. E. Hotchner, *Doris Day: Her Own Story.*
10. *Los Angeles Times,* 26 October 1979, Part 2, p. 1.
11. Ibid.
12. Ibid., 14 May 1980, Part 2, p. 1.
13. "1,189 Psychiatrists . . . ," *Fact,* September–October 1964.
14. Lurie, p. 19.
15. Suzannah Lessard, "Kennedy's Woman Problem, Women's Kennedy Problem," *Washington Monthly,* February 1979, pp. 12–13.
16. *Los Angeles Times,* 13 April 1980, Calendar section, p. 6.
17. Ibid.
18. Ibid.
19. Pilat, p. 203.
20. Faulk, p. 45.
21. Perls, pp. 174–75.
22. *Los Angeles Herald Examiner,* 20 March 1980, pp. 1, B6.
23. *Village Voice,* 3 March 1980, p. 51.
24. Norman Mailer, "An Appeal to Lillian Hellman and Mary McCarthy," *New York Times Book Review,* 11 May 1980, p. 3.

25. Kelner, p. 35.
26. Ibid., p. 26.
27. Ibid.
28. Ibid., p. 109.
29. Ibid., p. 254.
30. Ibid.

Chapter 7

1. Strick, pp. 15–17.
2. *Los Angeles Times,* 6 March 1980, Part 2, p. 1.
3. Ibid., 19 March 1980, Part 2, p. 1.
4. *National Law Journal,* 19 November 1979, p. 10.
5. Ibid.
6. Fred Danzig, *Advertising Age,* 8 January 1979, S-9.
7. *National Law Journal,* 9 June 1980, p. 3.
8. Ibid., 1 June 1979, p. 39.
9. *Los Angeles Times,* 28 August 1978, p. 3.
10. *Columbia Journalism Review,* May/June 1980, pp. 89–100.
11. Ibid.

Chapter 8

1. *New York Times,* 10 January 1979, p. 1.
2. Ibid.
3. *Los Angeles Daily Journal,* 21 June 1979, p. 1.
4. *National Law Journal,* 9 July 1979, p. 16.
5. Ibid., 30 September 1979, p. 1.
6. *Savvy,* February 1980, p. 42.
7. *National Law Journal,* 3 September 1979, p. 9.
8. *New York Times,* 22 July 1980, Sec. C, p. 10.
9. *New York Times,* 29 October 1979, *Week in Review,* p. 6.
10. Ann Northrop, "Otto Passman and Shirley Davis," *Ms.,* January 1978, p. 57.
11. Florence Isbell, "Congress as Ol' Massa," *Civil Liberties Review,* January/February 1978, p. 46. See also *Newsweek,* 18 June 1979, p. 52.
12. *National Law Journal,* 2 August 1979, p. 2.
13. Ibid., 14 January 1980, p. 2.
14. Tamila C. Jensen, "Title VII as an Employment Discrimination Remedy: Assessing the Costs and Benefits" (work in progress), p. 12.
15. Wallace, p. 190. See also *U.S. News & World Report,* 14 August 1972, p. 66.

16. Ralph R. Smith, "A Third Rate Case Shouldn't Make Hard Law," *Juris Doctor*, February 1978, pp. 22, 31.
17. Bringhurst, p. 3.

Chapter 9

1. *New York Post*, 4 June 1975, p. 23.
2. *Los Angeles Times*, 31 July 1980, p. 1.
3. Ann Taylor Fleming, "New Frontiers in Conception," *New York Times Sunday Magazine*, 20 July 1980, pp. 14–20+.
4. *Los Angeles Herald Examiner*, 12 December 1979, p. A3.
5. *Village Voice*, 14 April 1980, p. 35.

Selected Bibliography

Ansbacher, Heinz L., and Rowena R., eds. *The Individual Psychology of Alfred Adler*. New York: Harper Torchbooks, 1956.

Ardrey, Robert. *The Social Contract*. New York: Delta Books, 1970.

Aubert, Vilhelm, ed. *Sociology of Law*. Middlesex, England: Penguin Books, Ltd., 1969.

Baltzell, E. Digby. *The Protestant Establishment*. New York: Vintage Books, 1964.

Bancroft, Hubert Howe. *Popular Tribunals*. San Francisco: The History Co., 1887.

Bartlett, Irving H. *Daniel Webster*. New York: Norton, 1978.

Benedict, Ruth. *Patterns of Culture*. Boston: Houghton Mifflin, 1934.

Bloomfield, Maxwell. *American Lawyers in a Changing Society, 1776–1876*. Cambridge: Harvard University Press, 1976.

Bohannan, Paul, ed. *Law and Warfare*. Garden City: Natural History Press, 1967.

Boorstin, Daniel J. *The Americans*. 3 vols: *The Colonial Experience; The National Experience; The Democratic Experience*. New York: Vintage Books, 1950.

Bowen, Catherine Drinker. *John Adams and the American Revolution*. Boston: Little, Brown, 1950.

Brandon, Ruth: *A Capitalist Romance: Singer and the Sewing Machine*. Philadelphia: J. B. Lippincott, 1977.

Bringhurst, Bruce. *Antitrust and the Oil Monopoly*. Westport: Greenwood Press, 1978.

Cortner, Richard C. *The Apportionment Cases*. New York: Norton, 1970.

Cribbet, John E.; Fritz, Wm. F.; and Johnson, Corwin W. *Cases and Materials on Property*. Brooklyn: Foundation Press, 1960.

Curran, Barbara A. *The Legal Needs of the Public*. Chicago: American Bar Foundation, 1977.

Dolbeare, Kenneth. "The Supreme Court and the States." *The Impact of Supreme Court Decisions.* Edited by Theodore L. Becker and Malcolm M. Feeley. New York: Oxford University Press, 1973.

———. *Trial Courts in Urban Politics.* Huntington: Robt. E. Krieger Publishing Co., 1976.

Erikson, Kai T. *Everything In Its Path.* New York: Simon & Schuster, 1976.

Eslinger, Victoria L. "A Case Herstory: A Legal Suit." *Women Winning.* Edited by Virginia E. Pendergrass. Chicago: Nelson-Hall, 1979.

Faulk, John Henry. *Fear on Trial.* New York: Simon & Schuster, 1967.

Fehrenbacher, Don E. *The Dred Scott Case: Its Significance in American Law and Politics.* New York: Oxford University Press, 1978.

Fleming, Donald, and Bailyn, Bernard, eds. *Law in American History.* Boston: Little, Brown, 1971.

Foner, Philip S. *History of the Labor Movement in the United States,* vol. 3. New York: International Publishers, 1964.

Ford Foundation. *New Approaches to Conflict Resolution.* New York: Ford Foundation, 1978.

———. *Public Interest Law: Five Years Later.* New York: Ford Foundation, 1976.

Friedman, Lawrence M. *A History of American Law.* New York: Touchstone Books, 1973.

Gilmore, Grant. *The Ages of American Law.* New York: Yale University Press, 1977.

Glick, Ira O.; Weiss, Robert S.; and Parkes, C. Murray. *The First Year of Bereavement.* New York: John Wiley & Sons, 1974.

Graham, Fred P. *The Self-Inflicted Wound.* New York: Macmillan, 1970.

Handler, Joel F. *Social Movements and the Legal System.* New York: Academic Press, 1978.

Handler, Joel F.; Hollingsworth, Ellen Jane; and Erlanger, Howard S. *Lawyers and the Pursuit of Legal Rights.* New York: Academic Press, 1978.

Hotchner, A. E. *Doris Day: Her Own Story.* New York: Morrow, 1976.

Hughes, Graham. *The Conscience of the Courts.* New York: Anchor Press, 1975.

Huizinga, Johan. *Homo Ludens: A Study of the Play Element in Culture.* Boston: Beacon Press, 1950.

Hunting, Robert Bryant, and Neuwirth, Gloria S. *Who Sues in New York City?* New York: Columbia University Press, 1962.

Jensen, Tamila C. "Title VII: Costs and Benefits." Documentary film. March, 1977.

———. "Title VII as an Employment Discrimination Remedy: Assessing the Costs and Benefits." Work in progress.

Josephson, Eric and Mary, eds. *Man Alone.* New York: Dell, 1962.

Keesing, Felix M. *Cultural Anthropology*. New York: Holt, Rinehart, and Winston, 1967.

Kelner, Joseph, and Munves, James. *The Kent State Coverup*. New York: Harper & Row, 1980.

Kessel, John H. "Public Perceptions of the Supreme Court." *The Impact of Supreme Court Decisions*. Theodore L. Becker and Malcolm M. Feeley, eds. New York: Oxford University Press, 1973.

Kluger, Richard. *Simple Justice*. New York: Vintage Books, 1977.

Knightley, Phillip, et al. *Suffer the Children*. New York: Viking, 1979.

Kubler-Ross, Elisabeth. *On Death and Dying*. New York: Macmillan, 1969.

Levin, Meyer. *The Obsession*. New York: Simon & Schuster, 1973.

Lewis, William Draper, ed. *Great American Lawyers*. Philadelphia: John C. Winston, 1907.

Lurie, Leonard. *The Running of Richard Nixon*. New York: Coward, McCann & Geoghegan, 1972.

McDonald, John. *Strategy in Poker, Business and War*. New York: Norton, 1950.

Magrath, C. Peter. *Yazoo: The Case of Fletcher v. Peck*. New York: Norton, 1966.

Marke, Julius J. *Vignettes of Legal History*. South Hackensack: Fred B. Rothman, 1965.

Miller, Arthur Selwyn. *Social Change and Fundamental Law*. Westport: Greenwood Press, 1979.

Nader, Laura, and Todd, Harry F., Jr., eds. *The Disputing Process in Ten Societies*. New York: Columbia University Press, 1978.

Noonan, John Thomas, Jr. *Persons and Masks of the Law*. New York: Farrar, Straus, and Giroux, 1976.

Nye, Russell. *The Unembarrassed Muse*. New York: Dial Press, 1970.

O'Connell, Jeffrey. *The Lawsuit Lottery*. New York: Free Press, 1979.

Peck, David W. *Decision at Law*. New York: Dodd, Mead & Co., 1961.

Perls, F. S. *Ego, Hunger and Aggression*. New York: Vintage Books, 1969.

Pilat, Oliver. *Pegler: Angry Man of the Press*. Boston: Beacon Press, 1963.

Pospisil, Leopold. "The Attributes of Law." *Law and Warfare*. Edited by Paul Bohannan. Garden City: Natural History Press, 1967.

Pound, Roscoe. *The Lawyer from Antiquity to Modern Times*. St. Paul, Minn.: West Publishing Co., 1953.

———. "The Causes of Popular Dissatisfaction with the Administration of Justice." *Landmarks of Law*. Edited by Ray D. Henson. New York: Harper, 1960.

Prosser, William L. *Handbook of the Law of Torts.* St. Paul, Minn.: West Publishing Co., 1964.

Pruetzel, Maria, and Barbour, John A. *The Freddie Prinze Story.* Kalamazoo: Master's Press, 1978.

Reisman, David. "Law and Sociology." *Abundance for What?* New York: Anchor Press, 1965.

Rochlin, Gregory, M.D. *Man's Aggression.* Boston: Gambit Press, 1973.

Sandburg, Carl. "Lincoln the Lawyer." *Voices in Court.* Edited by William H. Davenport. New York: Macmillan, 1958.

Sheingold, Stuart A. *The Politics of Rights.* New Haven: Yale University Press, 1974.

Schwartz, Bernard. *Law in America.* New York: American Heritage, 1974.

Seavey, Warren A. "Principles of Torts." *Landmarks of Law.* Edited by Ray D. Henson. New York: Harper, 1960.

Shneidman, Edwin S. *Deaths of Man.* New York: Quadrangle/New York Times Book Co., 1973.

Spiegel, Yorick. *The Grief Process,* trans. Elisabeth Drake. Nashville: Abingdon Press, 1973.

Stern, Gerald M. *The Buffalo Creek Disaster.* New York: Vintage Books, 1976.

Strick, Anne. *Injustice for All.* New York: Vintage Books, 1950.

Sullivan, Mark. *Our Times,* vol. 2. New York: Scribner's, 1927.

Tapp, June Louin, and Levine, Felice J. *Law, Justice and the Individual in Society.* New York: Holt, Rinehart, and Winston, 1977.

Tocqueville, Alexis de. *Democracy in America.* New York: Vintage Books, 1945.

Unger, Robert Mangabeira. *Law in Modern Society.* New York: Free Press, 1976.

Van Kamm, Adrian. *Envy and Originality.* New York: Doubleday, 1972.

Wallace, Phyllis A., ed. *Equal Employment Opportunity and the AT&T Case.* Cambridge: MIT Press, 1975.

Weisbrod, Burton A.; Handler, Joel F.; and Komesar, Neil K. *Public Interest Law.* Berkeley: University of California Press, 1978.

Wiltse, Charles M., ed. *The Papers of Daniel Webster, Correspondence,* vol. 2. Hanover, N.H.: University Press of New England, 1976.

Witkin, Bernard E. *Summary of California Law.* 8th ed. San Francisco: Bancroft-Whitney, 1970.

———. *Summary of California Procedure.* 2nd ed. San Francisco: Bancroft-Whitney, 1970.

Wolford, Thorp L. "The Laws and Liberties of 1648." *Essays in the History of Early American Law.* Edited by David H. Flaherty. Chapel Hill: University of North Carolina Press, 1969.

Index